Indian Port and Shipping Industry

*Five Decades of My Involvement
in its Holistic Growth*

PROBIR MITRA

Printed in India

ISBN: 978-93-6045-025-0

First Printing, 2024

IndiePress

A division of Nasadiya Technologies Private Ltd.

Koramangala, Bangalore

Karnataka-560029

http://indiepress.in/

Edited by Pooja R

Typeset by PageMajik

Book Cover designed by Keerthipriya PH

Publishing Consultant – Chris

I'd like to dedicate this book to my wife Purnima, my continuous spiritual strength and support, and my daughter Sramana who is a famed and successful IT Professional in Silicon Valley, California.

Probir Mitra as he is known in the world of shipping, but for me it was always Probir Da.

It was about three decades ago I met Probir Da, at the SAIL office in Kolkata, where I had gone for a meeting to discuss shipping matters and logistic issues with regards to the movement of Coking Coal from Australia to India, with a focus of optimizing coal into Haldia. Due to draft restrictions at Haldia and tidal bottle necks of navigation in the Hooghly river, it was always a formidable challenge to optimize the transport of coal across the high seas, keeping in mind the need to maintain the economies of scale for maximizing and delivering this lifeline raw material for steel production to SAIL.

It was at one of these Brainstorming sessions that I realized the enthusiasm and passion Probir Da possessed, and his ability to always think out of the Box and come up with innovative solutions – He was a man ahead of his times. New ideas and new schemes in a Bureaucratic environment 3 decades ago and subsequently, were never received with open arms due to a certain mindset in a system, but that never deterred him from pushing his Ideas and pursuing his Goals and dreams.

He has stood tall in the shipping fraternity and is well respected both in the Private and Public sector shipping industry. He brought to the table the concepts of transloading at Saugor roads coal operations, by forging consortiums and spear heading open house discussions with Logistic players, Port authority, Environmentalists, Shipping Companies, and SAIL/end users – By no means an easy task to get such a diverse mind set Group of people to walk the talk. Succeed he did, by firmly planting the seed and concept of such an operation, the benefits of which are being reaped by various commercial, logistical and industrial organizations. Transhipment operations are now being regularly conducted at the Saugor roads/ anchorages, there by impacting/reducing the Ton Mile rate for the coal that is delivered to the steel mills. A very valuable contribution indeed both in terms of scale of economy for product delivery, as well as Logistical Innovation.

Kolkata Shipping and Probir Mitra are synonymous, and there is perhaps hardly any facet of this industry, where his presence and contributions are not felt. I for one have enjoyed my years of association with him, and I would like to wish him the very Best of Health and may he continue to Enrich the lives of those around him with his Expertise, Knowledge and Never Say Die attitude.

Lalit Badhwar
Former MD /CEO,Western Bulk Carriers,/Belships As,(Indian Continent)
Former MD/CEO, BOCIMAR INTL (Indian Continent)
Currently CMD – L.B.Consultants Pvt.Ltd.

LALIT BADHWAR: MOB +91 9810194294

L.B CONSULTANTS PVT. LTD.,
A-33/12, DLF PHASE – I
DLF CITY. General
GURUGRAM - 122002,
HARYANA, INDIA

EMAIL: Lbadhwar@hotmail.com
WEB: www.lbconsultants.in
Email-Chartering@lbconsultants.in
OFFICE TELEPHONE: +91-124-2567825

I feel very privileged to be asked to write a few words of my memory and experience working with Probir. Probir is a man of great experience and foresight, started his shipping career in 1960. As in most business especially in the field of Shipping, experience and vision is an asset, bearing in mind over 80 pct of the volume of international trade in goods is carried by sea. Probir always recognized India's vast coast line and the need to look for innovative means where shipping costs could be reduced and efficiency could be improved for the various end users and exporters he had contacts with. I had the privilege of working with Probir over 30 years and of taking part in some of such projects Probir had identified. What stood as lasting memories while dealing with Probir prior my retirement, was his never ending enthusiasm and drive. I also had the benefit of learning and tapping into Probir's vast experience. Probir's humour coupled with his deep understanding on the Spiritual side always found a way to remain calm and positive at all times. I wish Probir all the success and being able to impart his knowledge and wisdom into an industry very close to him.

Ram Nair
Former Director
H. CLARKSON & COMPANY LIMITED
London

Capstan Shipping: Probir Mitra

My introduction to Probir Mitra(Probir Da)started in 2009. I was the President of Seabulk Inc, a Canadian Marine Bulk specialist involved in Ship-to-ship(STS) operations around the world. Seabulk had learned about the constraints at Haldia Port in Bengal and Seabulk considered a lightering solution of bulk cargo delivered in large OGVs and lightered into smaller vessels for delivery to a shallow-draft port at Haldia. Probir Da was introduced to Seabulk as a local expert who had been involved with Kolkata port Trust and had extensive knowledge of the requirements in Haldia. During my first visit to Kolkata, I met Probir Da for dinner at the famous Oberoi Hotel in Kolkata. A tall, immaculately dressed Probir Da introduced himself and we spent the evening talking about matters of mutual interest, which went beyond Shipping. Probir Da was a great disciple of Vivekanada and hence a spiritual man. This further extended to classical Music and our common experiences about the music scene in Kolkata. By the end of the evening, I had met a true friend who had impressive credentials in Business and a life experience worthy of many more meetings. This we have done for almost fifteen years and this has been truly enriching The Haldia project required an innovative Transshipper design but the real challenge was the ability of the shallow-draft port to deal with transit from the anchorage to the port and timely and efficient discharges of the shuttle vessels. Probir Da handled all this and also all the negotiations with the Port on tariffs and support services. At all times, Probir Da showed a complete understanding of the challenges in delivering 'just-in-time' deliveries of millions of tones to a shallow- draft port. The solution developed for Haldia and Probir Da's role was truly exemplary In life, when a chance business meeting with a man leaves such an important mark in your life, this is what makes it all worthwhile. Probir Da is an inspiration and has made a difference to my life. May he continue to do more of this.

Sid Sridhar
President of Seabulk Inc,
Marine Bulk specialist
Vancouver
Canada

I am very happy to know that Shri Prabir Mitra has decided to pen down his illustrious journey, spanning well over six decades in the maritime sector. I have known Prabirda, as I call him since I respect him as my elder brother, for nearly five decades. I have found him to be a visionary who has always been far ahead of his time. Shri Mitra has worked relentlessly to solve the acute problem of draft in the riverine port of Kolkata by innovative approaches like transloading for bulk transportation and hub and spoke network for containers. Under his dynamic leadership, the Himalayan shipping company, which he founded along with his elder brother and the Bose's of E C Bose, emerged as a very prominent player in the East Coast India/ West Asia Gulf sector. His innovative approach helped his company to negotiate with the ports to beat the acute congestions prevailing then in the WAG region and thereby make his company financially strong and a fast growing concern. After Himalayan Shipping had to be wound up due to the unfortunate conflict between the Bose's and Mitra's, for which Prabirda was not directly responsible, he founded Capstan Shipping, a very successful maritime consultancy firm and continued his innovative approach in providing solutions for maritime problems to his customers. I'm confident that his memoirs will be an invaluable asset for all the maritime practitioners by inspiring them to think out of the box like Prabirda himself and will help them to deal with success and failures in the business with equanimity. This philosophy of life of Prabirda comes from his lifelong devotion to Thakur Ramakrishna Paramhansa. I pray to Thakur for a very long and healthy life of Prabirda so that he can continue to inspire others in the maritime sector and serve the society as a true Rotarian. Thakur bless.

Sabyasachi Hajara
Former Chairman
The Shipping Corporation of India

I'm delighted to know that Probir Mitra, my very special friend for over 6 decades, is penning down a memoir of his illustrious shipping career. He is respected professionally and socially as a deep spiritually splurged person. I'm happy to write and share my long association with him.

Probir Mitra, after his study of global shipping and undergoing training in international operations at the World's leading Baltic Exchange in London, joined the Birla Group Company Ratnakar Shipping as a senior executive to gain intimate knowledge about the problems and prospects of

Indian shipping. He had fierce ambition for the Indian Shipping Industry to gain a competitive edge in the global marketplace. He spent about 3 years at Ratnakar and made significant contributions in widening the horizons of the corporate operations. The landmark during his tenure was Ratnakar's acquisition of a new building 67000 DWT Crude Oil Carrier, which was given on a 12 years' time charter to Shell International Marine Ltd., UK. It placed Ratnakar in a different league through the successful time charter operation of the largest crude oil carrier on the Indian registry. Another significant contribution of Ratnakar Shipping during his tenure and active initiative was in the Marine Insurance sector of Indian Shipping. During the 1965 Indo-Pakistan war Marine Insurance of the entire Indian fleet was serviced by Lloyds Exchange, London and they put up a high war risk premium load on the Indian shipping. As the front man of Ratnakar Shipping, it was my predicament to handle a very complicated claim of our good vessel 'Ratna-Jyoti.' The impact of the high war risk premium was affecting the entire Ratnakar fleet. Following Probir's advice, I could convince the Indian ship owners' community and the Govt of India to form the hull committee and special war risk insurance division in the Finance Ministry and Indian shipping came out of Lloyd control.

Probir's ambition was much higher and he was restless to take a plunge in ship-owning himself. It led him to start his own company Himalaya Shipping with a well-thought strategy to build and acquire his own fleet over the years progressively. He always had on the radar prime focus on improvement of port infrastructure and enhancement of productivity to international standards.

Above all, he distinguished himself for his innovative thinking about linking Ocean, River, Rail and Road for a robust transport supply chain logistics. *It was, indeed, the key to enable operations at optimum cost.*

He tried his level best as circumstances permitted.

I'm sure his shipping memoir and eventful entrepreneurial journey will benefit the future generation in the port and shipping profession.

Ramesh Maheswari

Former President
Texmaco Ltd, Belghoria, India
And
Former Managing Director
Ratnakar Shipping Co Ltd

I have known Mr Probir Mitra for more than three decades. First, as a leader in the shipping industry and their after as a dedicated leader in rotary, inclined always to serve the humanity.

Over the years I have seeing him take up major initiatives through various institutions including Ramakrishna mission and rotary.

At times he intrigues me – how does he get such energy to not only pursue his dreams but follow up meticulously with a plan, implement the same by leading a team or motivating them to finally achieve the goal. He has done this with me time and again and I am very happy that he has cajoled me into taking up some more service projects in my already overflowing plate.

His perseverance, patience, tenacity especially at his age is remarkable. I wish him strength to keep doing this till he completes a century with good health and great service to humanity.

Regards,

Shekhar Mehta
President
Rotary International (2021–2022)

Indian Port and Shipping Industry: Five Decades Of My Involvement In Its Holistic Growth

When I stepped into the Stelp & Leighton Shipping office at Fenchurch Street in the city of London in March 1960, I was 20-year-old greenhorn just arrived from Calcutta to join this company as an intern to study shipping with specialization in ship chartering. I was enrolled in this program at the Institute of Chartered Shipbrokers. The institute had its headquarters near the Baltic Exchange in the city of London. This company was a multi-discipline shipping agency group spread over agency departments for various major shipping lines, including India Steamship Co., Calcutta, Hansa Line of Bremen, Germany, and many other major shipping lines from across the globe. Ship chartering and sale and purchase divisions, marine insurance, and an exclusive department for handling P&I claims and legal issues of the vessels under their agency. There were more than 10 ship brokers regularly attending the floor at the Baltic Exchange to do chartering business, with separate engagements in ship sale and purchase broking. In the marine insurance division, senior brokers were attending Lloyd Exchange for marine risk insurance of vessels covering hulls and machinery, particularly average, general average, total loss, and constructive total loss. The chartering division was looked after by Mr. Louise Hoare, one of the senior directors of the company, a legendary name in ship chartering who was also a senior director of Baltic Exchange.

The director-in-charge of the marine insurance division was Mr. Blake, and the company had a high-end specialization in this most important area of the shipping industry.

Mr. Norman Leighton and Mr. Pizzy were two other senior directors handling agency business and attending to vessels in port and all their marine requirements.

Mr. Archer, as senior GM, was running a team for specialized P&I club claims handling and associated legal matters.

Sir Bijoy Prasad Singhroy, Chairman of India Steamship Co., and their British Chief Executive, Mr. Chris Smart, introduced me to this company. They assigned me as an intern to receive training in all major divisions of shipping, with a specialization in chartering. This arrangement involved a reciprocal exchange of trainees with Stelp & Leighton, and it led to young James Felton being sent to Calcutta for an internship at India Steamship Co. My first engagement was with Mr. Archer in the P&I Department, and during more than three years of my training tenure, I went around all the departments, with the maximum time spent in the chartering division, where I received personal parental care from Mr. Louise Hoare, who introduced me to Baltic Exchange.

I was attending twice-a-week ship-broking classes at the institute in the evening. I was also enrolled in a shipping education course at City of London College, a 3-day-a-week evening course. Within this three year period, I appeared and did well in the institute examination and became a Fellow of The Institute of Chartered Shipbrokers at the recommendation of my mentor, Mr. Louise Hoare, after passing my intermediate and final examinations. Louise was not only my 'Guru' in chartering but also harboring high hopes for me to scale heights in the Indian shipping industry.

After spending over three years in London, I joined Karl Geuther & Co. Bremen, Germany, who was agent for India Steamship Co. and the Shipping Corporation of India, apart from holding many other European shipping line agencies. In this company, I could gain experience in liner shipping cargo booking and client servicing, stevedoring, and stowage of cargo in the liner vessels with optimum space utilization.

I befriended Peter Blumbach in Bremen and received much affection from his mother during my one-year stay in Bremen, Germany. Peter later promoted Amsbach Shipping in Singapore and still continues to be its chairman.

During my near-five-year training period in shipping, I managed to do the intermediate and final part one of the Institute of Chartered Secretaries course by enrolling in the institute. I did not pursue this further after my return to India. It was my mentor Louise Hoare who instilled in my mind the spirit of entrepreneurship for serving the Indian shipping industry through the conceptualization of innovative port and shipping-related projects with the promotion of a start-up shipping company with forays into liner shipping, bulk carriers—tramp shipping, containers, tankers, and inland water transport in the riverine terrain of India, linking coastal ports with the vast hinterland.

When I returned to India in early 1965, Indian shipping was just maturing. I boarded a cargo ship of India Steamship Co.—Indian Splendour at Liverpool, and the company offered me accommodation in the owner's cabin.

British Master Capt. Pitt was on command, and the voyage was for almost one month, covering many ports in the Mediterranean, Adriatic, and Red Sea. The initial European port's stay on the vessel was reasonably long. The interaction between agents, various service agencies, shipmates, and officers was interesting to observe. There were give-and-takes in terms of money and entertainment. Capt. Pitt was one of the last British Master Mariners of the ISS, and I found him a non-interfering leader of the Indian officers on board. He never touched any drinks when at sea and was a strict disciplinarian for the watch-keeping officers while stitching hand embroidery in his cabin when he was not on duty at the bridge. He was always drinking heavily in ports and entertaining all of us with his naughty marine stories. Cargo booking, loading, and stowage at earlier ports of call occasionally used to eat away cargo space designated for the following port of call bookings, which always figured in the competitive negotiating negotiations between port agents.

I narrate the above period of my shipping career building as an introduction to my entry into the Indian shipping industry which in the early mid-sixties was at its nascent stage of development. In fact, Transchart was formed by Govt of India in New Delhi when I was in London and I remember the big commotion it created among the Baltic brokers when a huge volume of Govt of India chartering business got shifted from London to Delhi. There were only three Indian liner shipping companies—Scindia Steam Navigation Co. and India Steamship Co. from the private sector with The Shipping Corporation of India just entering the liner shipping scenario as a public sector Govt of India undertaking. They were all running under conference with a cargo pool system to protect revenue from freight undercutting and avoid competition. In the bulk sector, Great Eastern Shipping was a prominent big-name efficiently competing with the international giants including the Greeks and Norwegians. Many Indian shipping ventures were sprouting primarily in the bulk and oil sector who were never allowed entry in the conference pool by the biggies. The government was overactive in protecting cargo share for the Indian shipping companies without much thought on fleet development through encouraging private and public investments to make Indian shipping adequately armed to combat global hawks in international shipping. Bureaucratic red tape on various licensing for ship acquisition and different trade route operations was rampant.

Ship acquisition financing was always needing foreign exchange clearance from the RBI and specialized tie-ups between Indian banks and leading foreign banks for accessing foreign exchange loan funding at a competitive interest rate. To incentivise adequate investment in the shipping industry from private investors, an innovative concession model on the debt-equity ratio and collateral securities was needed as government policy guidelines.

Through the reading of international shipping publications and extensive discussion with my mentor during Stelp & Leighton days and later in Germany, when I visited major German ports like Bremen, Hamburg, Bremer Haven, etc., my young mind developed scattered concepts of ship operation, port handling, and the shipbuilding industry. In the early 1960s, global shipping was going through a major evolution process of linking trade and transportation through the establishment of innovative cost and logistics optimization. Ship chartering market evaluation depended much on the global economy in terms of regional export-import movement of cargo between nation-states, bringing the basic comparative cost of the economic system in sync with purchasing power parity and another extraneous political and high-level diplomatic relationship between developed and underdeveloped countries in the global community of nations. Unitization of cargo, multi-modal transportation, and infrastructure building with supporting bulk cargo requirements in the areas of energy, steel, cement, oil, and food were all on the desk of the global shipping research and development experts for robust and systemic growth and development of the shipping industry as a whole. My scattered shipping mind was continuously seeking logistic concept integration for the Indian shipping industry and was looking for first-hand exposure in the industry for consolidation of my thought process.

When I stepped out of the 'Indian Splendour' at the port of Bombay, I was looking for an Indian shipping company that would give me adequate exposure in the Indian shipping industry with the freedom for innovative thinking in project and concept development. I did not find the assistant manager offer of SCI congenial for my exposure dream. After coming back to Calcutta, I hesitated to join the ISS Port Operation Department as there was hardly any element of chartering expertise requirement. After almost three months of waiting, I went for an interview with Sri Ramesh Maheswari, who was the MD of Ratnakar Shipping Co., of the K K Birla Group, a start-up in the shipping industry. Ramesh pleasantly surprised me by offering a cup of tea and asking me to share my insights on shipping and port industry development. When I asked him if I was answering his interview call for engagement with this company, he casually replied that he had gone through my bio-data and that, as a newcomer to shipping, he wanted me to educate him about my experience and exposure in global shipping. Besides sharing my ideas about the shipping industry for nearly 20 minutes, I also connected with him emotionally. Despite the pay packet offer being much less than the ISS offer, I accepted it.

I got started with Ratnakar Shipping which only had four dry cargo vessels and one tanker. One of the twin Decker vessels Ratna-Manjusree was on period charter with SCI and other vessels Ratna-Chandralekha, Ratna-Sovona, and Ratna-Jyoti were engaged in coastal coal transportation. Tanker Ratna-Jayasree was on long-term charter with Burma Shell.

There were regular Coastal coal movements from Calcutta to Tuticorin to service TNEB mainly and other southern power plants and occasionally we were bringing back Salt Cargo to Calcutta always discharging over-side in the Calcutta moorings. During Bore tides these ships were shifted inside the docks for safety. Coal Docks of Calcutta Port were very active in mid-sixties with one mechanical berth and two other manual handling coal berths in the KPD Mominpur area. My cousin Kalyan Mitter was the Coal Dock Superintendent and his very able Deputy Superintendent was Suniti Bhose. It was very important to secure open wagon coal cargo allocation from the Coal Controller office in Dalhousie Square for our vessels to secure mechanical Berth allocation for our Ships which was designed to handle open wagon coal traffic only. It was my daily routine to attend berthing meetings in KPD and then visit the Coal Dock Super office. Despite draft restrictions our vessels like Ratna Chandralekha could load an average of 10k tons of cargo in Calcutta port those days in mid-Sixties. The Coal Controller was

Amal Sircar who was my senior friend from Table Tennis as a player and official of BTTA from my playing days. For the port operations i.e., berthing, river pilot and harbor pilot calling coordination, and mainly coal dock lobbying for early loading and dispatch of the vessels, I was sharing the load with my colleague Mr. Shiva. My morning calls at the coal dock used to be very enjoyable with two delightful persons Kalyan Mitter alias Manik Da and Suniti da. Kalyan Mitter was a very knowledgeable and much respected Calcutta Port officer and besides his front role as Coal Dock Super, he was also part of a trusted group of officers enjoying the confidence and respect of the then Chairman B B Ghose for planning and development. He was my cousin and an intellectual personality with a broad mind and multi-layer interest in literature, art, and culture. He married a Brahma family Lady without succumbing to the pressure of the staunch Brahma family pressure to turn Brahma by giving up his own faith and belief. His deputy Suniti Bhose was also another very knowledgeable Port officer with intellectual depth and 'stealing the show' personality with his ready wit and sonorous voice. He was always the kingpin of any party or small group adda. He was also a part of the Chairman's selected team of officers for planning and development. Suniti Da also married a charming Lady from a staunch Brahma family against the will and consent of his own and the girl's family. Unfortunately, after the birth of their only child, she got totally incapacitated to move around due to an incurable ailment. There was no support from either family and Suniti Da carried his own cross and love lotus giving his heart and soul to keep her happy and cheerful and taking full care of their only child.

I was fortunate to receive a warm welcome from senior officers during evening planning sessions for Haldia Port. During my initial months with Ratnakar Shipping, I gained valuable insights and experience in port infrastructure development over a period of 9–12 months. Suniti Da was always a humorous smiling face never allowing any pain of his heart to surface. He was a storehouse of humorous stories and a repertoire of dramatic story telling with loads of jokes and anecdotes which he used to share with us in his immaculate humorous presentations. Suniti Da was a great theatre personality and he always attracted all in any 'adda.' Manik Da (Kalyan Mitter) narrated in our 'adda' one of his hilarious experiences when he went to a Greek Ship with Suniti Da in the dock after receiving a call from the Captain who was in a rage for not receiving some essential port services. When they met the Captain he was swearing and shouting at them in Greek language with Chief Officer by his side who could speak English. After 10 minutes of continuous blasts from the Captain, Suniti Da replied in Greek without waiting for the Interpreter with an equal velocity of the blast for five minutes and everyone went silent. When they came back to the office Manik Da asked in amazement, "Suniti, I didn't know you could speak Greek." Suniti Da smilingly replied, "I have replied by lip reading to match his swearing and this was not Greek but enough to calm them down." These coal dock days started for me a very long-lasting friendship with Suniti Da and in later years we staged a number of voice plays under his direction. Unfortunately, we lost Manik Da at a very early age while working. He had a massive heart attack after driving home from the office and collapsed in his drawing room just after garaging his car. At the time of B B Ghosh as Chairman of the Port, Haldia port planning was on the drawing board. Senior port officers like Robin Roy, Pama Roy, Kalyan Mitter, Suniti Bhose, and other senior engineers used to assemble at the Strand Rd headquarter of Calcutta Port on the 5th floor of the new building. My Ratnakar office was at the Mackinon Mackenzy building on Strand Rd close to the Calcutta Port office. I was fortunate to be welcomed affectionately by all these senior officers in the evening planning session for Haldia Port for almost 9–12 months during my initial days with Ratnakar Shipping. This gave me a lot of insight and experience in port infrastructure creation.

To make productive use of my specialized chartering knowledge, Ramesh Maheswari and my immediate boss, Keshab Mathur, introduced me to the Transchart operation in Delhi. Mr. S. N. Banerjee, popularly known as Aku Banerjee, and Mr. P. I. Mehta were the officers in charge, and both of them gave me a lot of affectionate respect and eagerly shared my chartering knowledge for a huge volume of government chartering activities involving the chartering of mostly foreign vessels, as Indian vessels were not always available in position due to the scarcity of suitable Indian vessels for tramp operation. There were panel brokers of Transchart with a strong broking house backing them from primarily London and also limited participation from New York, Tokyo, Greece, Hong Kong, Singapore, etc. Ratnakar Shipping collaborated with Harris & Dickson as their London broker for chartering, sale, and purchase activities. I maintained communication with Mr. David Reed, Senior Director of Harris & Dickson, to plan and develop various chartering and vessel acquisition projects. During my Delhi visits and interactions with Aku Da and Mr. P. I. Mehta in Transchart, I presented my innovative thoughts on their chartering requirements for the import of PL 480 wheat cargo from the USA and Canada to India.

An upsurge in India's food imports, particularly PL 480 grain, created an upswing in the voyage freight market, and Transchart was compelled to fork out substantial foreign exchange towards freight payments to foreign vessels. I proposed the time chartering of foreign vessels by the Indian shipping company and negotiated with Transchart regarding their voyage chartering inquiries. The help I needed from them was to give me the inquiry a day in advance so that I could line up a time charter and offer the same to them on a voyage basis when they officially came into the market. They were convinced that there would be substantial foreign exchange savings by way of surplus from the deal for the Indian shipping company. Even after convincing them, it took me a little time and effort to convince Ratnakar management of the mechanics of this chartering operation. Ramesh Maheswari was highly intelligent and quickly grasped my proposal of investing in a short-term charter hire of 15–30 days. This strategy involved collecting 90% of the voyage freight upon issuance of the Bill of Lading after loading and sailing of the chartered foreign vessel from the USA east coast or Canadian load port to India.

Unfortunately, my immediate boss Keshav Mathur raised various negative queries like most Greek vessels offered to Transchart for voyages are ballasting from Europe to the load port and it would not be possible for us to find owners to deliver the vessel to us on time charter at the load port. I countered this by stating that 'we shall pay ballast bonus for such owners to give us delivery at the load port.' There was apprehension about DG Shipping's objection in allowing foreign exchange approval to pay time charter hire which I wanted to justify by projecting foreign exchange savings in the differential of voyage freight Transchart paying to us in Indian rupees and the substantial margin between voyage freight and time charter hire. Finally, we went up to Chairman K K Birla, and the project was approved. We alerted David Reed / Harris & Dickson to establish contact with Greek Ship owners for finalizing quick-time charters on sub-India Govt approval basis. The subject was to be lifted in 24/48 hrs time after fixing the Transchart voyage charter. I had to park myself at a Janata Hotel suite with telex facilities as the best communication available those days and we fixed during the next 3/4 months more than 60 vessels with the cooperation of Harris & Dickson in London and Transchart in Delhi. There was a fat earnings and cash flow generation for Ratnakar with meagre investment which excited Chairman K K Birla to suggest to me a London assignment to do this kind of Trans-Atlantic cross chartering.

During my Ratnakar days, Ramesh Maheswari encouraged me to engage in cleaning up ship supply frauds going on between ship chandlers and the off-shore and on-shore officers of the company. I could catch one of our leading ship chandlers, Aziz & Co., supplying huge volumes of wire ropes through fake invoices and challans. I uncovered this by creating a rift between the master or chief officer and the second officer. Although effective, it strained relationships with senior colleagues and was not a pleasant experience.

I will narrate another story of major ship acquisition and chartering-out project of Ratna-Jyoti, where the company acquired this vessel in poor condition. Furthermore, at the recommendation of next-door broker neighbor Blacker & Co., Jardine Henderson supported a fake company called G K Shipping without checking their antecedent. It was a long voyage under their time charter from the east coast of India to the east coast of Canada, and the vessel encountered several mechanical breakdowns and ultimately ended up in Canada with litigation on cargo that the charterer was facing, coupled with a huge repair bill for the vessel and G.A. claims. There was a huge impact on the insurance premium of the entire fleet of Ratnakar. The time charterers and the man concerned, Mr. Habul Mukherjee, vanished from the scene. Jardine took the position that they were only agents of G.K. Shipping. The lawyers' visit to the G K Shipping office address revealed a locked room and a sign board.

Repair and dry dock expenses of the vessel were substantial. Time Charterers had P&I Club cover for the cargo but P&I Club lawyers, like us, were finding no trace of the time Charterers. Indian Exporters and their cargo insurance got involved in litigations with Canadian consignee and there was obvious General Average adjustment surfacing. In the absence of Time Charterer, Ship owners were dragged into the mess with owner's P&I Club and vessel Insurance brought into the scene to protect owner's interest. My Insurance experience with Stelp & Leighton was fully tested for a complicated case handling. I was fortunate to meet Mr V K Bhandari at this point who was a Colossus in Insurance knowledge. VKB was representing P&I Club in India and was also attached to Ruby Insurance which was in Birla Group on those days when Insurance was private. This was 1965 and due to India Pakistan war Lloyds London imposed hefty war risk premium on Indian vessels. Working with VKB and Average Adjuster M K Jani I could gather in depth insight into International Marine Insurance and exploitation in terms of hefty premium and foreign exchange outgo on insurance of Indian Ships. Insurable Interest in the vessel like Hull & Machinery and Cargo broken up into Particular Average, General Average, Total Loss and Constructive TL were under holistic premium load for Indian Vessels in Lloyds with bunch of agencies with vested interest making a feast. India Govt intervention was necessary and fortunately India Govt rose up to the occasion during this time and special hull committee and War Risk Insurance dept was created in the Finance Ministry.

Coming back to Ratna Jyoti Insurance claim document finalization which was before formation of the Hull committee, VKB laid out before Mr Maheswari comprehensive distribution of premium impact on each of the Insurable interest and heavy repair expenditure claim was attracting maximum premium. In sum total premium payable on entire Ratnakar fleet was far exceeding the repair cost to be incurred for Ratna Jyoti. I asked VKB in the meeting what happens if we drop our Particular Average repair claim and do not allow any premium hike on our total fleet. VKB got a shock and felt I was naive and this kind of decision would seriously damage our International Insurance Market credibility. Ramesh was always high intellect person with quick reflex and he caught on to my idea and said he would go to the Ministry on behalf of Indian Shipping Industry for protection against such premium hike in the International Insurance market for Indian vessels. It was at Ramesh's initiative and aggressive lobbying at the Govt level direct war risk insurance coverage was provided by the Ministry and Hull insurance committee was formed which got strength and structure from Indian Insurance Companies after Insurance nationalization.

During my little over three years tenure with Ratnakar Shipping, I was approached more than once by Swapan Dasgupta of Sinclair & co who were essentially freight brokers but Swapan Da was seriously pursuing entry into Ship Chartering and Sale & Purchase broking business and formed Sinclair Freight & Chartering Pvt Ltd as extended wing of parent Sinclair & co which was originally a British partnership firm where Swapan Da acquired controlling share after British partners except one British sleeping partner, left. Swapan Da took 2/3 Indian partners including Kersi Dastur from a Shipping Agency and Stevedoring group who had some knowledge in Chartering and Shipping in general in addition to traditional routine freight broking. Sinclair was house broker for India Steamship and

Swapan Da was personally very close to their management. My first interaction with Swapan Da was when as ISS broker he fixed Ratna Chandralekha of Ratnakar on time charter to ISS for 3/6 months for India-UKC round voyage on their conference liner route. There was clause in the Charter party that at the time of delivery, vessel was to be fully fitted for ordinary cargo service. The vessel was not having adequate cargo battens in the holds and we engaged contractor to supply and get vessel fully cargo batten fitted. When I went on board to get the delivery certificate signed by the Time charterers, J L Puri and Capt Ronnie Ghose of ISS refused to take delivery as the vessel was not fitted for ordinary cargo service. My sincere pleading with them that this was not hampering their immediate loading plan and my contractor was advised to complete the Job simultaneous with loading operation, did not cut ice with them. After coming back to my office, I sent the Delivery Certificate to their operation Manager N K Sen stating that standard ordinary cargo for the owner is coal and the vessel is fully fitted for ordinary cargo service and time charterers had taken the vessel on hire with full knowledge of the vessel's past voyages cargo history. I also stated that cargo batten fitting work to meet Charterer's requirement was being carried out on Charterers account. This letter raised a tempest in ISS office and Swapan Da as broker requested me to come for a meeting with Mr Chris Smart at ISS office. I had high regards for Chris and it was he who introduced me to shipping initially and assisted me in London and Germany in my training days. Chris, N K Sen and Swapan Da were present in the meeting and I politely narrated my encounter with his officers on board. He smiled and stated 'Probir, you are smart and I feel good that I encouraged you to study Chartering.' He advised N K Sen to sign the delivery certificate and requested me to withdraw my claim for cargo batten expenses reimbursement. Coming out of his office we completed all formalities and between N K Sen, Swapan Da and me a long lasting bonding of mutual respect and affection developed since then.

Swapan Da, almost within a few months of this incident, requested that I join Sinclair Freight & Chartering with a good pay packet and take on the lead role to take this company forward. Although this offer was substantially higher than my then-remuneration with Ratnakar Shipping, I could not make up my mind straight away until I had a frank discussion with Ramesh Maheswari.

I advised Ramesh that my dream of a path-breaking journey in the Indian shipping industry is more industry-centric than employer-centric, and I opted for serving Ratnakar at a low salary level compared to other offers I had from SCI and ISS for exposure and experience in a start-up shipping company.

I found Sinclair and Swapan Dasgupta's offer attractive not merely for a better pay packet but more as an opportunity to build a chartering and sale-and-purchase broking house, which would add value to my overall industry exposure.

Ramesh advised me about the limitations of a ship-broking house like Sinclair as a player in comprehensive shipping industry development at the macro level. In the shipping industry, ship management, port management, innovative ship design for servicing global trade with strong multimodal transport logistic service products, etc. are involved, apart from ship financing and macro-economic exposure in global shipping. Swapan Dasgupta was senior to Ramesh in age, but Ramesh diplomatically warned me about the risk of my getting exploited in a broking house where vision and mission limitations were not likely to offer me any sustainable pathway to pursue my Indian shipping industry development dreams.

Ramesh at the same time appreciated my concern about getting choked in the routine rigmarole of Ratnakar Shipping Management, where my immediate bosses had both knowledge and vision limitations. He admitted that his own dual role as MD of Ratnakar and President of Texmaco does not have any balance and is tilted more towards Texmaco than shipping. He was a super competent administrator with a high intellect and an innovative mind, always eager to learn, digest, and make quick decisions for implementation. Ramesh narrated to me his first interview with K. K. Birla before joining the group as KKB's trusted 'Man Friday.' He advised me that KKB Group was in the advanced stage of concluding a takeover deal with ISS from J.N. Bhan and Khemka Group. This was an offer of genuine long-term scope for pursuing my shipping industry dream.

Although I honored Ramesh's request to delay my decision by one more year, I finally joined Sinclair in early 1969 after following my hunch that working for a big group like KKB, be it Ratnakar or ISS would provide too many management hurdles for me to pursue my dreams and innovative project visions for the Indian shipping industry. I fully realized that an entrepreneur's pathway in life with dreaming eyes will not be strewn with roses, but I reconciled myself to accept the password PPP—**Patience, Perseverance, and Purity**—for my long-term journey in the shipping stream.

In Sinclair, my seniors were Swapan Dasgupta and Kersi Dastur, and I was given adequate freedom and space to develop innovative sale and purchase projects and chartering activities.

During my three-year stint with Sinclairs, I could build a young team of interns with the full support and backing of management. I closely coordinated with Sinclair offices in Bombay and Delhi, headed by Jayant Mehta and Bal Vashist, respectively, in addition to my own posting in Calcutta, where I interacted with and made decisions in close proximity to my seniors. The Delhi office was very effectively and profitably servicing Transchart, and we had the benefit of having David Bruce & Co. as our London broker associate. My old friend from my Stelp & Leighton days, James Felton, was the MIC and senior partner of David Bruce, and they had almost monopoly control of Greek tonnages, which were mostly offering and getting fixed for Transchart business.

Vashist was the lead broker representing Sinclair in the Transchart panel and was efficiently and aggressively fixing vessels ahead of all other brokers. Management used to get occasional confidential complaints from Akuda (SNB) about Vashist's drinking habits and extramarital activities, which we handled with tact and tolerance. Jayant Mehta was a very pleasant leader for the Bombay office and was a popular man with most of the Bombay ship owners for servicing chartering and the S&P market. A number of new shipping enterprises were emerging those days that needed consultancy support, and between Kersi, me, and Jayant, we had good teamwork in servicing such consultancy and S&P inquiries.

We decided to take on 6/8 management trainees to strengthen our service network by giving them training and exposure in shipping, taking cues from my own experience at Stelp & Leighton London. After interview and contact recommendations, Subodh Joglekor, Udayan Sen, Sujit Dutta, Samir Dasgupta, Sankar Narayan, and Chadrasekhar were initially picked up, who were later joined by Ravi Chopra and Anees at the near end of my tenure. They were posted between the Calcutta, Bombay, and Delhi offices. They were all encouraged to enroll in the Institute of Chartered Shipbrokers, London, exams. We also considered giving them London Shipping Market exposure through our Associates through a reciprocal exchange arrangement.

Apart from David Bruce's chartering business, we could also tie up a valuable London associate at H. Clarkson & Co., one of the largest shipping consultants and brokers in the shipping world, for S&P and chartering at Swapan Da's initiative. Clarkson was very keen on the emerging Indian shipping industry, particularly project developments and S&P market harnessing. John Wheeler Clarkson, MD, was a very knowledgeable and dynamic professional, and we worked well to develop our strong image in Indian shipping consultancy and S&P projects, even to the extent of servicing Indian port infrastructure through innovative projects. Young David Penn was sent by John to our Calcutta office to work with us on projects involving consultancy, S&P, Port, and IWT projects.

Sinclair Freight & Chartering's brand image in the Indian shipping industry was soaring, and we were approached by many big industrial houses that were considering foray into the Indian shipping industry. Swapan Da was ever-ready to explore uncharted territory, and I was encouraged to pursue my diversified interests and connections in IWT, port, and river infrastructure development. In Calcutta Port, although Kalyan Mitter-Manik Da was no more, my bonding with Suniti Bhose, Robin Roy, Pama Roy, Tikku, P. N. Sen, and others continued. One of my old friends, Manab Pal from London Shipping Days, who was working for SCI, left SCI and established contact with the Nepal Royal family to start the Royal Nepal Shipping Corporation as an independent conference member in the UK-Continent liner trade.

In spite of raising the eyebrows of three prominent Indian players in this trade, Manab, with his astute shipping knowledge and craft, ensured the entry of RNSC into the conference as a national shipping line. During my Bremen days in shipping, I had the privilege of befriending Col. Helm, owner of the famous Hansa Line in Germany, and after returning to Calcutta, I met the trusted custodian of Hansa business in India, Mr. Sunil Baran Roy, in his large Hansa Line Calcutta office. Sunil Da liked me instantly, for divine reasons. Purnima and I got very closely attached to Sunil Da's family, and we were never allowed to say no to attending any of his many parties at home or onboard Hansa Vessels in port since then.

I came to learn about Manab Pal's RNSC story from Sunil Da. Sunil Da introduced Manab to Hansa management to capture additional market share of high-freighted India/UK-Cont trade by allowing RNSC to use Hansa vessels on some kind of internal charter arrangement. Manab was given office space for RNSC in Hansa's office and marketing support for trade development by Hansa until RNSC acquired vessels under their ownership. Manab, from his SCI days, had the reputation of a fun-loving bachelor, and his allotted SCI bachelor's flat on Rowland Road was notorious for rowdy entertainment parties. He was very smart and convincing in his marketing guises. I met Manab in his RNSC Calcutta office on Brabourne Road, along with David Penn. He gave us a warm reception and laid out before us the big ship acquisition plan of RNSC in the presence of S. B. Roy.

He had already helped the Nepal Royal family set up the RNSC head office in Kathmandu, and adequate Royal family funds had been allocated for buying 5/6 suitable liner vessels during the next 12/18 months, not only for servicing the UK-Cont conference pool with Hansa holding hands but also to claim a slice of other conference liner trade routes like the USA, Far East, etc. as the rightful share of Nepal as an independent landlocked country. Through Hansa's support to Manab with one of their liner vessels on charter, he was able to secure full load booking for the inaugural voyage from Calcutta only, even before the formal acceptance of RNSC in the cargo pool.

I could see his ploy for rate-cutting without any pool obligation to fill up his vessel. He was to visit London and Bremen with his vessel acquisition plans, and Hansa, with their experience and expertise, was always to be his techno-commercial support. He agreed to give us an introduction to his RNSC Kathmandu Royal family owners and encouraged us to visit Nepal to cement a strong shipping consulting relationship between Clarkson-Sinclair and RNSC. Sunil Da praised him as a very aggressive and knowledgeable young shipping professional and young David was thoroughly impressed. I was also impressed, but with some knowledge about his background and nature, my mind was looking for flaws in his game plan. Back in the office, David sent out a report of our RNSC meeting to his bosses in Clarkson, London, where he mentioned, in connection with Manab's London visit, that rumor has it that "Manab Pal is a fun-loving bachelor."

Swapan Da and Kersi insisted that I visit Kathmandu with David Penn for first-hand verification of the project status, as they could find some doubts in my mind. After a few further interactions with Manab, it was decided that Manab would visit London after sailing out of the vessel on her inaugural voyage. He introduced us to the RNSC Royal family owners, and a meeting date was fixed in their office, which I preferred instead of meeting in the hotel. There were three people, including a Royal Family member, who welcomed us into their office and were eager listeners to our backgrounds and narration of the RNSC acquisition plan and development story as we heard from Manab. They frankly admitted that they had no experience in shipping and were totally dependent on Manab's professional experience and expertise.

They were lucky to have a tie-up with Hansa Line and would consider investing in ship purchases after doing a few successful voyages with Hansa's vessels initially. We could not dig out any banking details or business plans with ship purchase financing planning, as all these were confidential and not to be divulged without Manab's consent. Young David was satisfied with this stand, but I was not. Meanwhile, Manab was given royal treatment in the Clarkson office, and they were very impressed with his shipping knowledge and development growth plan for RNSC. After about a little over one month from sailing out of the Hansa Vessel from India, I was advised by Sunil Da that after the collection of full freight, Manab had packed up the RNSC Calcutta office, and Hansa was left with the vessel and cargo to complete the voyage formalities at their own expense.

During around 5–6 weeks of training for David Penn in Calcutta, I gave him exposure to ship financing and ship management exercises, which I was always doing for my clients as a consultant. I also introduced him to one of my senior Calcutta Port Trust friend and mentor, Robin Roy. As I mentioned earlier, Robin Roy was a very knowledgeable port officer who was a lead member of the Haldia Port planning team. He was a man of dreams and visions for the integrated development of Indian port infrastructure as a multimodal cargo transport network with links to the sea, river, road, and rail. He had a British wife, a delightful lady with wits and poise, and we often met socially at Calcutta Club for pure *adda*.

He found in me an ardent learner and listener of his dreams and visions, with active participation. We were discussing mechanization of cargo handling in port to cut down on port stay of the vessels, unitization of cargo pallets and packaging, innovative customized ships and barge designs to optimize cost and supply chain logistics, dredging and building of deep sea port infrastructure, etc. This intense learning in my early few years in Indian shipping was of great value to me during my later days. Young David participated in a few of our longish discussions in the Calcutta Port office, sometimes extending till very late evenings. Watching him, I thought this would help our building bridge with a strong Clarkson Consultancy and R&D team in the future.

During this time Robin Roy introduced me to an American old man in the shipping profession, Gordon Duke, who was in Calcutta interacting with Calcutta port and CIWTC for lightening PL 480 grain vessels at Sandheads through excavator machines on board capable of giving reasonably high discharging cadence for over-side transfer of cargo from the mother vessels to barges and relatively small lighter vessels. There was berthing congestion in Calcutta Port those days due to the substantial volume of food grain imports by the Indian government. I already narrated my Ratnakar day's participation in this trade with chartered foreign vessels, although I skipped my handling experience of these vessels in Calcutta port to secure priority berthing with suggested innovative methods and assistance from my friends in Calcutta port. There was no Sandheads' clause in Transchart C P, and it was very important to get the vessels brought up to Garden Reach anchorage by the River Pilots so that vessels were within port limits and NOR could be served on Charterer's Agents by the vessel for lay-time counting.

Barring a few, most of the Ratnakar Chartered vessels avoided the impact of Sandhead's congestion, and we stopped chartering when the bunching of vessels became significant and unavoidable. Even after the introduction of the Sandheads clause in the charter party later, lightening operations at Sandheads during the calm winter months were explored to ease port congestion and mitigate waiting for the owners. Naresh Kotak of J. M. Baxi had almost a monopoly over most of the grain-carrying Greek vessels. I befriended him to assist Gordon with his machines, CIWTC barges, and lighters to do a good volume of lightening business. Sinclair could secure a reasonable volume of short-term charter business by fixing daughter vessels for lightening. Capt. Okha of Everett Shipping and Gopal Bose of E.C. Bose Co. were my close friends and allies in this operation for finding suitable daughter vessels and cargo handling operations at Sandheads and Saga.

Ship-owners under J. M. Baxi Agency filed a huge demurrage claim against Transchart and FCI, which the Government of India refused to entertain as they were not obliged to accept a Notice of Readiness until the vessels were within the port limit at Garden Reach. Owners argued that it was the charterer's responsibility to bring the vessels in, and demurrage would have to be paid if they failed, as owners were left without any option but to wait. A group of shipowners under the J. M. Baxi Agency filed arbitration proceedings against the government importer FCI. Govt. of India's London Solicitors, Stocken & Co.—if I remember the name correctly—it was Mr. D'Silva who was handling the case. He came to India seeking help from a knowledgeable chartering consultant and met S. N. Banerjee (alias Aku) in Transchart along with FCI officers.

The case was to be heard at the New York District Court in the later part of 1971, and Akuda requested that I assist the government as an expert witness in court. Sinclair was doing substantial Transchart chartering with David Bruce. The James Felton (D.B.)/Bal Vashist (Sinclair) combination worked very effectively. Both Swapan Da and Kersi agreed to my taking this government consultancy assignment with no cost to Sinclairs for my travel, stay, and allowances for my nearly two-week stay in New York. Mr. D'Silva came to Calcutta and briefed me with papers. After a good study of the papers, I took him to Calcutta Port, DMD Capt. Prem Batra, to seek his help in giving expert evidence on Calcutta Port's inability to bring those vessels down the rivers for various complicated riverine technical reasons, despite FCI Agents repeated requests to bring the vessels into the port.

Capt. Batra agreed to join the team for New York court proceedings, and we were booked at the Sheraton Hotel for the entire period of 15 days. Naresh Kotak was there as the opponent's principal witness. We structured the case on the premise that port pilots provided owners with an estimated waiting time based on calling priority. According to the governing Charter Party and Carriage of Goods by Sea Act, owners had the discretion to decide whether to proceed to the nearest port for cargo discharge and sail out. This decision aimed to mitigate losses, as owners were fully aware of the Charter Party obligation to be within port limits before tendering and accepting NOR. Based on my legal interpretation and Prem Batra's evidence from the Calcutta port pilot side, which lasted almost 10 days of hearings of examinations in chief and cross-examinations, the government succeeded in avoiding any demurrage payment.

Mr. Pranab Sen, the legendary CP of the Calcutta Police, joined Sinclair as Chairman of the Board in 1970. He had a delightfully positive personality, and I enjoyed his very special affection and appreciation for my shipping knowledge and dynamic, positive approach to deal-making. We were enjoying our excellent teamwork as a close-knit family, and Sinclair became enviably cash-rich during my three-year tenure with them until the end of 1972. Swapan Da committed investment in supporting my shipping project for owning and operating vessels with a business plan for long-term scaling with the implementation of various port and shipping-related innovative logistic projects. I projected 10-year financials with IRR and ROI. Phase-wise target milestones with equity investment and self-generation were planned with frugal starting capital and an optimal mix of owned and chartered tonnages. Swapan Da agreed to offer me sweat equity, fifty percent of my family holdings in the venture, and full freedom to run the venture as the CEO for my dream realization. Pranab Da and Kersi were parties to this discussion when our business was flourishing.

I was impressed with Swapan Da offering me shares in the company to give me a feeling of ownership. I also got a formal award with reasonable money as the outstanding "Shipping Consultant and S&P Broker" from the management. I was enthused to give my best entrepreneurial initiative for growth and development, with a target focus on my Indian shipping industry dream realization.

I befriended Capt Bill of Andaman Shipping Line operating single ship service between Calcutta- Port Blair and introduced to him Mr Narasimhan of Heaur Trading Madras through my Consultancy services to both for an amalgamated Shipping project Heaur Shipping Lines and sold two small Ships. Sinclair Bombay office was also doing well in tonnage chartering of most of the leading Ship-owners and doing substantial Shipping Consultancy and limited S&P activities with Clarkson support and cashing on their International reputation. Subodh Joglekar was sent out to London to have exposure and training both with David Bruce and Clarksons for a reasonably long span of time. This was the time when me and BalVashist had a major difference of opinion with Swapan Da when he decided to cut off relationship with David Bruce for Transchart Business and have Clarkson in their place for Transchart business servicing. Our Delhi office was always giving us maximum revenue through fixing of Greek vessels where my friend James Felton and David Bruce had excellent market hold. Swapan Da felt Clarkson with their size and International image as one of the largest Shipping Consultant and Broker would have much larger outreach for tonnage support if they could be convinced to invest in Delhi Transchart panel broking as Sinclair Associate. We already had R S Plateu as our Oslo, Norway Associate. They were also big name in International Shipping. We had other Associates in New York, Hong Kong, Singapore etc but none of them were as effective as David Bruce in Transchart business. I explained to Swapan Da that principal reason for this was that most of the reputed Shipowner clients of these big broking houses were focused on custom built vessels for servicing long term International cargo servicing with standard charter parties and compatible conventional clauses equitably balanced between owners and charterers. Both Time Charter Parties and Voyage C Ps were found to have clauses leaning towards owners or the charterers but shipbrokers' (owners as well as charterers) after fixing main terms negotiated balancing by introducing clauses as addendum. Executed proforma CPs between reputed owners and charterers were often mentioned as 'per executed proforma with necessary modification' in negotiating main terms. Transchart Standard CP was non-negotiable grossly tilting in charterer's favor. This was not acceptable to the reputed international Ship-owners. There were limited owners under mostly Greek tonnages who developed expertise in Transchart business. We could not convince Swapan Da to change his mind and he went to London personally to do the change by convincing John Wheeler of Clarkson. Ultimately this decision proved disastrous for the company. Kersi agreed with my views but was dwarfed by Swapan da. Kersi was not as aggressive and sharp as Swapan Da but was a conservative broker with honesty and integrity ever willing to admit and learn from his mistakes. I will narrate one incident where Kersi and I went to Ramesh Maheswari's residence at Trivoli Court in connection with an S&P deal involving sale of Ratna Chandralekha of Ratnakar to ISS. At that time ISS was in take over process by KK Birla group and we went to negotiate and arrive at a price agreement. From Buyer's side we offered a very reasonable price and Ramesh tried to use his ego centric marketing skill to give us an inflated value of the overage vessel by emphasizing why the vessel should be treated at par with any modern vessel always mentioning 'Probir will know the vessel better than anybody else.' Ultimately we came to no agreement and Kersi got up to leave and went up to the door to find me still sitting. I requested Kersi to wait and advised Ramesh why I considered our offered price reasonable from my knowledge of the vessel's condition and diminishing market demand for such vessel in coming years. Finally I convinced Ramesh to accept our price offer and the sale was completed. Coming out Kersi smilingly congratulated me and jokingly mentioned 'two of us must not come together for meeting clients in future.'

Within the first-quarter of 1971, my comprehensive shipping project report with 10-year projections, vessel acquisitions, ancillary support port development, and IWT projects with collaboration links and financials was fully ready and given to the Sinclair Board for investment consideration. Frugal start-up equity capital was proposed based on 6:1 debt equity to qualify for the Shipping Development Fund Committee (SDFC) and bank support. Revenue generation from the deployment of the vessels in the bulk tramp market, both for period contracts and spot market fixing, specific liner services, project-oriented barge services for riverine linking, etc., was on the 10-year road map for scaling and growth of the venture. If I remember correctly, we were actively pursuing a jute import project for the Jute Mills Association members from Bangladesh and East Pakistan before the Bangladesh War in collaboration with Bhagwan Kotak of J. M. Baxi and Khargu Singh of Eastern Navigation. This was from Narayangunge to Calcutta, which was successfully completed before the Bangladesh War. There was adequate fund generation for the company, and my shipping project start-up equity demand was within Rs. 30 lacs. Swapan Dasgupta had a one-to-one meeting with me and informed me that management is impressed with the shipping project and the board has to decide whether to take an investment plunge either in the shipping industry or diversify into the hotel industry as per an attractive proposal received from a hotel management consultant who has been interacting with Swapan Da on this project for some time.

In either case, there would be an independent corporate management entity to be run under the Sinclair Board with a full-time CEO and management team. I was to accept a paid CEO assignment without any equity commitment. I reminded Swapan Da that this was a departure from his earlier commitment, based on which I had worked on a holistic team building on a happy family platform to make Sinclair Freight & Chartering investment and management ready for entering the Indian shipping industry with a long-term industry development mission with global outreach. For this, my plan was not only to go for an IPO after the first few years of operation but also to encourage the equity participation of key personnel with a sense of ownership in the growth and development of the planned project. Somehow or another Swapan Da was inclined to go for the hotel project and asked me to wait for a second-phase investment opportunity. My strong argument that hotel investment will make the 'very successful shipping consultant' image of Sinclairs completely defocused did not cut much ice with Swapan Da.

I was disappointed and separately discussed this outcome with Chairman Pranab Sen and Kersi Dastur. Both of them agreed with my view but were too shy to seriously protest Swapan Da's decision. Pranab Da was always very affectionate to me and appreciative of my shipping knowledge and innovative initiatives. He was also a close friend of my bachelor uncle, Mr. Arun Mitter, and was playing tennis with my uncle at Calcutta South Club. Pranab Da gave me parental advice to look for an investor to pursue my shipping dream, even if this means parting company with Sinclairs.

As a working professional in my early 30's, I was in a predicament to find an angel capital investor who would fully trust me to implement my dream shipping project as per the DPR already drawn. Mr. Gopal Bose of E. C. Bose & Co. was not only a business friend when working with Capt. Okha of Everett Shipping and Mr. Gordon Duke for the Sandhead/Sagar Lightening Project, as I already narrated, but also both Bose and Mitra families were closely related. Capt. Okha suggested I meet Gopal Da to explore investment. When I met him, he heard in detail about my shipping project and long-term dream and instantly committed to investing. I was surprised that he did not find it necessary to get my project report examined by any reputed shipping consultant firm and advised me to go ahead with the initial equity within Rs. 20 lacs and assured me that if I and the Mitra family wish to take 50% equity, he will give me time to mobilize such funds by laying out the initial upfront.

My bond with Gopal Da since then became intimate and strong, as this remarkable businessman in the stevedoring profession with a strong heritage and almost 16 years older than me is full of affection and humor. He had no ego or vanity to openly accept his lack of intricate shipping knowledge. In his own humorous expression, he called himself *Coolir Sardar*—a labor supplier for ship cargo handling. My own dada, Salil Mittra, was an electrical engineer and was the promoter of an engineering enterprise, Samal Harand & Co., which he was very successfully running with a factory at Bondel Road in the early 1960s. In 1971, he was facing labor trouble and lockdown in his factory, starting with left-wing regimes coming into power for the first time in the late 1960s. He was badly run down on his cash reserves. He was fretting at home, with tension and worries impacting his mental and physical health. I spoke to him about my shipping project and the commitment I got from Gopal Da for a Bose and Mitra family shipping venture under my leadership to drive the project.

Dada was a start-up entrepreneur as an electrical engineer, and at that moment of crisis, he expressed his keenness to be a part of the proposal, although he had no shipping knowledge or resources to invest at that time. He was skeptical about Gopal Da laying out the upfront fund and not honoring his commitment later when we were ready to take our 50% share. He suggested we somehow mobilize 25-30% of the paid-up equity through about 15-20% sweat equity for me as promoter and consultant fees and mobilize another 15-20% within our family. My father encouraged me to start the venture, and he was confident of mobilizing the entire 50% through his friends and contacts, even if we could not mobilize the funds immediately within our family. Between my father, uncle, dada, Sejda-Malay, and I, we could mobilize Rs. 3.5 lacs, and my father was confident of mobilizing the balance of Rs. 6.5 lacs from his close friends outside the family. Dada and I went to Gopal Da with this capital structure proposal. Gopal Da did not agree to any outside participation beyond the Bose and Mitra family and suggested we keep the initial paid-up capital at Rs. 10 lacs instead of Rs. 20 lacs and agreed to contribute the balance of Rs. 10 lacs as interest-free working capital in the company.

We registered Himalaya Shipping Co. in 1971 as a Pvt. Ltd. company with an initial start-up equity of Rs. 10 lacs and the intention to go public 4–5 years after acquiring at least two vessels in our fleet. It was to be a very frugal and challenging tightrope operation with a ship financing arrangement for acquiring two second-hand vessels within the first two years for starting a Calcutta-West Asia Gulf liner service where a reasonably large market comprising of high-freighted general cargo like tea, jute, timber, glass, C-I goods, etc. was being serviced by a conference comprising members like SCI, Scindia, South East Asia Shipping, Malabar Line, Irano-Hind.

In 1971, I was still with Sinclair and decided to continue with Sinclair for Himalaya's first two vessel purchases through the Sinclair broking channel. This was to give Sinclair consultancy and S&P profile apart from adding Himalaya to their client list. During this period, the Himalaya Board was to have Gopal Bose and B S Bose as two directors from the Bose family, and Dada and my uncle Arun Mitter from the Mitra family until I formally joined as CEO after quitting Sinclair. Fortunately, I could negotiate and finalize the purchase of a small single-decker geared vessel of 3500 DWT at a very cheap price of USD 200000, equivalent to less than Rs. 20 lacs at the prevailing exchange rate at that time.

The vessel was under HSBC Mortgage from the previous owner, and it was an auction sale from HSBC, which Clarkson secured for the buyer. Mr. K. V. Rammurty was the Chief Manager of Indian Bank, operating from their Brabourne Road Office and looking after the entire Eastern Zone. He was a very dynamic and aggressive banker, and I introduced to him many of my shipping consultancy clients. By the grace of Thakur, Ma, and Swamiji, he developed strong faith and respect for me, and we always enjoyed our soul-raising spiritual discussions on Thakur, Ma, Swamiji, and Vedanta philosophy, often at his residence near Bengal Club. He found my shipping project DPR and long-term vision for the Indian shipping industry interesting, and apart from processing and sending my proposal to his head office in Madras for sanctioning a foreign exchange loan at a competitive labor plus interest rate, he arranged a special meeting for me with his CMD, Mr. Laxminarayan when he was on a visit to Calcutta. Our loan was instantly sanctioned with some collateral security backing.

In the meantime, I could convince my erstwhile Ratnakar colleague T. S. Shiva to join Himalayas as operations manager and Mr. Madhusudan Sarkar as engineer superintendent. Gopal Da got Capt. Savigny, an elderly, experienced British Mariner, to join us as Marine Super. Initially, we started office operations from our Elgin Road residence, using Dada's office room and our ground-floor hall for the first few months, until we moved out to our 18 Brabourne Road office at the PNB Building. Dada and Gopal Da were joint managing directors. We finalized the purchase of the first vessel for the Himalayas in the 2nd quarter of 1972 from my Sinclair Desk, and after completing all S&P documentation by Clarkson-Sinclair, the vessel was scheduled for delivery in Hong Kong in November 1972.

Capt. Sengupta was working for E.C. Bose stevedoring at the time, and we sent him with a full Indian crew and officers to take delivery of the vessels and bring them to Calcutta to load them for her maiden voyage to the West Asia Gulf ports of Dubai and Kuwait. Symbolic of climbing the first peak of the Himalayan venture, we named the vessel 'Nanda Devi.' We appointed Walem Shipping Hong Kong, a very reputed ship management, agency, and brokerage firm, as our agent. Mr. M. Sircar, our engineer, selected a senior chief engineer for the vessel while he himself went with the crew for the delivery voyage. All three of us—Gopal Da, Dada, and me—went to take delivery of our first vessel to Hong Kong. We took delivery of the vessel after dry docking and bottom inspection and were very ably supported by our agent, Walem Shipping.

This delivery saga will remain incomplete if I do not narrate an interesting experience with a Chinese ship chandler who was appointed by our agent to stuff the vessel with stores and provisions. After taking formal delivery of the vessel, we were introduced to this ship by Capt. Sengupta and our agent in the captain's cabin presented a very comprehensive quotation covering a total list of the vessel's stores and provision requirements amounting to a little over USD 60k.

Agents highly recommended him as a very resourceful and experienced party. Although the captain and the agents found their quotation reasonable, we felt this was very high and wanted to check with a few other parties independently. I took the quotation and asked him to see me at my hotel in the evening. Both Dada and Gopal Da left the matter with me to handle. After checking with a few other parties through my Sinclair contacts, I was convinced that the figure was highly overloaded. I discussed this with Dada and Gopal Da, and Gopal Da felt we should negotiate for a price reduction of 15/20%, and it would be unwise to upset a big agent like Walem by introducing any other supplier outside their panel. We were all convinced that there was a fat cutback for agents and captains in the price. The Chinese guy came to my hotel room and invited us for big entertainment and offered a 10% reduction in the total invoice without my asking. He enthusiastically highlighted the confidence he enjoys in Walem. I asked him bluntly if we bring in another supplier, how much commission this new party will be required to pay to the agent and the captain of the vessel?

The Chinese guy was visibly acting to not divulge his cards. He said to honor requests from his first time owners customer, he would discount up to 20%. I offered lumsum USD 15K against his little over USD 60K quotes. He almost fell from his chair and requested me to be reasonable, admitting that in his business it is customary to satisfy agents and captains, and in this case, the captain's demand was big. Finally, after horse trading, we settled at USD 25k on my confirming the order on his invoice and my assurance that the next morning we shall be present on board to ensure that there will be no difficulty in his getting the receipt challan signed. Gopal Da and Dada could hardly believe this, and I narrated my earlier experience in Ratnakar with Aziz & Co. in Calcutta port. Savings of Rs. 4 lacs for our frugal start-up capital were huge in our bootstrapping operation. Gopal Da was amazed at Capt. Sengupta doing such a deal, but apart from springing a surprise on the captain, we restrained from expressing any emotion.

Nanda Devi had Capt. Arnab Sen as Master on her maiden voyage to the West Asia Gulf, primarily with the steel billets of my friend Surendra Pal of APJ and Tea of G Randerian, plus some general cargo of C.I. Goods and Gunny. We were operating service outside the West Asia Gulf Conference, and my friend, Mr. M. K. Tanna of Malabar Lines, assisted me a lot in cargo mobilization. I picked up D. K. Choudhury from APJ to assist Shiva. Ashis Mitra (Babul) from TT stable was also picked up to join the Himalayas. Dada's friend Bula Da and his charter accountant firm were assisting us in all financial matters. Our uncle, Mr. Ajit Mitra of Solicitors Firm Bose & Mitra, was assisting us in all legal matters. We could collect reasonably decent freight for Nanda Devi's first voyage, but the vessel experienced problems with the generator on her return ballast voyage to Calcutta. After temporary repairs, we could send out the vessel for her second voyage. However, realizing the vulnerability without the import and replacement of particular spare machinery, we had to place an order for the supply of these parts from the manufacturer's branch center in Singapore. The additional freight collection helped us meet our cash drainage for these supply and repair bills, but it was very tightrope walking.

In the meantime, I was negotiating with Ramesh Maheswari for the purchase of their vessel Ratna Manjushree, a 10,000 DWT twin-decker vessel over 15 years old that was due for a special survey in 1974. Our engineer, Mr. Sircar, knew the vessel well, serving as chief engineer of the vessel under Ratnakar. Mr. Sircar, after inspection of the vessel, gave a report that, as per the class record of the vessel, special survey expenses should not exceed Rs. 20 lacs with a 3–4 week lay-up time for the vessel. The market valuation of the vessel after SS was nearly Rs. 1 crore. I could finalize the purchase on 'as is condition' for delivery at Calcutta in March 1973 at Rs. 30 lacs.

Mr. Rammurthi from the Indian bank side financed the vessel with a 20% margin and mortgaged the ship to the bank without any further collateral. We obtained the necessary DG Shipping approval for the change of name and the ownership of the vessel for global operation. While I concluded this deal as my last S&P performance under Sinclair, I parted company with Sinclair and joined Himalayas full-time as CEO and Executive Director/Permanent Invitee on the Board. Dada and my uncle continued to be represented on the board from the Mitra family side. We named the vessel 'Gouri Shankar,' another peak of the Himalayas, and fixed her maiden voyage under the Himalayas from Calcutta to Port Sudan with full-load jute contract cargo. The vessel was to load over-side Gunny Bales presented from Jute Mills by barges.

We planned to complete loading in 10 days and sail out. Unfortunately, our trial time started after taking delivery of Gouri Shankar. First, our Engineer Super got the vessel involved in unforeseen repairs and messed up with two or three Marine Engineering firms, delaying the readiness of the vessel to start loading. Ultimately, Mr. Sircar resigned and left us in the middle of a mess. By the grace of Thakur, Ma, and Swamiji, I could find and line up Mr. S. N Roy at this juncture, an extraordinarily competent engineer with administrative and leadership skills who was to remain my lifelong friend and shipping industry colleague later. SNR controlled the repair situation with astute handling and made the vessel load-ready in 7 days. He brought in his friend Debanshu Rakshit as Chief Engineer for the vessel, who was a super-efficient senior engineer with a spiritual mindset. Through the introduction of my Sejda (Malay Mitter) from his Shalimar Paints Marine Paints supply connection, we could rope in another spiritually splurged Master Mariner, Capt. Vijay Barve, as Captain of Gouri Shankar.

After loading almost 90% of our Port Sudan cargo and even issuing B/L at the request of some of the shippers within the next 5–6 days, we got a surprise requisition notice from DG Shipping, Mr. Gopalan Nair, on the vessel for coastal coal loading to meet the urgent requirement of TNEB Madras. I went to Bombay to personally explain to him that we purchased the vessel with DG clearance for a global operation license, which was the vessel's earlier status under Ratnakar ownership, and we were already 90% loaded with our Port Sudan export cargo, which was also an important export promotion for the nation with foreign exchange earnings. He bluntly stated that as a new shipping line, we were indulgent in unhealthy freight rebating to take away already booked cargo from an established national line, and we must unload the cargo and place the vessel for coastal coal loading. He made me aware of his power under the Merchant Shipping Act to requisition a vessel to meet an emergency government requirement. In this case, TNEB is a government power supply entity. All my arguments and pleading failed to cut ice, and finally, as the last stroke of his vendetta, he issued instructions to Calcutta Customs and port authorities not to give port clearance for the vessel to sail out. After coming to my wit's end to make him see reason and equity, I decided to complete the loading of the vessel and seek the intervention of Shipping Secretary Mr. Pimputkar in Delhi to resolve this. All my seniors in the shipping industry, like Mr. Gokuldas and N. M. Trivedi of Scindia, N. K. Sen, and P. K. Mullik of ISS, had sympathy for my predicament but were skeptical about our new company's ability to fight government ruling due to unequal power and sustenance capacity. I always suspected S. K. Sen of SCI and his artificial statements of concern. Dada and Gopal Da's confidence level was very shaken. I assured them that Thakur Ramakrishna is holding my hand to fight this gross injustice and vindictive behavior of Gopalan Nair, and the truth will prevail even if it means going to court against the government to challenge the Merchant Shipping Act. I saw a glimpse of hope in my initial interaction with Secretary Shipping when he gave me a patient hearing and accepted that injustice had been done. He called Gopalan Nair to Delhi and chided him in my presence saying that it was unjust and unfair for him to interfere with the commercial decision-making of any private ship-owner. However, in his final verdict, he found fault with my arrogance in defying the government order and gave me a penal condition to do two coastal voyages before starting global operations as per the vessel's trading license. I pleaded that the vessel was already loaded and ready to sail out, and I would be happy to do two coastal voyages after completing this voyage to honor his verdict. He was not ready to budge, and that made me lose my calm when I told him in an agitated voice that he was respected by me as an honest and fair IAS officer, and I thought he had practical ship operation knowledge, but his ridiculous verdict was giving me doubt about this. I also said I was not left with much option but to go to the court for justice and order against such whimsical behavior from government officers. Mr. Pimputkar shrugged his shoulders and said, "The government will have to obey court orders in that case." I expressed my concern that the government would carry vendetta against me and my start-up company to hinder our growth and development. He replied instantly by saying that, on the contrary, the government would hold me in high esteem if I proved the government wrong, and he would be the first person to congratulate me. There was some sincere honesty on his face, which made me trust him intuitively.

Back in Calcutta from Delhi, I found the vessel had completed loading and was already waiting for a couple of days. On the same evening, our uncle, Mr. Ajit Mitra, solicitor, took us to his friend, Senior Barrister R. C. Deb, and I was ready with my full brief. R. C. Deb was also my former president of the Bengal Table Tennis Association and had both affection and respect for me. He opined we needed to move a fundamental right petition under Sec. 226 challenging the use of the requisition power of the government on unreasonable grounds. He suggested we go to Somnath Chatterjee to move an aggressive, strongly drafted petition emphasizing the urgency for an order on DG Shipping to withdraw their unjust and illegal intervention on our fundamental right, which was causing delay and waiting for a loaded vessel in the port, incurring huge losses to the company. Somnath Da was Dada's class friend and our close family friend. He involved our cousin, Barrister Anindya Mitra, as his junior to draft a strong petition and moved the matter to

Justice Sambhu Ghose's court on the original side within 24 hours. The Somnath Da-Anindya Da combination was lethal, and although senior counsel Sankardas Banerjee was holding a brief from the government side, we got an order in our favor in the trial court when the government went on appeal at the joint bench of Chief Justice Sankar Prasad Mitra and Justice Sabyasachi Mukherjee.

Somnath Da was to go to Delhi for the parliament session and could not appear for the appeal hearing. At his advice, we requested R. C. Deb (Sona Da) to kindly appear for us at the Appeal Division Bench. Justice Ghose's order was upheld by the joint bench, and we could sail out of 'Gouri Shankar' within the next 48 hours after completing all clearance formalities. I was pleasantly surprised when Assistant DG Mr. D. N. Phool, who was present in the court, very warmly congratulated me and gave wholehearted cooperation with customs and port for expediting the sailing of our vessel. He confidentially endorsed my decision to send one of our junior officers to Bombay with the court order and paste it on Mr. Gopalon Nayar's chamber door. This was somewhat childish, but after getting a feel for the senior DG Officers' thoughts on the whimsical decisions of Gopalon Nayar, I felt encouraged to take such action.

There was great relief and joy in our office, and apart from genuine encouragement from my seniors in shipping like Mr. Gokul Das of Scindia, N.K. Sen of ISS, Vasant Seth of Great Eastern, etc. I was flooded with congratulatory phone calls from all in the industry as this order brought change to the Merchant Shipping Act.

These delays of over 20 days had a very adverse impact on our company's cash flow and profitability. Our frugal capital bootstrapping was strained to its bones. Thakur's blessings flowed incessantly through my friend, Mr. Rammurthi of Indian Bank, by way of working capital support beyond our originally sanctioned limit. Gouri Shankar returned to Calcutta after loading rock phosphate at the Aqaba Port of the Red Sea for two ports on the east coast of India, with the second port discharge ending in Calcutta. Although we had reasonably good freight revenue generation from the round-trip voyage, our ultimate profitability suffered due to the long initial wait. We did one short coastal coal voyage as SNR was considering sending the vessel for special survey dry docking and repair at the Hindustan Shipyard, Vizag, before putting her in our regular West Asia Gulf liner service. The cost and time estimate for this was Rs. 25 lacs and 3 weeks duration layup. Gopal Da and Dada were hesitant to take this decision because of our fund shortage, but I took the plunge as per the SNR recommendation, depending on my friend Mr. Rammurthi's hope and assurance that, based on our 6-month financial projections from the operation of the vessel after SS and repair, he would be able to convince his management to give us a 6- or 9-month short-term loan of Rs. 30 lacs. Following the saying, "when it rains, it pours," our other vessel, Nandadevi, was also experiencing technical issues that were impacting our operational profitability. In consultation with SNR and Debanshu Rakshit, I decided to lay up the vessel at Mazagon Shipyard, Bombay, for 7 days, committing another Rs. 7 lacs in cost estimates as indicated by SNR. I was confident that with Rs. 30 lacs in loan finance and good trade support from our West Asia Gulf service, we should be able to get both vessels repaired and conditioned for providing monthly scheduled liner service and earning market confidence for reliability.

Gopal Da and Dada by this time became familiar with my faith-driven optimism for our company's growth and progress despite the hassles and hurdles in our challenging pathway. We were committed to pursue our dream realization with frugal start-up capital and tightrope walking on Bootstrapped finance management. My unflinching faith in Thakur Sri Ramakrishna and my unwavering belief that Thakur is holding my hands to make a mark in the shipping industry made me see many apparent miracles in life to validate this spiritual splurge in my being. My experience of adversities was all accepted as divine design for the good of my elevated existence and my detached karma for large canvas dream realization.

In this turbulent time of trials and tribulations, for some unknown reason, I was experiencing a vibrant spiritual current of bliss and peace in my being to lessen my tension and stress and inspire hope and optimism. In the shipping circle, my dada was addressed as 'Dada' for all, and only Gopal Da affectionately addressed me as Chordada.

In early 1974, when both of our vessels were in repair yards and I was frantically pursuing our short-term loan application with Indian Bank, Gopal Da asked in Dada's presence, What will happen if the loan application gets turned down? Did I not feel there was at least a 10% chance of this happening? I promptly replied that there was more than a 10% chance of this happening, and I would consider such an event as per divine design for something better than this for our long-term good. Gopal Da said he wished he could have such faith and mentioned that miracles like the Gouri Shankar court case victory were not often repeated. Dada felt even if we got the loan, it would be difficult to repay this within six months, as trade support to fill up a vessel of Gouri Shankar size under a non-conference line like us would be a daunting task.

During the later part of Gouri Shankar's repair completion time at Hindusthan Shipyard, SNR camped himself at Vizag to supervise the wrap-up of vessel repairs and the cost review of all repairs. It took less than 3 weeks to complete SS and repair, and SNR negotiated with Hindusthan Shipyard management to get the vessel released on payment of Rs. 18 lacs against their submitted invoice of nearly Rs. 25 lacs and pay the balance within the next 15 days after scrutiny and final settlement of their invoice. It was sometime in early March 1974, when 1975 World TT was just allotted to Calcutta. I went to Mr. Rammurthy with the hope of loan sanction and fund release. His Chief Zonal Manager office at Indian Bank was near the Gariahat Kwality restaurant. I found him genuinely sad and depressed to tell me that our loan application had been turned down by his head office. He was looking more worried than me about finding some way to bail me out. I was talking spiritually to thank Thakur for giving me a friend and well-wisher like him and said Thakur's divine intervention would surely come if I was on the right path. I will never forget in my life his words when he said, "Mr. Mitra, you are a face of divine faith to me, and that is solid security." When I left his office, he came down with me, chatted till my car came, and said my faith would pull me out of this trouble as I got in the car. I was emotionally moved, and his empathy was filling up my mental space to sidetrack my acute, immediate problem. Gopal Da and Dada were anxiously waiting in the office, and when I broke the disturbing news, they were helplessly upset. Gopal Da, as an expression of his anguish, said, "Do you still feel this setback is for our good?" Before I answered, Dada asked Gopal Da if he could arrange a private loan from his sources. Gopal Da chuckled and said a few lacs may be arranged, but mobilizing Rs. 30 lacs and that too within such a short time span would be practically impossible. My mind was still filled with Mr. Rammurthi's face, seeking sourcing solutions from the trade while silently listening. When Dada finally stated, "Probir, we all respect your faith and dynamism, but for running a shipping company, we are hopelessly short in our capital base," I responded with full conviction, "This is our trial time to somehow mobilize this fund, and once both vessels are back in trade, we will achieve full turnaround and won't look back on our growth path." It was more to allay their worries and tensions and kindle confidence in their disturbed minds. I never believed in praying to Thakur for any material boon, but I only prayed for His blessings to keep my faith and surrender unshaken. I went back to my chamber, leaving them to discuss and making phone calls to a few influential freight brokers to explore the West Asia Gulf freight market.

It was about 1 p.m., just before I was leaving with Dada for lunch at home. I had a visit from a very big transport company, Ashok Leyland, Local Chief Manager (a client of Mr. Rammurthi/Indian Bank), who handed over a cheque for Rs 10 lacs, stating that this was a corporate loan at the ruling bank rate of interest for six months, fully secured by Mr. Rammurthi's personal guarantee. I accepted the same with profuse thanks. Tears were rolling out of my eyes, and it took me more than ten minutes to control my emotions before

I could hand over the check to Dada and Gopal Da, who were still in Gopal Da's chamber. For a fleeting moment, I physically felt the divine touch of Thakur on my head, which filled my mind with bliss unspeakable.

In the car driving back home for lunch, Dada expressed his deep gratitude to Mr. Rammurthi. I said that with Thakur holding our hand, we were destined to see many such miracles, and Ma planted this seed of faith and surrender in us, and so long as we did not waiver in our faith and surrender, Thakur would always be with us. Dada admitted that such worries and tensions make him brood and impair his mental health, and he wondered how I could keep my calm. I suggested, "You talk to Ma when in tension and feeling distressed, which I often do to fuel my strength." Dada confessed that Ma always advised him to make a total surrender, but it was easier said than done.

After lunch in the office, I found my good friend Gajen Bhai of freight broker Devcurn Company waiting for me. He advised me that due to the almost six-month berthing delay in the ports of Khorramshahr, Iran, and Basra, Iraq, none of the conference lines were placing any vessels, and there was huge accumulated cargo for these ports looking for the conference to intervene with the member lines. He felt the Gouri Shankar-sized vessel would get easily filled up with high-freighted cargo if I risked the berthing delay and managed berthing at the discharging end by some kind of arrangement. It was clear to me that this high-risk decision was necessary to get the trade and market on our side for the long haul and mitigate our acute cash crisis.

I advised him that I could declare Gouri Shankar in the port for Basra and Khorramshahr loading on the condition that shippers pay a 300% congestion surcharge on the conference freight rate and pay me 50% advance freight on booking confirmation. Gajen Bhai requested that I give him 48 hours with assurance to give his own shippers priority booking, and he was confident that it would work. He confidentially advised me that G Jerambhai & Co., one of the most reputed jute mill owners and export houses known to me from the Sinclair days, was sitting with a large export order for Basra, and if I trusted them to place their cargo barges alongside the vessel immediately on her arrival and agree to issue a B/L to meet the LC date, then 100% freight could be paid. He wanted me to back him on this booking in preference to Sinclairs, which had a strong hold on this shipper. I thought for a while and then suggested to him that he confidentially bring my friend Dungarsibhai, one of the owners of this group, to my office with him to finalize this deal with me, and I would have no hesitation in solving their B/L issue. If Sinclair came to me after this, I would be able to tell them that Dungashibhai came to me with Devcurn (before Sinclair) and finalized the booking. The next morning, Dungarsibhai came with Devcurn and expressed his pleasure to see me at the shipowners' desk. He happily agreed to pay a 300% surcharge on freight for congestion risk and deeply appreciated my friendly cooperation in issuing him a freight prepaid B/L on the same day. He assured me to place his cargo of jute in barges alongside the vessel immediately upon berthing. The total cargo was ready for loading on barges. We collected nearly Rs. 20 lacs in freight from this one shipper alone.

Next morning, Gouri Shankar appeared in the Daily Shipping list to open bookings for Khorramshahr and Basra, and our operation manager, Mr. Shiva, opened carting at the allocated berth by port. Our operation team of Shiva, D. K. Choudhury, and B. K. Banerjee were experienced and strong in documentation, port, and customs handling. SNR, after settling with Hindustan Shipyard, got the vessel to Calcutta port within the next four days to berth and commence loading. Gouri Shankar, as a five-hold geared twin decker, was an ideal liner vessel for assorted general cargo loading, and apart from collecting 50% freight in advance for a load of steel, tea, gunny, plywood, glass, the CI Goods vessel sailed out with Capt. Barve as Master and Debangsu Rakshit as Chief Engineer within the next 10 days, with Gopal Da personally supervising loading and stowage from the E.C. Bose side. We collected over Rs. 1.2 crore in freight for this voyage, which made both Dada and Gopal Da happy and tension-free.

This was a big break and turn round for Himalaya Shipping, and it served multiple areas of the company's future growth graph. Firstly, the West Asia Gulf Shipper community got embedded with me and the Himalayas with immense gratitude and appreciation for my very personal concern for the trade in this area. When I assured regular placement of vessels in this trade for 3 weeks frequency to start with and then increased the frequency of sailings as per trade requirements and responses, they all acknowledged this as a great service to the trade. I also got the opportunity to get our other vessel, Nanda Devi, from Mazagon Dock and her placement for West Asia Gulf loading after the sailing of Gouri Shankar. For a smaller single-decker vessel, we declared for Dubai and Kuwait loading after getting assurance from the shippers for a full load. This was the beginning of Himalaya Shipping's real growth march in the shipping industry.

Himalaya Shipping was still not accepted as a member of the West Asia Gulf Conference, which had only 5 members, namely the Shipping Corporation of India, Scindia Steam Navigation, India Steam Ship, South East Asia Shipping of the Dhanjibhoy family, and Malabar Shipping Lines. Out of the member lines, although Mr. N. M. Trivedi of Scindia was the conference chairman, the placement of Scindia vessels in the trade was infrequent. South East Asia Shipping was very regular, as was SCI. Malabar Lines, with Mr. M. Tanna as their Calcutta manager, was placing one vessel every two months.

When I applied for conference membership for Himalaya Shipping, objections came from SCI and South East Asia Shipping only, and Conference Chairman Mr. Trivedi was very keen to admit us, and he was a very affectionate friend and admirer of my bold shipping venture. Mr. N. K. Sen of ISS was always very fond of me from my Ratnakar and Sinclair days, and ISS was not placing any vessels for West Asia Gulf Ports loading. Muljibhai Tanna of

Malabar was a good senior shipping friend and my neighbor living on Elgin Road. Immediately after my placement of Gouri Shankar for Khorramshahr, Basra loading, I had a call from Mr. S. K. Sen, Regional Director of SCI, who offered unsolicited elder brotherly advice that my vessel would be stuck for the whole year in Shat-el-Arab river ports and would ruin my new venture. I politely asked him why he was not taking this risk as a member of the National Shipping Line and a prominent member of the conference to come to the rescue of the shippers in this trade. He said that as a member of the National Shipping Line, he had acted as a prudent shipping professional to advise fellow members in the conference not to place any vessel to protect their interests. This he cited as the reason for his objection to admitting inexperienced and irresponsible new shipping lines as members of the conference. I conveyed this message to Mr. Trivedi as Conference Chairman and also to the entire shippers' community to facilitate the entry of Himalaya Shipping as a conference member. We not only got admitted to the conference after loading and sailing our second vessel, Nanda Devi, under the shippers' pressure and with the support of all other member lines except SCI but also got a breakthrough with the shippers' community and the market to monopolize this trade for the next 5 or 6 years.

Through my friend Mr. Tanna, I established a long-term relationship with Mr. Mustafa Mouaket of Al-Mouaket Shipping Agency, Kuwait Port, who had very strong connections spread throughout the entire West Asia Gulf region, including UAE ports, Iraq ports, and Iranian ports. I used his network to appoint our agents in Dubai, Abu Dhabi, Khorramshahr, and Basra. In Dubai and Abu Dhabi, he was operating through his own subagents, but in Khorramshahr, he introduced me to an outstanding Iranian gentleman, Mr. Mehdi Karoon, owner of his shipping agency, Karoon & Co. In 1974, it was still the Shah Regime in Iran, and Mehdi had strong connections with the Royal Palace in Tehran. Basra Port in Iraq was under the National Government Agency, where Mustafa had very intimate government contacts.

Within a few days of sailing Gouri Shankar from Calcutta Port, I flew out to Kuwait to meet Mustafa and then visited other ports in the UAE, Iran, and Iraq to set up efficient handling arrangements and present them with our long-term liner shipping service plan in the region. It was essential for me to know firsthand the various cargo consignees who were to be made comfortable and happy by our agents to satisfy our shippers' clients, mostly those servicing export orders on C&F terms. Mustafa fully understood me and my immediate requirement to establish a permanent berthing arrangement for Gouri Shankar and other vessels to follow at Khorramshahr and Basra. He could immediately tie up arrangements with his Basra port contacts for priority berthing of our vessels, and I agreed to pay his special fees for this job on a vessel-to-vessel basis. For Khorramshahr, he suggested I visit Khorramshahr and discuss arrangements with Mr. Mehdi Karoon directly. I found Mehdi Karoon living in a colossal Persian palace, and he gave me a royal reception. He knew most of the consignees well, and his contact with port officers was very intimate and personal. Mr. Karoon hosted a mega party in his palace, which all the port officers and a large number of consignees were invited. He announced with aplomb Himalaya Shipping's long-term plan with fortnightly frequency calls of vessels to service the trade, which will need priority berthing cooperation from the port. All the consignees were suffering in the absence of regularly scheduled liner service and wholeheartedly welcomed me for introducing Himalaya Shipping Liner Service. The party went very well, and when Mehdi personally dropped me off at my hotel, he confirmed to me that Gouri Shankar would berth within 3–5 days of her arrival in Khorramshahr, and he had made appropriate arrangements long-term at a price of berthing fees per vessel, which I agreed to and requested he include in his pro forma invoice for us to remit port disbursements. It was the start of a very long-term arrangement that lasted for good 5–6 years until the Iran–Iraq war broke out during the 3rd quarter of the 1980s.

After coming back to Calcutta, we arranged for our operation manager Shiva to visit Khorramshahr and Basra during the discharge time of Gouri Shankar to ensure smooth implementation of the arrangements made for berthing and quick release of the vessel. This voyage of Gouri Shankar was extremely rewarding for us, and she did subsequent consecutive voyages of 45/50 days on average to achieve a major turn-around for the company.

As a conference member, we looked at the trade for establishing a long-term win-win relationship through servicing their export orders and improving our service profile with scheduled frequency and reliability. Combining the West Asia Gulf ports of Dubai, and Abu Dhabi, and the Saudi Arabian ports of Dammam, Kuwait, Basra, and Khorramshahr, market demand justified the placement of more vessels to gain and retain 75/80% of the market share. Except for Southeast Asia, none of the other member lines, including SCI, were committed players on this route. To improve our revenue turn-round, I approached Ratan Da (N.K. Sen) of ISS to see if he would be willing to collaborate with us with two of his R-class vessels, almost 14–15k DWT, ideal for liner loading for joint service. He suggested that instead of joint service, if we are really confident in filling up vessels and ensuring quick turn-around, he would be happy to offer two R-class vessels on a short-term charter, and if our performance was good, he would consider giving some S-class vessels in the future. We negotiated a reasonable charter hire and took 'Indian Resource' and 'Indian Renown' on a 6- to 9-month charter in the 3rd quarter of 1974, and these vessels by mid-'75 gave us a huge dividend. During this period, our Bombay agent Vinoo Bhai was giving us constant market feedback from West Asia Gulf Shippers to start a regular Bombay-West Asia Gulf service by placing Nanda Devi in this trade. Voyage economics for a small vessel like Nanda Devi for Bombay-West Asia Gulf haul was always more economical, and I decided to start the service between Bombay and Dubai, Abu Dhabi, Kuwait, restricting discharge to a maximum of two ports after taking ISS vessels on charter to hoist 20-day frequency loading at Calcutta port with a bigger cargo capacity.

We were negotiating at this stage the purchase of another 5500 DWT geared single deck logger from a Japanese owner through my Sinclair-Clarkson broking channel. All in all, Thakur held our hand to lift us from the abysmal bottom of collapsing finance to the realm of comfortable mental space to plan growth and progress. We had already formed a strong management team, with Prasanta Ghose joining as our finance manager and Vijay Barve as marine superintendent. We had other backup junior officers like B.K. Banerjee, Ashish Mitra, etc., apart from Shiva and D.K. Chowdhury on the operation side. After winning our legal battle against DG Shipping and Gopalan Nair as the then DG, our respect and friendship with almost all departments of the DG Shipping office increased manifold. Our Bombay agent Vinoobhai's office was next door to the DG Shipping office, and by this time, my Sinclair colleague Jayant Mehta joined us as our Bombay rep, and he was given office space in our agent office. Jayant was a very popular man among the Bombay Shipping Circle. Between Jayant and Vinoobhai, we had a very personalized market representation in Bombay. Dada and I frequently visited Bombay and were also represented in the INSOA (Indian Ship Owners Association) as young members with progressive industry development thinking. I introduced Dada to all my shipping friends, and Dada soon became the Dada of the shipping industry, with both seniors and juniors as my dada. The teamwork of Gopal Da, Dada, and me was very prominently displayed in the entire Indian shipping industry circle during our rapid growth and development years. Dada's friend Bula Roychoudhury (Bula Da) was our finance consultant from the very start of our project. Bula Da was a very competent charter accountant, and he was running his own CA firm. Bula Da's contribution to our finance planning, bank loan applications with 5/10 year IRR projections, risk management analysis, reserve building in the balance sheet to expand the scope and outreach of loan capital access for vessel acquisition, determining a prudent mix of working capital needs, always keeping in view our frugal start-up capital, etc., was very profound and substantial. Both

Dada and I enriched ourselves with huge knowledge resources and financing engineering skills while working with him.

Dada's ego was sensitive, and he grew annoyed hearing from Bula Da about the financial engineering that kick started Samal Harand Company's growth trajectory in its early years.

For me, it was pure bliss to learn from a knowledgeable financial expert. Our uncle Ajit Mitra (Kutu kaka) was full of love and affection for both of us from our childhood and was like our legal guardian. With Thakur holding our hands and Swamiji incessantly whispering in my ear the mantras of 'Charai Beti and Avi,' I was moving forward in my shipping industry dream realization with supreme confidence and poise. The trust and support of both Gopal Da and Dada were total. It never occurred to me that Gopal Da could ever back out of his commitment to give the Mitra family group 50% ownership under any provocation. Dada and I were to hold 20% each and allocate 6/7% to Sejda (Malay). The balance of 3/4% was allocated to my father, uncle, and another maternal cousin who helped us with the initial seed capital. In March 1975, just after I finalized the purchase of our 3rd vessel to be named 'Nilkantha' another Himalayan peak, Bula Da advised me one-on-one that there was adequate reserve built up in our balance sheet to increase the paid-up capital base from Rs. 10 lacs to Rs. 18/20 lacs to get the agreed holding pattern established before we go for further growth and expansion. I shared with him my thoughts and future development of the company, for which the equity base of the company had to be substantially enhanced through an IPO 4–5 years down the line.

Second-hand vessel acquisitions with high maintenance costs were for initial reserve building and phase-wise equity enhancement to the maximum extent possible. It was the intention that over the next few years, the promoter's stake, as per our agreed holding pattern, could be kept at 25/26% when going for an IPO. The Law of Atrophy was inevitable in the growth graph of any dynamic organization, and I could visualize containerization of cargo in liner shipping was coming in a big way in the next decade, and our surcharge-centric high-revenue operation in the West Asia Gulf trade route was to witness sea change through unitization of cargo and cost logistics re-orientation plans already on the drawing board of International Shipping. I was already interacting with Clarkson, R. S. Plateau, and my other global contacts to establish shipyard contacts for new building ordering and acquisition at a low market cycle forecast in 1979/80. The development of a robust shipping agency and ship management division was also on my radar. Bula Da cautioned me about Dada's very narrow and conservative mindset and vision in thinking long-term and narrated his disappointing experience in Samal Harand, where Bula Da's views on financial engineering were ignored by Dada, causing serious cash flow crises. Even commitments on stake offerings to the directors were never kept, causing distrust and doubts in the minds of loyal friends like Bula Da and Mr. Choudhury.

I was disturbed and surprised but expressed my confidence that Dada would surely appreciate that shipping, as a capital-intensive industry, had no chance of thriving long-term with Rs. 18 lakh equity base. Also, between Gopal Da, Dada, and me, we developed good teamwork. We went to Japan together with family to take delivery of Nilkantha at the Tsenuishi Shipyard near Hiroshima. SNR went a few days early to complete crewing and delivery formalities. I discussed with both Gopal Da and Dada individually and collectively about the capitalization of reserves and the future growth plan of the company. Gopal Da was very upbeat and openly admitted that while he understood the nuances of stevedoring, chipping, and painting in the shipping industry, he invested fully with faith in my experience and expertise and would always go by my growth plan. He, however, gave me advice as an elder brother to personally keep a minimum of 30% of our family shares for my own interest and also for the long-term interest of the company. He strongly felt that the share of Dada and me should not be the same, as Dada is a non-shipping person with an egocentric nature, and in the future, as my prominence in the shipping industry grows, he will develop complex in relationships to create management conflict.

These were words of wisdom that I took note of but didn't want to discuss with Dada to create misunderstandings.

Dada appreciated my growth plan and vision but was skeptical about going public, which he felt we should discuss with Bula Da and other reputed consultants. I did not tell him that I had already discussed with Bula Da and left that for future discussions when we returned to Calcutta.

The Japanese owners of 'Nilkantha' booked us at a comfortable hotel near the shipyard, where we were to take delivery of the vessel at the dry dock. SNR was efficient and meticulous as always, and the delivery went very smoothly. I must narrate here a gala post-delivery dinner party hosted by the erstwhile owners of the vessel at a typical Japanese guesthouse, where we were supposed to sit on the floor with a decorative food display laid out on the floor-level table with a height of aesthetics of Japanese art, including gun carriages and other innovative artistic displays of food items. There were Geisha girls to serve food and entertain the guests. To my dismay, practically all the food was served as raw fish, meat, etc., except fruits and vegetables. There were Japanese drinks. Purnima and other ladies understood my predicament, and I was mostly eating fruits and some vegetable salads. In spite of having interpreters, we were having language problems, and Gopal Da was at his best by freely using all Bengali jokes and encouraging our interpreters to ask the Geisha Girls to take special care of me.

As a direct outcome, one of the girls pushed raw fish into my mouth, which was a Japanese delicacy: sushi. I could somehow gulp it with Saki drinks, but the smell stayed in my mouth till I went up to my hotel room and had a proper mouthwash. This incident became a favorite tease story for Gopal Da and our family for a long time. After sailing out the vessel for Calcutta, our full family team, including S. N. Roy, went to Tokyo, where we had a meeting with Mitsubishi Group shipyards. This meeting was set up by Sinclair-Clarksons and their Tokyo broker associates. John Wheeler, MD of Clarksons, and my friend BAL Vashist of Sinclair were also in Tokyo. We discussed our future container vessel acquisition plan to start a container feeder service between Calcutta, Madras, and Singapore from 1980 onwards. The indicated price and delivery time were not very comfortable for me at that time, and John from his broker's crystal ball recommended that I wait until 1977 when the market was expected to be somewhat down.

We came back to Calcutta via Hong Kong. Gopal Da and Boudi went to Manila at the invitation of Capt. Okha for an extended holiday.. As per our discussion in Japan regarding reserve capitalization and equity leveling, Dada wanted to keep 51% for Mitra Group and do same before Gopal Da's return from holiday. I objected to this as our agreement with Gopal Da was 50:50 holding and Gopal Da kept to this commitment unflinchingly. I advised Dada that Gopal Da even told me that he had pressure from his nephew Tutu and son Partha to keep 51% holding for Bose family and he advised them that for healthy growth and development of the company and its business, trust and harmony are of extreme importance. Dada finally agreed to keep 50:50 holding but wanted to allocate 1% to Bodhon Bose in Bose family holding. Both Bula Da and I suggested not doing anything till Gopal Da's return and without consulting Gopal Da. In a heated argument Bula Da said 'Salil, this is a very wrong attitude and earlier created misunderstanding in Samal Harand and you should not cause this kind of indiscreet disharmony between the partners at this point of healthy growth path of the organization.'

Dada was infuriated to hear this from Bula Da in my presence and insisted that he had talked to his friends Bodhon Da and Chandi Da in the Bose family, and they promised to suitably explain this to Gopal Da. In his defense, he explained that if the company were to go for an IPO for the new building acquisition we discussed in Tokyo, then we were to start a dialog with the bank and SDFC immediately with enhanced equity capital, keeping our 26% promoter's holding. We were all against this decision, including our uncle Ajit Mitra (Kutu Kaka), who was our legal guardian.

To our surprise, Dada acted arrogantly and emotionally, insisting that Bula Da perform reserve capitalization on the company's balance sheet for the fiscal year ending March 31, 1975, immediately. This hasty, unjust, and imprudent decision later became the root cause of hindering growth and ultimately led to the downfall of the company due to a lack of trust and harmony among the partners. In my spiritual mind, I often thought of Oscar Wild's epic literary piece 'The Picture of Dorian Gray,' where the innocence and beauty of the face in the picture started getting distorted with Dorian Gray's descent from innocence and purity towards the abysmal pit of greed, lust, and falling values. Himalaya's spiritual security in the strong grip of Thakur Ramakrishna, Ma, and Swamiji was affected by a degradation in the value system. As we expected, Gopal Da on his return was very upset, and he could not and did not resist Tutu and Partha from starting litigation and unhealthy battling for an unequal balancing in shareholding. When I tried to calm Gopal Da down, he told me very frankly that although he wanted me to hold a minimum of 30% of Mitra Group shares, he never intervened in Dada and me deciding this, but Dada had no business to allocate shares to Bodhon Da in the Bose Group holding without consulting Gopal Da. I had no answer but only pleaded for his magnanimity and good sense to prevent serious damage to the dream expansion plan that I envisioned for the company. Gopal Da wanted the board to be restructured with Gopal Da as Chairman, me as Managing Director, and Dada was not in the management. I explained to him with all humility that this would create a big rift in our family, and this was the last thing desirable. Gopal Da appreciated but frankly advised me that he invested in this shipping venture with affection, full trust, and confidence in me as a dynamic shipping professional and spiritually splurged person. He was consciously aware that, without my free hand, the growth and development of this highly potential shipping venture would badly suffer. He stated with conviction that there was bound to be a serious clash of ego and jealousy with the misguided ego of Dada as a non-shipping person, and this would hinder growth and progress. While appreciating his sentiments and words of wisdom, I requested that he resist Tutu from influencing Partha, Gopal Da's elder son, and at the same time bring his younger son Bubai to the Himalayas as a management trainee so that I could train him in professional shipping with some international exposure for a future leadership role. Gopal Da confided that Bubai was more intelligent and suitable for a larger shipping position than the stevedoring business, but he was worried that it would take a lot of time for Partha to understand and realize Tutu's game plan to take control of E.C. Bose & Co. in Gopal Da's absence.

Tutu, I found at that time, was a highly intelligent, shrewd, and competent young entrepreneur with very sharp reflexes and a good understanding of the greed and need of the corrupt government machinery at the central and the state, which he used to his advantage. Tutu was very focused on his agenda, and Gopal Da was relieved of much work. Tutu's initiative, competence, and dynamic business acumen achieved growth and expansion for E.C. Bose Co. in Calcutta, Vizag, and Paradeep. Gopal Da used to spend the first half of the day in the E.C. Bose office and the second half in the Himalaya office. Himalaya's West Asia Gulf Service vessels greatly benefited from Gopal Da's personal supervision of efficient stevedoring, both in minimizing port stays and the agreed cost matrix linked with productivity. With the increase in our operation frequency and vessel calls, Gopal Da delegated this to Capt. Sengupta and Tutu's charge.

I found this was resulting in an increase in port stay for the vessels, and the cost per ton for 5 or 6 vessels was going up substantially. After discussing this with Gopal Da, I took some time to compare these stevedoring bills with an equal number of earlier vessel bills that we had paid by making some on-account payments. Also at the same time (with Gopal Da's consent), I took a competitive per-ton rate quote from Mr. Mahalingam of T. P. Roychoudhury & Co. The difference was substantial, and the per-ton rate of Mahalingam was matching the rate per ton we achieved for our earlier vessels under E.C. Bose Co. when Gopal Da was personally supervising. After placing the facts and figures before Gopal Da, I requested that he give his decision for the settlement of ECB's outstanding invoices of nearly Rs. 18 lakh. Gopal Da very sincerely explained that he fully appreciated my cost control philosophy in ship management, which I stated to him in Hong Kong. I was of the firm belief that ship repair, victualing and stores, inventory control for supply planning alongwith stevedoring, stowage, turn-around etc needed special attention as cost control measures which were to be effectively implemented to have an incremental impact on our revenue. This was the reason for the in-house services of ECB and Capstan (under Purnima's management) to be introduced. SNR joining our company also substantially controlled Vessels R&M expenses. Gopal Da advised me to settle ECB outstanding invoices at the TPRC quoted rate, which meant a nearly Rs. 7/8 lac reduction. Tutu came to my office and said Mahalingam under quoted, knowing fully well that he would not be required to work at this rate as per the understanding between the stevedores working in the port. He was sure to back out if asked to perform. Mahalingam confirmed that he would not touch our business unless Gopal Da gave consent.

Gopal Da unhesitatingly consented and advised Tutu in my presence that if ECB cannot match the TPRC rate, Himalaya Business will go to TPRC. Tutu surrendered the business to TPRC and offered me an incentive to pass his existing bills without any deductions. Gopal Da felt highly embarrassed and advised Tutu to accept without arguement the management decision. SNR implemented a standard cost matrix system for stores, provisions, and bonded supply fronts. Purnima closely monitored this system at both the Himalaya office and the Capstan office.

SNR also introduced a similar cost matrix control system on board and onshore, which gave us outstanding results. SNR knew that Samal Harand as an engineering unit was not doing very well and suggested to Dada to form a Marine Engineering division in Samal Harand where SNR and two other senior engineers, Debansu Rakshit and M Sircar, will form a team to generate business and provide reliable service not only to improve the Himalaya Vessels cost matrix but also to secure repair jobs from other clients like ISS, Scindia, SCI, and other Indian and foreign line vessels. Dada signed an MOU with the engineers to share profits, and after the first year of performance, he agreed to allot a stake in the Samal Harand Marine division to three of them. In less than two years, SNR, through this team, not only improved the cost matrix of Himalayan vessels but also secured substantial marine engineering business for Samal Harand. Dada was very happy that his own engineering company was revived and looked after efficiently by this team.

During this period, a few important events happened in the company to accelerate its growth. We developed a strong shipping agency division in the company and secured the agency of Bangladesh Shipping Corporation's East Coast USA Liner Service and a few other foreign lines agencies. A Dutch company was exporting poppy shells to the Calcutta-based corporate house 'Organon' on C&F terms. My very dear old friend Vizzy Iyengar was the MD of Organon at that time. They had regular monthly vessel calls with full-load cargo, and we were agents for the Dutch ship owners. Bangladesh Shipping Corporation's very challenging and lucrative business opportunity came to me when Swapan Dasgupta invited me to meet Capt. Safi, BSC CMD, for lunch at the Bengal Club. The BSC agent in Calcutta was SCI and Capt. Safi indicated their interest as a National Shipping Corporation to start East Coast USA liner service to Mr. S. R. Prasad, the then Regional Director of SCI Calcutta. Mr. Prasad discouraged him as this route was highly competitive, with prominent lines like Brocklebank, Waterman, APL, Helenic, Scindia, and SCI as conference members and BSC as a new entrant having no chance of securing even one ounce of cargo. Capt. Safi approached Swapan Da as a friend and leading freight broker for help. Swapan Da, knowing my hold on the shippers and client servicing reputation, recommended me and Himalaya Shipping for their agency for aggressive marketing.

I explained to him the necessity of overcoming strong policing by the USA Federal Marines against rebating to score over competing lines. It was also essential to provide good-spec liner vessels for monthly frequency call. For this at least four vessels to be placed for scheduled monthly service. If he was ready to meet these two vital conditions, then with a month's notice, we could start service with a good prospect of securing full-load cargo between Calcutta and Chittagong. Capt. Safi secured four ships for placement on this run and advised me to announce the scheduled service. We started the service with Banglar Maan as the first BSC vessel placed in East Coast USA liner service from January 1976. This vessel was fully booked with carpet backing and jute cargo, primarily high-freighted volume cargo. We had a gala party on board with all shippers, trade, and port officials. Shippers were very happy, and we never looked back thereafter for the next 4 years. In fact, in the very first year, BSC ranked joint No. 1 performance-wise with Brocklebank, where BSC was higher on revenue than Brocklebank Line (BL) while BL was higher on tonnage. SCI was lower than Waterman. This result, when announced in the conference meeting, infuriated SCI Management. SCI Chairman Admiral Kishen Dev moved at the Ministry his proposal for the Freight Bureau as adopted by Sri Lanka at that time, where more than 60% of the cargo was to be allocated to the National Line. Before taking any decision, the ministry wanted to know trade and shippers reactions.

Mr. Sanjay Sen, President of the Eastern India Shippers Association, convened a meeting of all the shippers, freight brokers, and shipping lines at the Bengal Chamber, where SCI CMD was to place his proposal for seeking trade support. From the freight broker's side, Swapan Dasgupta from Sinclair, the lead member of the Freight Brokers Association, hosted a party of the shippers before the Shipper Association meeting, to which I was invited. The Boons and Banes of Freight Bureau proposal was discussed, and service logistics based on cost and quality were debated. Most of the shippers were sceptical about SCI's intention to establish a monopoly without offering efficient service to eliminate competition.

They liked me for my personalized service to address the comfort level of both the shippers and the consignees on the other end. USA marketing was a very different brand from West Asia Gulf, and there was strong policing and vigilance from US Federal Maritime against rebating. To capture this market, BSC was paying us special marketing fees outside the books and also to Swapan Da. It was suggested in the party by the shippers that I should speak in the Bengal Chamber meeting after Admiral Kishen Dev to highlight the shippers' concern strongly, as none of them were finding the courage to openly resist him.

In the meeting, the SCI Chairman played the patriotism card for the National Line, and without taking my name, he decried the anti-national marketing activities of some Indian shipping lines to promote our neighbouring National Line. There were questions asked about the necessity of providing vessels at the scheduled frequency, transit time accommodation, timely document release, and other sensitive areas of the USA market.

At the end, I stood up to say that protecting the interests of the Indian exporters is also necessary in the national interest, and I was just doing that in marketing and servicing the trade by vessels of the national line of Bangladesh who were compelled to change their earlier agency arrangement with SCI. I also emphasized that I do not believe in going to my shipper clients with a begging bowl to support my vessels, but try to earn their support through my service quality. I had a standing ovation from the whole house of shippers and brokers. This infuriated my almost 20-year-older than me SCI chairman. He was heard openly saying to all at the end of the meeting that some policing at the Indian end would also be introduced against rebating by less reputable operators. My mission was accomplished. I thought to myself when this bane of having high-ego bureaucrats (without any in-depth knowledge of trade and shipping) at the helm of the Indian shipping industry would end to allow space for its growth and maturity. SCI did ring the alarm bell for USA policing during the last quarter of the 1976–1977 financial year, and there was much harassment caused to many of our clients in the USA. I had to undertake a reasonably elaborate USA and UKC marketing tour in 1977 along with BSC General Manager Afzal Khan. I will come to that episode later.

Dada and Gopal Da were very happy with the lucrative BSC Agency business and out-of-book marketing fees that were coming to three of us. Both Dada and I paid 10% of our fees to Sejda (Malay) against the seed capital support he provided initially. This continued until the third-quarter of 1981. Coming back to the Himalayas of 1976, we had over 70% of the Calcutta West Asia Gulf Market and a very substantial share of the Bombay West Asia Gulf Market through our two vessels, Nanda Devi and Nilkantha. We were servicing the Calcutta market by Gouri Shankar and two 'R' Class Chartered vessels of ISS. We occasionally chartered foreign vessels for short durations with conference support and DGS approval to meet trade demands. At this stage of our venture, I was feeling inclined to introduce an additional fairly large-size 13/14k DWT vessel in Calcutta-West Asia Gulf service as all our ships were going full and I was getting pressure from the trade to make our sailing frequency bimonthly. My good old friend Raman of Great Eastern Chartering brought me a sale inquiry from Great Eastern Shipping for their tween-decker 14k DWT vessel 'Jag Laxmi' which was in Dubai at that time with some bulk cargo. Raman informed me that the vessel, though 16 years old, had just passed the Special Survey and was fairly well maintained for another 4–5 years of trouble-free service in our Calcutta–West Asia Gulf service. Debanshu Rakshit was to reach Dubai the next day as Chief Engineer of Gouri Shankar by divine coincidence. I requested DR to inspect the vessel and give me a report on her condition. Raman got us permission for an inspection. The Rakhsit report was good, and he said that without spending much money on vessel maintenance, we can safely trade for 4–5 years. He, however, emphasized that after 4 years, we should scrap the vessel and view the vessel value at a near-5,000-ton LDT. This way, we should fetch a reasonably good price for the vessel from the demolition market. When I asked him whether we should go for an inspection of the class record and go for a bottom inspection, Rakshit did not feel it was necessary if we decided to run for 4 years only and then scrap the vessel. I calculated a scrap value of Rs. 80/90 lacs as per the then market and got convinced that if we bought the vessel within a Rs. 1.5 crore price range with 25% down payment and balance in four years, we should be able to generate substantial revenue and cash surplus for the company in four years.

By this time in 1976, we were using three banks: Indian Bank for our first two vessel loan financings, but after our working capital loan application was turned down, Mr. Rammurthy personally suggested to me that we build relationships with one or two other banks. For future vessel acquisitions, we got SBI to loan finance our Nilkantha acquisition. We also opened dedicated operation account for our chartered vessels of ISS with United Industrial Bank. Like Mr. Rammurthy, UIB CMD Mr. J. N. Biswas was a friend of mine and, at my request, became Vice President of BTTA. Mr. Rammurthy was transferred to Bombay in 1976, and our relationship with Indian Bank lacked the personal warmth of Mr. Rammurthy. I consulted Dada and Gopal Da about my intention to purchase Jag Laxmi on deferred payment terms from Great Eastern Shipping against Bank Guarantee and got our Chief Accountant Prasanta Ghose to present a four-year projection to the board with cash flow and profit generation and taking Rs. 80 lacs as scrap value after 4 years.

In working out vessel operating costs SNR estimated monthly R&M costs on the assumption of our scrapping the vessel after 4 years. The figures were very promising, and I got the formal board clearance. Gopal Da advised me that Dada told him confidentially that I was moving very aggressively and taking their consent as granted for post-decision ratification. I reminded both Dada and Gopal Da that although West Asia Gulf Market was building our foundation with reserve creation in the balance sheet, this would not last permanently as containerization of liner cargo would rapidly make ordinary break bulk service with tween decker vessels obsolete in the next 3/4 years. We therefore needed to move fast while the going was good to be able to raise public capital, ensuring a minimum 25% holding for us. I had a plan ready for acquiring container feeder vessels for starting Calcutta-Singapore and Calcutta-Colombo scheduled feeder services.

The bulk cargo market of coal, iron ore, food grains, fertilizers, etc. was also on my radar through acquisition of Handymax and Panamax Bulk carriers. There were also other innovative projects like the Sandheads transloading operation, the round-the-world container service for achieving unit cost reduction through multiple slot handling, and another innovative LASH barge with Becket 1 and Becket 2 lash ship designs that my Danish friend Gustav Drohse brought to me from Federikshaven Shipyard. All these dreams I elaborated to Dada, Gopal Da, and my entire Himalaya Team. Gopal Da appreciated them and frankly admitted that they were beyond his limited shipping knowledge. He was always ready to hold my hand with trust and confidence in my Indian shipping industry dream realization. SNR, as a technical man, was a dreamer like me with entrepreneurial drive.

From the finance side, Bula Da and Prashanta encouraged and assisted me in preparing the next 20 years financial planning and projections with compatible phase-wise 3/4 tranches of IPOs in gaps of 4/5 years. The central idea was to keep our holding of 25% in the company as far as possible and simultaneously create a strong techno-commercially proficient management team with talent hunting and honing as a continuous process in the system. Bula Da always believed that in a robust industry-building model, even small holdings of technocrats would be congenial for the management efficiency. Dada was still nursing his wound with Gopal Da, and I suspected Tutu's astute and intelligent hand play on Dada in influencing his mindset against Gopal Da and me. As a very competent charter accountant, Prashanta Ghose was exceptionally good in his planning and presentation of financial projections, and he was always in sync with my thoughts and plans. Both SNR and PKG were fully convinced about my game plan for scrapping our old vessels before their next SS in three to five years for the generation of sufficient reserves in the balance sheet and then acquiring new buildings from Japanese and Korean shipyards in the early 1980s low shipping market.

I was targeting the start of container feeder service of weekly frequency between Calcutta-Madras and Singapore in the early 1980s with two 500 TEU capacity geared NBs from Japanese yards, as I had earlier discussed with John Wheeler of Clarksons and Mitsubishi in Tokyo. With both container cargo support and fast turn-around in port, this project, with an investment of USD 5 million each for two vessels and a conservative per TEU revenue projection with less than 70% capacity utilization, was giving a 25% IRR and attractive ROI in Prasanta's 10-year projection. My further plan was to place an order for two Panamax bulkers of 75k dwt with a broad beam and a reasonably shorter LOA for draft flexibility for mid-80s delivery, with one of the order-hungry Far Eastern Shipyards. We were expecting the tram market to improve by then. The next two decades of our fleet expansion plans were clear in my mind. I was trying to build a balanced fleet of container vessels to capitalize on our existing hold on the liner cargo market—both feeder service and main line service—by joining the International Main Line Consortium. Different infrastructure development projects in developing nations like India, Africa, the Middle East, Australia, and other Far Eastern nations were dictating the trend of the bulk carrier market, both for spot and period charters. Supply chain logistics needed composite integration of total multi-modal transport service both in bulk and container shipping in the areas of sea, river, rail, and road to establish optimum cost and logistics benefits for source-to-destination cargo delivery on a real-time revenue, cost, and profit model. There was always an industry preference for long-term contracts to mitigate price fluctuation risks in their raw material procurement and keep product costs stable.

Innovations in ship design and building in international shipping were constantly going hand in hand with innovative port infrastructure development to achieve economies of scale. My long-term vision for Himalaya Shipping was to invest in port and shipping industry development through a consortium of multiple players picking up IWT, rail, and road development activities independently and collectively, with assured returns on all sectors for the consortium players.

I was also actively interacting with BSC, Dhaka, CSC, Colombo, ISS, and a few other Hong Kong, Singapore, Tokyo, and Korean ship owners who were starting large-scale all-route container service to consider consortium formation for round-the-world container service with Panamax and post-Panama-size container vessels.

Multiple slot handling in one round voyage by such big size vessels was bound to create per TEU cost reduction and sufficient space for the ship owners to cope with rate fluctuations in the competitive global container shipping market. Round-the-world container service with efficient feeder service backup and a Port-net system in the port container terminal was a win-win future for trade and shipping.

Separate agency and ship management divisions for the company as independent profit centers were also well thought through between me and the technical team. Overall, the spirit of futuristic growth and expansion was soaring in our management team.

I finalized the purchase of 'Jag Laxmi' with delivery at Calcutta in May 1976. If my memory serves right, the present owner agreed to ballast the vessel back to Calcutta from Dubai with clean holds and fully fitted cargo battens for our West Asia Gulf general liner cargo loading. I spoke to Mr. Vasant Seth in Bombay in the presence of broker Raman of Great Eastern Chartering and fixed an appointment for the next day afternoon to discuss price and payment terms. VS was always affectionate to me and assured me of his cooperation to close matters quickly. 'Jag Laxmi' was their real 'Laxmi' for a good 15 years, and he would like Himalaya's to make a fortune out of her. I met VS at 3:30 p.m. the next afternoon in Bombay with Raman.

The Great Eastern Shipping Secretary, Dr. Sakhlecha, was present at the meeting. Dr. Sakhlecha was the only doctorate in shipping in India and had many publications providing deep insight into the shipping industry, covering a very wide spectrum of shipping knowledge ranging from operation, chartering, insurance, S&P, etc. It was almost a ritual for me to spend some time with him whenever I was in Bombay to enrich my own knowledge bank. It took us 15 minutes to finish our job. I requested VS to allow me to pay Rs. 1.25 crore for the vessel purchase with a 25% down payment and a balance in 5 yearly installments against a BG from UIB. His asking price was Rs. 1.5 crore, and he wanted me to close this at Rs. 1.3 crore. I surrendered to him as a respected senior in the industry to say that I had indicated my comfort level to buy the ship and had no courage to do any horse trading, and it was for him to decide. VS looked at Dr. Sakhlecha, and both smiled. He got up from his chair and shook hands with me to say, 'Probir, you get what you want, and the deal is closed.' We got into stimulating discussions on the global shipping scenario vis-à-vis the Indian shipping industry, where both VS and Dr. S gave me space to narrate my futuristic vision for the next 2–3 decades for my company and then gave me a glimpse of Great Eastern history and their exciting journey down the years. Both of them gave me inputs of wisdom by pointing out possible roadblocks down the roads that were to be overcome.

We named this vessel 'Kedarnath' after another Himalayan peak, symbolizing the fourth climb on our growth path. With its rapid turn-around, minimal days of repair layup, and high voyage freight generation, the vessel indeed became our 'Laxmi' for four years, generating significant cash for the company.

In the 3rd quarter of 1976, SNR frankly advised me that he and two other senior engineers got into an agreement with Dada about creating a profitable Marine Engineering Division not only to help Samal Harand but also to create strong competitive technical management for our proposed Ship Management Division in the future on a profit-sharing basis. This also provided an incentive for the engineers to introduce and monitor cost control measures by eliminating the impact of kickbacks and favoring money prevalent among the mariners. This project started in 1975 with an agreement between the engineers and Dada and was very successful during the first two years SNR requested the conversion of their profit share into a stake in the company as per the agreement. SNR advised me that Mr. Chowdhury of Samal Harand was dragging his feet on this subject, and he requested that I speak to Dada to resolve this matter.

When I spoke to Dada, he was visibly upset and mentioned that SNR is very ambitious, and due to my indulgence and dependence on him, SNR was thinking he was indispensible for the company. Dada also cautioned that soon SNR will demand stakes in the Himalayas. I tried to explain that we had a strong and efficient management team working in harmony, and this was the prime driving force behind the phenomenal growth and progress of the company, with a very positive growth graph for the future. I explained my vision plan for the next three decades for the company, where some stake-holding by the competent management team was an important element to strengthen the commitment, confidence, and involvement of the competent officers as participants in our dreams and visions both at the micro and macro level. Dada felt that with limited capital resources, our growth and progress so far were a miracle to him, and he was not as confident as me to believe that Thakur was holding our hand and we should overcome all hurdles at all times. He mentioned that many times in the past we came to the brink of closure due to acute financial constraints and got out of such situations miraculously, but we took such miracles as granted at all times.

Dada also confidentially briefed me about Tutu's badmouthing about Gopal Da and Tutu's plan to speak out through Partha about my autocratic management style in the company. My decision to take Bubai into Himalaya's operations team and train him abroad was also, as per Dada, not liked by Tutu and Partha. I got worried that Dada's mind was getting polluted through brain washing, and this, coupled with his ego-centric nature and frog of the well vision, was becoming a threat to the Himalaya's future growth potential. I discussed this with Gopal Da at length and frankly advised him that unless we had frankness and transparency between the three of us and discussed or determined our respective roles, our phenomenal growth story was destined for a tragic end. Gopal Da appreciated and was very frank in admitting that between his two sons, Bubai, he felt, was more intelligent and capable of running industry with training, and it would take a long time for Partha to understand Tutu's cunning design to take over control of ECB after Gopal Da, and he wanted Bubai to be trained under me to flow in the development stream of Himalaya Shipping in sync with my visions and dreams. This was the reason for his keeping Bubai away from ECB for independent sailing in the shipping industry and leaving Partha with the stevedoring business of ECB. He agreed with me that it would be disastrous to lose SNR from the management or make any break in the smooth and harmonious teamwork we were having with motivated involvement of all. Dada in his opinion was a non-shipping person and not at all a team man.

He further predicted that in the Samal Harand dispute, Dada would not care if SNR left. The internal cost control measure that we were following under the supervision of SNR and Bodhon Da as the full-time director in charge in the areas of stevedoring, repair, maintenance and ship handling would be seriously bruised. Dada would appoint some other Marine Engineer in Samal Harand as his profit center, and there would always be an inclination to siphon out money from Himalaya Shipping, which was going to be of secondary interest. Gopal Da appreciated my hesitation to get into any conflict with Dada to avoid any disharmony in the family, but he advised, as an elder brother, that such conflict would happen after my father's certain demise. I told Gopal Da that Babi (my father) advised me at the start not to take Dada into a shipping venture and got into a big argument with Kakababu, my uncle, on this issue. Gopal Da suggested that I speak with Babi and Kakababu, mentioning his name. He proposed now that Samal Harand has turned around, Dada should return full-time to his engineering business. Additionally, he recommended restructuring the Himalaya Board with Gopal Da as Chairman and myself as Managing Director. There were five board members at that time: Gopal Da, Bodhon Da, Partha from the Bose group, and Dada and Kakababu from the Mitra group. I was ED and CEO and was a permanent invitee to the board meetings. Gopal Da wanted me to join as MD and 6th member of the board to make representation even. I did not speak to Babi, as he was having a pacemaker installed in his heart by then and did not want to disturb his mind. But I spoke to Kakababu in detail. He wanted to resign and make room for me in the board and said that Gopal Da was trying to create rift between me and Dada. According to him, Dada had no jealousy or complexity in accepting my lead role in the management and was always appreciative of my shipping knowledge and aggressive expansion drive. He mentioned that Dada had high praise for me for securing the BSC Agency. He also asked me not to talk to Babi about this, which would create complications. I requested that Gopal Da have a joint meeting with Dada in his chamber. Dada took this meeting as a confrontation and got into arguments with Gopal Da for creating rifts and disharmony between two families in his effort to take control of the organization. Gopal Da obviously blamed Dada for this. Dada highlighted his own contribution to this company at the cost of his own Samal Harand's interest. Without allowing this to go to a point of bitterness, I intervened to lay out my own big dream for the Himalayas and Indian shipping industry, for which I had my 2/3-decade forward plan ready for phase-wise execution. With frugal paid-up capital, we had invested in old, almost-over-age vessels to trade in the relatively less competitive market of the West Asia Gulf and successfully captured almost monopoly market share.

This kind of high revenue turnover with a frugal equity base was building up substantial reserves in the company's balance sheet to help future expansion, but still, there would be a requirement for a substantial increase in the equity base, which we could achieve only through an IPO. To continue this West Asia Gulf Service for another 4–5 years, we might require the acquisition of one or two more modern vessels, as all four vessels in our fleet would require heavy repair and maintenance expenses, and I planned to scrap them before they were due next SS. From the early 1980s onwards, all liner services would be container-focused, and this would require a complete reorientation of our fleet acquisition plan. However, if we had no harmony in our management and a continuous threat to break our well-built harmonious teamwork with quality personnel, there was no chance of my dream realization. It was therefore important for me to take a call on my future career growth path. Dada slipped out that Tutu was always warning him regarding the risk of Himalaya Shipping being run by me in an autocratic manner, and by going for an IPO, other directors and promoter investors would lose total control. On the Samal Harand and SNR issue, Dada did not want us to interfere in his own company business, and he did not feel SNR quitting the company would cause any major damage. He mentioned Kakababu had talked to him about the board restructuring proposal of Gopal Da, which he would consider accepting after three years. Gopal Da candidly stated that the internal cost control system for the vessels on repair and maintenance, supplies of stores and provisions, and stevedoring and chipping painting as introduced and controlled by SNR and his department assistant Ashis Mitra was working very efficiently under Bodhon Da's supervision as director in-charge, and if SNR left, this system would be seriously impaired. The meeting did not end very happily, and I could see Dada was sulking. Later, when we were returning home for lunch, Dada told me that Gopal Da was trying to create a rift between me and him. Although Gopal Da was smooth and fair on the surface, he was scheming with Tutu to take control of the company by side-lining him. I suggested to Dada that I place my futuristic plan for board approval where more than one IPO for the company is in phases in our financial projections. If this plan and proposal got blocked by Bose Group, then Dada's view on Gopal Da's intention would be clearly established. My futuristic plan was approved by the board unanimously in the next month board meeting which proved Dada wrong in his assessment of Gopal Da's intention.

I had to take SNR in confidence and requested that he continued for another couple of years. I assured SNR that I'll keep insisting on Dada to act as per their signed agreement. SNR agreed but advised me that if Dada did not do anything during these two years, then he would resign. He assured me that for all of the post-early 80's expansion plans for the company, he would come back to me and join a restructured board, which was to essentially happen.

Coming back to business, Dada and I, in one of our joint Bombay visits, finalized the purchase of an office flat of 1600 sq ft more or less at the proposed Jolly Maker Chamber 2 in Nariman Point in 1976 for delivery by the 1977 third-quarter at a very cheap price when booking just opened. Our Bombay rep, Jayant Mehta, helped us with this with his local contacts. While continuing with our Bombay agent, Vinoo Bhai, we decided to open our new office in Bombay in 1977. Jayant Mehta was already working for us, and we took on my friend C. R. Kelekar from table tennis as the second man in the Bombay team.

We finalized the purchase of our 5th vessel through Sinclairs-Clarkson, which was a 5-year-old City Line 3 decker vessel that we renamed 'Sri Kailash' as a mark of our climbing another Himalayan peak. We took delivery of the vessel, as far as I remember, in early 1977 in Hamburg. SBI financed this vessel, and we sent out SNR a few days before the delivery. We were planning a visit to Hamburg for delivery and then followed it up with a London visit to meet Clarkson and a few other chartering brokers, including my friend James Felton of David Bruce. When I called the travel agent to book our tickets, Dada insisted that one of Dada or Gopal Da should stay back, which was unlike our previous few delivery trips. Gopal Da volunteered to stay back, but I could sense that he was not at all happy with this suggestion from Dada. Gopal Da told me that he was always interested in getting acquainted with my international contacts, particularly James Felton of David Bruice London, where

I was sending Bubai for his internship in shipping. Other than this, Dada was right that neither he nor Dada had any role in the delivery except the ornamental honor of formal coconut breaking and flag change. In any case, he would wait till 78 or 79 for Dada to step down in the expectation that I would take some proactive steps if Dada did not step down.

We took delivery of Sri Kailash at Hamburg, and I could meet my chartering guru, Louise Hoare, in the Hotel Four Seasons, where Louise was also staying like us. Louise was superlative in his praise for me and predicted a big role for me in the growth and development of the Indian shipping industry. Dada reciprocated warmly, stating that Himalaya Shipping's ambitious long-term growth plan under my skilled project innovation and dynamic leadership was destined for big delivery. I poured out my heart to Louise to narrate plans and strategies for the Himalayas. He heard me with interest and patience in Dada's presence and offered some valuable strategic guidance. He wanted me to meet Col. Helms of Hansa Line in Bremen, which was already on my travel schedule. I also had a plan to meet my old firm, Karl Geuther, in Bremen to discuss agency business and future container trends in international shipping. In Bremen, Col. Helms gave me and Dada a very warm welcome and greatly appreciated our container vision for the 1980s. He confidentially advised that Hansa was considering a merger with another German major, Hapag Lloyd, which had a big container focus for the future.

In Karl Geuther, both Mr. Geuther and Mr. Schnitger were excited to know about the Himalaya's ship-owning, ship management, and shipping agency combination and promised to recommend us for the Indian agency of their European clients.

In London, we met John Wheeler, Hugh Maccoy, and John Okeefee in Clarkson and explored container vessels and the Panamax Bulk Carrier New Building Market in Japanese and Korean Shipyards.

The market was on a downward path, and Hugh and John Okeeffee suggested that the appropriate time for us to finalize a block deal for two 500 TEU container vessels would be the first-quarter of 1978 for 1980 delivery. They promised to suitably explore a few reputed shipyards for this. Bulk Carriers New Building Market was also down, but to suit our plan for low market order placement and high tramp market delivery, the best strategy would be 1981/82 order placement for 1984 delivery. Dada participated in almost 4 hours of intense interaction with Clarkson, with lunch hosted by John Wheeler. Later in the hotel, when we were discussing it between the two of us, he expressed his appreciation for my ambitious plan and securing the support of such knowledgeable brokers and consultants for supporting us, but he wanted to know my fund mobilization plan for investments of nearly Rs. 70 crore in equivalent USD between 1980 and 1982. I explained to him in detail the financial projection I discussed and structured with Bula Da and Prashanta Ghose. Dada accepted my projection of a Rs. 3/4 crore reserve building in company B/S by 1980 for capitalization, but he was sceptical of my IPO plan for a Rs. 16 crore public issue.

I advised him that I had been interacting with the Grindlays Bank Merchant Banking division with financial planning and projections for the next 10–20 years, with each vessel acquisition project as an independent profit center. With 25% promoters holding, Grindlays would gladly underwrite Rs. 16 crores. I was confident that our issue would be oversubscribed. Moreover, with subsidized SDFC funding at 3% interest and a 6:1 debt-to-equity ratio, our opportunities would expand, allowing for up to Rs. 100 crore of investment. Dada had apprehension about Bose Group, particularly Tutu, agreeing to such equity dilution through a public issue. I reminded him that the Himalaya's Board had approved this expansion plan which Bose Group had a majority. I knew Tutu was in close touch with Dada. I tried to give Dada my own estimation of Tutu as a young entrepreneur with a sharp intellect and an uncanny assessment of the greed and need of the politicians and bureaucrats in the corridor of power. Tutu's quick reflexes and business sense were no match for Partha or even Gopal Da. Tutu was, however, not an industry man and a quick cash, no-risk business frame with a contractors' mind-set. Gopal Da was fully aware that ECB would flourish under Tutu but perish under Partha because of his experience and astute business sense. He was keeping Bubai away from Tutu, anticipating clashes and conflict through confrontation. On the other hand, as Tutu told me later, I was projected as Tutu's No. 1 adversary so that both the Himalayas and the ECB grew independent of each other with the least chance of any collaboration between Tutu and me. Tutu was playing on Dada's egocentric nature with a definite design to retard Himalaya's rapid stride in the Indian shipping industry.

I advised Dada in London that if any such negative decision came from Bose Group, I would put it in my papers and quit the company.

Dada was with me when I met James Felton of David Bruice and discussed Chartering Market. I was often chartering suitable Greek vessels through DB to satisfy shippers' demand in the West Asia Gulf Market. James was also in agreement with me on the recovery and turnaround of the global tramp market for bulk carriers from 1984 to 1985.

We fixed 'Sri Kailas' for Transchart Cargo of Rock Phosphate from Casablanca to E.C. India, and SNR went back to Calcutta after the vessel sailed out for Casablanca in ballast. Capt. Khandakar, if I am spelling his name correctly, was in command.

We reached Calcutta after our Bremen and London trips, 5 or 6 days before the vessel reached Casablanca.

Our operation manager, Mr. Shiva, advised me that while I was in London, EEPC members were requesting that we place a spot vessel for the Dubai and Kuwait loads of an accumulated volume of CI Goods cargo, for which they had given a letter to West Asia Gulf Conference Chairman, Mr. N. M Trivedi. I received a spot-trip TC offer from a Greek vessel, Marietta E, through my friend James Felton of David Bruice. I requested that James take a firm offer from the vessel and gave him a price range to trade for a few days until I returned to Calcutta.

Mr. Trivedi called a conference meeting to discuss the EEPC letter, which I was to attend only a day after our return. We needed a letter to be given to DGS from the conference to approve the foreign vessel charter. Marietta E was a prompt vessel, and we needed early DG clearance to finalize the fixture and place her in the berth. Unfortunately, I was stuck at home with a fever, and Dada volunteered to attend the meeting to get the charter clearance. All conference members strongly objected to our chartering a foreign vessel, and Dada got into an uncomfortable situation. Dada advised me that except for Mr. Trivedi, no other conference member supported us. We had decent bookings for CI Goods, steel, and tea cargo to make the vessel full. Mr. Trivedi advised me that Dada lost his cool and advised other lines to deal with EEPC, and Himalaya would step back. This gave no scope for further discussion, and he was calling EEPC members to meet the conference members to address the issue. I advised Mr. Kejriwal, who was EEPC Chairman at that time, if my memory serves right, to attend this meeting in full strength and demand the placement of a vessel within 7 days, and then request Mr. Trivedi to push DGS to clear our Marietta E Charter as the vessel was in Calcutta port. This strategy worked, and we could finalize the charter and place the vessel for loading. Pratul Mukherji of Pramukh Agency, who was an agent for South East Asia Shipping in Bombay for the Dhajibhoy Group, was a close friend of Gopal Da. His office was on Brabourne Road, opposite the PNB Building, where we had our office. Pratul Da used to often walk across to have the *adda* with Gopal Da, where Dada and I always joined to discuss conference and market gossip. We had rented his flat near Deshapriya Park for SNR residence. Pratul Da, in one such *adda* when Marietta E was still loading in the port, told Gopal Da and Dada humorously and affectionately that I knew some market magic and control conference chairman with my magic. He said Marieta E charter permission was outright declined by all the conference members, including him, and Dada, being cornered, left the meeting in frustration.

In two days after this, 'Your Chordada got us back to the conference meeting with EEPC members and invited and trapped us to swallow our own bitter pills' he stated in Bengali. Gopal Da added further spice to this, but I noticed Dada's face dropping with an element of complex. I covered up by stating that Dada did the right thing by leaving the meeting, which paved the way for EEPC intervention, but I realized that such unintentional innocent remarks were a potential danger zone for the company management.

During this time, on a very late evening, when me, SNR, and only a few others, like our telex operator Swami, my secretary Sudhis Bose, and Ashis Mitra, were in the office, the master of 'Sri Kailash' called from the Casablanca agent's office to advise that on arrival at Casablanca, a 'L'-shaped gush on the starboard aft of the vessel had been found. SNR could not figure out from the master how this happened except for a statement that Lloyd Surveyor boarded the vessel on his call and advised repair locally before the vessel could be placed at the loading berth. There was no log entry during voyage time of any accident or foreign body contact. A detailed telex from the agent came within 30 minutes, giving a quote of over USD 75K and an estimated 10 days of port time for repair. We could smell collusive corruption, and it was necessary for SNR to fly out. Unfortunately, in those days, lots of travel formalities were involved with RBI, and immediate action as required was not possible. I contacted one of my German engineering consultant friends, Hans Kuhne, from Hamburg, who was a very experienced and close friend from my Karl Geuther working days in Bremen. Hans agreed to fly out immediately to Casablanca. SNR advised the Master to hold back any action until Mr. Kuhne's arrival. Hans arrived the next morning and called me to advise me the same evening that the agent, repairer, and Lloyd's local surveyor were all in collusion to hold back the vessel and extract money. According to him, if this work was done in Cadiz, which was the nearest Spanish port, it should not take more than 36 hours within USD 15/20K cost. I authorized Hans to make the best decision when he told me that, fortunately, the vessel was in the anchorage, but agents were trying to take her in the next morning to start repair work. Lloyds Surveyors advised him that the vessel was out of class until it was repaired, and he would not allow the vessel to sail out to Cadiz. Hans' next phone call came at 1 a.m., waking me up. He simply informed me that he had decided to sail out to Cadiz, which was an 8/10-hour voyage, but during this period, the vessel would be out of class.

He wanted my clearance to sail out immediately before the agent or Lloyd Surveyor got a chance to intervene. In my half-asleep state, I immediately responded with a 'go ahead' without thinking. The following day, I was tense until late afternoon as the vessel was out of class. In the evening, Hans called to confirm the vessel's arrival at a Cadiz shipyard, expressing hope that it would sail out the next morning.

The total cost of the repair, including Hans's fees, was less than USD 15K. 'Sri Kailash' had to ballast back to Calcutta to be placed in our West Asia Gulf liner service.

In 1977, we started BSC East Coast USA liner service as BSC Agent, and this was an entirely different brand of marketing with adequate service and cost incentives, as I stated earlier. Bubai and my nephew, Amit, joined as management trainees. Another marketing and operations man, Ranjan Mukherji, was hired by us, coming from Brockle Bank Line. We also recruited young Pinaki Ghose as a trainee. We also had a very senior shipping professional for port operation S Chakravarty. In fact, when Dr. Sakhlecha of Great Eastern came to our office after we purchased Great Eastern Shipping's Jag Laxmi, he mentioned to us that the excellent Himalaya team and the management enthusiasm were reminding him of the early days of Great Eastern Shipping. Our Bombay office at Jolly Maker Chamber 2 in Nariman Point also got started in 1977. I had to make an extensive marketing tour of Europe and the USA for BSC at Capt. Safi's (CMD BSC) request, where I covered my friend Gustav Drohse's requested visit to Federikshavn Shipyard for Becket LASH ship project integration with IWT in India. Both Dada and I were making frequent trips to Dacca and Chittagong. My travels to West Asia Gulf ports were also substantial. Gopal Da and Boudi joined me on such trips a few times. If my memory serves right, Bubai was sent to London in 1977 to work with James Felton and David Bruce around this time.

I had extensive travel during 1977, sometimes alone and also at times with Dada, Gopal Da, and our family.

In the long round-the-world marketing trip covering Europe, the UK, the USA, and the Far East for BSC specifically and also on various vessel acquisition and chartering/agency activities in the Himalayas, Purnima and our daughter Soma (who was 7 years old) also joined me on my own account. As I stated earlier, I was actively pursuing order placement for new container feeder vessels with Japanese yards within mid-1978 for delivery to emerge by the last quarter of 1980. Afzal Khan, GM, BSC, and his wife were also present with me in the UK and USA for various extensive meetings we had with BSC foreign agents and USA importers. After our success in the USA east coast liner service for BSC, they were considering the changeover of their UK continental liner service agency from SCI to the Himalayas. This ultimately happened in early 1978, and our 1977 UK groundwork with BSC agents and shipper/consignee clients proved very productive and useful.

I will state a few interesting anecdotes during the trip for my readers to slightly deviate from the core business.

In our travel schedule, we kept the first 4 days for holidays in Rome and Paris. Both me and Purnima had a profound interest in the classical paintings and sculptures of artists like Bernini and Michael Angelo (in Rome), as well as the works of classical painters at the Louvre and also at the Modern Impresario Museum D'Orsay. We were both amused and delighted to find little Soma showing intense interest in such artworks and flooding us with her inquisitions. We visited Versailles Palace, where stories of French history from the guides were entertaining for Soma, and many questions were asked later in the hotel, which were not easy for us to answer. Bernini's sculptures in Rome, covering a wide spectrum of Greek mythology and stories of the Iliad and Odyssey, were very intellectually stimulating in their contents and aesthetics. Soma had read and knew most of the stories. Even the Vatican City Pieta of Michael Angelo and the painting on the Sistine Chapel wall, she found interesting. While discussing the sculpture of Moses at the church of 'St Peter's in Chains' and the Michelangelo story from the novel 'The Agony and the Ecstasy,' she expressed curiosity about the details.

Our next business meeting was a visit to Frederikshavn, Denmark. We were received at the Copenhagen airport by shipyard representatives. We saw him waiting with my name board at the entrance as we came out with our luggage trollies. After the exchange of greetings, I naively asked him, 'What time do we fly?' He politely answered, 'As soon as you are ready, sir.' He was the pilot of the shipyard's private small plane, and Soma was mighty pleased when he allowed her to sit in the cockpit. Gustav Drohse and Yard's MD drove us to the hotel. We spent two very productive days discussing the Becket LASH Vessel project concept and its unique potential and scope to integrate IWT river routes with ocean route for bulk cargo movement of substantial-high-quality low-ash content import coal demands of various power plants. There were many river-side power-plants which had potential benefit from this project. Various technical issues, like jetties at the riverside power plants with mechanical LASH barges discharging arrangements, were on the power-plants drawing board. We visited the shipyard, where Purnima and Soma also joined me out of their own curiosity. Gustav was a passionate promoter of the LASH concept, and I was trying for CIWTC and the government IWT sector to get into a PPP model project structured between a Danish-Dutch dredging company and Himalaya Shipping for long-term industry development.

Gustav was actively pursuing this with Dutch and Danish parties. We were invited for dinner at the residence of Mr. Bach, MD of the shipyard.

Mr. Bach and his wife was a delightful couple with a son of Soma's age. It was a very enjoyable evening at their home, where their son and Soma got engaged in playing together with fun and frolick so naturally without knowing each other's language. Among the parents, we were wondering if children had their own language of bonding.

We were in Copenhagen for two nights and saw Little Mermaid and visited Trivoly Gardens, which was fun for Soma, before flying out to London. Apart from a brief business call at the A.P. Moller office discussing both – container shipping and bulk carrier tramp markets, this short visit was spent mixing business and sightseeing with family. An interesting experience happened in our hotel room on the first night of our stay. We kept all the window curtains open to watch the sky and display of light in the Tivoli Gardens, which was next to our hotel, before retiring to sleep. Just after midnight, we were surprised to find that the room was full of daylight in Denmark.

Our London stay was for a longer duration. Afzal was already there before my arrival, and we spent quality time with the BSC Agent and some of my old contacts to explore the UKC Liner service and existing pool and conference systems for improving BSC UKC service, which was till then under SCI control in India. John Wheeler, John Okeefe, Hugh Maccoy of Clarkson, James Felton, etc. were my routine contact names.

My cousins Gautam and Dheera had their first child, Leela, Purnima, and Soma spent a lot of time with them. Our very close friend Dilip Choudhury and his Belgian wife Christine, along with their two sons Ambar and Ravi, invited us to their home. The two boys pampered Soma as a little sister, and we ended up with a late-evening dinner at a Chinese restaurant. Soma was tired and fell asleep, and the two brothers got her comfortably lodged on the table next to our table and looked after her very tenderly.

We stayed at the City of London Tower Hotel and made time for sightseeing and shopping. Afzal's wife flew out to New York alone as she wanted to meet a few of her relatives living in New York. USA agents of BSC were advised to receive her at the airport and reach her at her relative's place. Afzal got an alarming call from BSC New York agent to inform them that they could not find her at the airport on flight arrival. We were all worried, and Afzal had a harrowing 2 hours of exchanging phone calls with her relatives and NY agents before she could be located and reached to her relative's place. Apparently, when she was originally asked by Bill, the NY Agent, whether she was Mrs. Khan, She answered no, as Bill's language and accent she could not follow.

Afzal reached New York earlier than us, as our SAS flight was via Copenhagen.

We had three full days of very intense and constructive meetings with USA shippers and consignees, both independently and collectively with the agents, to address issues raised about port handling logistics and documentation. We could dig out information on our major competitor's strengths and weaknesses. There was strong policing by the Federal Marine on freight rebating and marketing logistics on integrated cost and freight formula. This needed deft handling by American parties' marketing agents in the UK and Europe. Our competitors in the UK, USA, and Helenic Line, with their own setup in New York, were scoring heavily over Indian Lines in the marketing logistics handling in the UK and Europe. The aggressive onslaught of BSC in their hidden reserve of freight market ammunition as a newcomer not only caught them off guard but they were also found holding hands with weak Indian shipping lines in conference meetings to point the policing guns of the Federal Marine on BSC. My marketing trip with BSC GM was primarily to counter this ploy and make our American clients aware of this ploy. I took this opportunity to discuss with Eastern, Southern, and Western USA shippers and consignees both immediate and future market logistics with container service for door-to-door delivery and optimization of transportation cost logistics.

We meticulously planned the listing of influential clients in New York, New Orleans, San Francisco, and LA, and our travel schedule covered all four cities in the USA. Land bridges with rail and road freight corridors were getting developed fast in the USA, and I could visualize their immense development scope in India.

In New Orleans, apart from meeting a few shippers and consignee clients for logistics discussions linked to handling and door-to-door delivery concepts through container introduction (which was happening fast in global liner shipping), I was probing Inland Water Transport in the USA. The detailed comparative cost and logistics efficacies between self-propelled barges and dumb barges flotillas with tugs were discussed with relevant authorities. I was fortunate to have interaction with Plimsol Club members researching load lines, oceanic zone-wise winter and summer draft charting, river draft, fresh water draft, salt water draft calculation for optimization of loading capacity, etc. Afzal came with me up to New Orleans and then went back to NY, where his wife stayed back with her relatives. We combined the business trip with sightseeing and a holiday for the family. Visits to French Quarters in New Orleans, Fisherman Wharf, Golden Gate Bridge in SF, Disney Land, Hollywood, and Queen Mary Passenger Ship in LA were covered along with a number of sea beaches in our USA trip. It was a round-the-world trip, and we came back to Calcutta via Honolulu, Tokyo, and Singapore. This trip and various interactions with shipping clients, associates, and agents gave me lots of insight into the future of international container shipping, which is to emerge in the next decade.

Back in Calcutta, I got busy in serious interaction with the then Grindlays Bank Merchant Banking Division (before their takeover by Standard Chartered later) regarding our future IPO, and with help and guidance from Bula Da and Prasanta, we got an IPO planned for the last quarter of 1978 or the first-quarter of 1979 with Grindlays MBD confidently underwriting the issue. With our next 10-year acquisition plan and financial projections, we could also get an SDFC loan lined up for the purchase of new building container vessels. We released our inquiries for two 500 TEU container vessels and started getting regular visits from a number of Japanese and Korean shipyards when the market was dipping downward. While West Asia Gulf liner service was vibrantly thriving with 10 days of frequency sailings from Calcutta and Bombay between our five own and a couple of charter vessels, there were gatherings of smoke in Iran and Iraq, with Khomeini taking over power from the Shah of Iran and a continuous spat between Tehran and Baghdad. Both our Calcutta and Bombay marketing teams were very active under Shiva in Calcutta, along with S. Chakravarty and B. K. Banerjee (who joined us from Gladstone as agents of City Line UK), looking after port operation, marketing, and documentation.

The Bombay office, under Jayant Mehta and Kelekar, built up a small but very effective team for marketing, documentation, and port operations. We were emboldened to accept further agency business from BSC and other foreign lines for both Calcutta and Bombay. For BSC client servicing and port operation in Calcutta, we took Ranjan Mukherji from Brocklebank, and my nephew Amit was tagged up with him in this. I was enjoying this creative workload with strong faith and surrender to Thakur, Ma, and Swamiji to guide me in the right direction.

My passion for table tennis was a jealous mistress of my professional passion for shipping. The early 70s and early 80s were my very busy days in table tennis, with equal, if not more, work pressure on my entrepreneurial commitments. I always got divine guidance and direction from Swamiji's Karma Yoga and my mentor Swami Lokeswaranandaji's vibrant presence in my being to practice detached Karma and instant switching of mind focus training. Creating mental space for intense rest in the midst of intense activities was Swamiji's prescription for generating creativity and productivity in human life. Dada often asked me while dropping me off at the Great Eastern Hotel in the evenings on his way back home how I was managing the time-sharing in pursuing these two passions of equal vibrancy. My hectic travel time (in the flight, airport transit, or hotel rooms) hardly had any space to feel lonely, as I had reading, writing poems and articles, and meditation as my constant companions. With growing children at home in our joint family, I always enjoyed engaging them in creative activities like play-acting, recitations, paintings, sports, and even writing poems. Amit and Renee were the son and daughter of my elder cousin 'chorda' Tarun Mitra, and they were older in age than my other 5 nephews: Arijit (Dada's son) and Avik (my *sejhdi* Manju Ghose's son), who were older than others like Ananjan and Raja (Nilanjan) (my *sejda* Malay's sons) and Ronty (Ritankar) (my *Chordi* Dipti Pal's son). My 3 nieces, Mita (my cousin Barda Ashok Roychowdhury's daughter), Ruma (my *sejhdi* Manju's daughter), were slightly older than Chandreyee (Dada's daughter) and Soma (my daughter). In our joint family ambiance, all these children were growing up together, playing, quarreling, and loving each other under the joint supervision of the elders. Treatments they received from their grandparents were more indulgent than from their parents. Whenever I engaged them in any play staged at our house hall or lawn under my direction, there used to be a lot of fun for them and also the elders during the rehearsal days. I used to organize for them painting competitions, poetry writing competitions, sprint races, etc. Many times, Maharaj Swami Lokeswarananda and other monks attended plays staged by the children to encourage them. I remember receiving sweet letters from Ronty, Chandreyee, and Soma while traveling in London, asking me when the next play would be staged. There are always upsides and downsides to the joint family system, but this system is great for mind training and soul expansion to think of others beyond one's narrow precinct and to develop the power to adjust and rub shoulders between persons of different levels of nature and character.

We staged Parashuram's 'Bhushundir Math' under my script and direction, and all the children with about 6 weeks of rehearsal performed brilliantly. Maharaj always appreciated my introducing the events under the direction of the 'Jatha, kaka, baba, ma, kakima, pishima, mama, mami, and all the elders of the children.' I mention this to highlight the strong family bonding that, by the grace of Thakur, Ma, Swamiji, and my mother's faith and surrender, prevailed in our joint family. My father, as the eldest and the head of the family, with his social skills, spontaneous love, and empathy, was the prime force in keeping this bonding string intact.

When my father advised me not to involve Dada in my shipping venture, I didn't understand the depth of his wisdom when he was apprehending impairment of family harmony due to professional complexities. My uncle as a bachelor never understood this and advised me to ignore my father's advice.

The year 1977 brought many changes to my life. I lost my father this year. There was a chink in the Himalayan happy family team when SNR advised me with a heavy heart his decision to leave Himalaya. This happened when Dada through his Samal Harand colleague, Mr. Chowdhury, advised him without any ambiguity that no stakeholding in the Samal Harand marine division as a separate unit would be given to SNR and the marine engineer's team, and the earlier agreement had been rescinded by Dada unilaterally. SNR was aware of my long-term vision and design to go for public issues for the Himalaya Shipping, where I offered stake holdings for the entire management team. He advised me that Shiva, Capt. Barve and his engineering team were going for a ship management venture, and all three of them would be committed to joining the Himalayas if and when my roadmap for IPO and expansion with me as MD was on the stream in real terms. SNR was very bitter toward Dada, and at the risk of hurting my sentiments, he clearly told me that I was to face serious roadblocks in my visions and dreams if Dada continued in the organization. He reminded me that Samal Harand was introduced by him to keep repair bills for the company under control and ensure the smooth running of the vessels with minimum layup. Profit-sharing incentives for the engineers were the prime force in this exercise. Keeping in mind the intention of our management to replace the old vessels by 1980, when most of them would be due for special surveys, we had avoided any major repairs that could have opened floodgates of fund drainage, as had been the case with many big shipping companies. He predicted that Samal Harand working under independent hired engineers would pose a serious conflict of interest. He stated all these to Gopal Da also. In a one-to-one meeting with me, Gopal Da expressed his anguish and concern with the simultaneous departure of three key persons and stated his apprehension that all my plans and projections would be halted if Dada continued. Gopal Da also told me that Dada was against our plan for a public issue and the modernization of the fleet by new building acquisitions.

Dada was also against my pre-planned decision to scrap Kedarnath in 1979 when she was due for a special survey. According to Gopal Da, since Kedarnath had performed exceedingly well financially and Great Eastern Shipping instalments were getting fully cleared by 1978, going for SS of Kedarnath would allow Samal Harand to take out money from the company. He also affectionately reminded me that when I earlier reduced the ECB stevedoring bill substantially and introduced TPRC and Mahalingam as stevedores, he did not object to or allow Tutu to disturb Himalaya's cost benefits through this decision, but he saw Dada's ploy to oust SNR as designed in the interest of Samal Harand and he had no intention to quit his Jt MD position in 1979 as committed. A serious management crisis in the company was looming large to scuttle my ambitious expansion plan.

Babi (my father) passed away in May 1977. During our mourning time, I requested SNR and two others to stay back until the first-quarter of 1978 to try and sort things out. They obliged me out of love and respect,

Babi's demise created a big void in our own joint family and also in our extended family in society. So many beneficiaries and friends enjoyed Babi's love and empathy. We were hearing touching stories from many of them, narrating with emotions and tears. This created a big void in our joint family. He always kept alive a strong harmonious bond between our uncles, aunts, and cousins through frequent family get-togethers during Durga Puja, Saraswati Puja,

Jamai Sashti, Bhai Phota, Kali Puja celebrations with fireworks, and other philanthropic events like Bhowanipore Sahajya Samity distributions of cloths, sweets, blankets, etc. to listed beneficiaries who were receiving financial support from the Samity. He was secretary of Sir Ramesh Mitter Girls High School and had active participation in much social work in the area of education and health. He was the Councellor of CMC for some time during Dr. B. C. Roy's time.

He was passionate about gardening, flowers, and particularly roses, and his rose garden in Mihijam and the beautiful house were very dear to him. His loss before I reached 40 was a big void in my life.

In July 1977, Gopal Da and I sat down with Dada to discuss SNR and two other resignation issues. I explained to Dada that with SNR, D. Rakshit, and M. Sarkar looking after the repair and maintenance of our vessels through their Samal Harand involvement, we could save time and money for repair and substantial repair costs. This was one of the main factors in Himalaya's success story with a frugal capital base. I also reminded him of our Nanda Devi Hong Kong experience, where our captain was in collusion with the agent and ship Chandler, which was going to cost us USD 50K in drainage.

Gopal Da was emphatic about protecting Himalaya's interests, and if Dada committed stake allocation in Samal Harand Marine to SNR and engineers, the breach of trust would not have happened and management harmony retained.

Dada was angry and complained that SNR was ambitious and, in the future, would claim stakes in the Himalayas as well. He said M. Sarkar agreed with him to join the Himalayas to replace SNR and continue with Samal Harand without claiming a stake like SNR.

I was shocked and firmly stated that I had a plan to give senior management personnel a stake in the company when Himalaya Shipping was going public, and SNR replacement by Sarkar would be disastrous for us, and there would be a big conflict of interest if he continued with Samal Harand. Dada exposed his hidden agenda in anger to say that he was having second thoughts on a public issue, and he had been warned that this would take the management control of the company totally out of the owner's grip. I was very disappointed and explained that I brought both Gopal Da and Dada into the shipping industry with a clearly laid-out plan for long-term scaling and introducing innovative projects on our growth path. Running a shipping company with a frugal capital of Rs. 18 lacs would not allow us to replace our overage vessels with new buildings, keeping with the trend of international shipping demand, and that would be the end of our journey. If there was mistrust and a continuous breach of commitment, then there was no point in my continuing with the organization. I would rather consider a new start-up instead of pursuing agency business, ship management, and other innovative port and shipping projects in the Himalayas. I was pursuing two container vessel orders with Japanese Shipyards as per our board approval and definite expansion plan for the next two decades, and if public issues were not pursued, there would be no future for the company. Under pressure, Dada wanted some time to think. After this rather unpleasant meeting, Gopal Da advised me to talk to my uncle and inform him of these issues to avoid any misunderstanding in the family. He also advised me to pursue my plans uninterrupted, and he would lend full support. I discussed the matter in detail with my uncle but found him irritated to say Gopal Da was trying to create a rift between the brothers and corner Dada. He said Dada was very appreciative of my securing BSC Agency, which was giving us a high yield in revenue, and that Dada would never stand in the way of my expansion plan implementation. On the Samal Harand issue, Kakababu continuously emphasized that, as a non-shipping person, SH was Dada's core business interest and failed to understand the conflict of interest issue. About the breach of commitment to SNR and the engineers, he said he would discuss it with Dada, and if there was any serious management issue, he would ask Dada to withdraw the Samal Harand Marine Engineering division totally from doing any business with Himalaya.

Kakababu further appeased me by stating that I should join the board in his place immediately and take over as MD when Dada quits as JT MD by 1978, as agreed. I expressed my doubt if Dada would agree to withdraw SH from the Himalayas or keep his commitment to hand over the MD position to me in 1978. Kakababu, in his simplicity and lack of understanding of the intrigues, felt Gopal Da was creating wrong ideas in my mind about Dada. I agreed to wait for his further feedback after he had talked to Dada. However, if there were further breaches from Dada or Gopal Da, I would stand by my decision to quit the Himalayas.

It was a very hectic action time for the Himalayas from the 3rd or 4th quarter of 1977 to the first-quarter of 1978. I finalized with Koyo Shipyard of Mitsui Group Japan a block order for two 500 TEU capacity geared container vessels, New Building, through Hugh Maccoy and John Okeeffee, who were no longer in Clarkson and had their own independent outfit. The deal was done at USD 5 million per vessel, and the yard paid for the SNR visit to the yard to finalize technical specs. SNR gladly did this job, as he was expecting me and Gopal Da to sort out issues with Dada on SH.

I followed up on the SNR visit for contract document finalization at the Koyo Shipyard near Hiroshima and the signing of the final contract at the Mitsui Tokyo office. Hugh Maccoy also came from London to Japan for this and further discussion with Mitsui for our Bulk Carrier NB order exploration at a competitive price. It was a very constructive and productive seven days in Japan, including travels between Osaka, Koyo Shipyard, and Tokyo by bullet trains and three full days at the shipyard, all hosted by Mitsui. In a downward market, this relationship-building with Mitsui offered the Himalayas multiple opportunities for business development. Hugh Maccoy's knowledge and experience in the S&P NB Contract were of immense value. We signed the contract document of over 100 pages in Tokyo with a ceremony and press conference where we jointly declared our future collaboration intentions.

I came back to Calcutta very satisfied with Himalaya's name in the global shipping market soaring high as a dynamic and aggressive Indian shipping company. From 1978 to the first-quarter of 1979, there were ups and downs in the Himalayas' journey. We secured a number of agency businesses, including the entire Indian agency of BSC. There was a big jute fire on Banglar Moitree when she was loading for UKC Ports under the SCI Agency. I was asked by Capt. Safi whether I could help them deal with a very messy situation due to the jute fire spreading and SCI giving no tangible assistance as their agent. I could very well understand the reason for SCI apathy, as they had already written off BSC after Himalaya took over USA Agency. I teamed up with my Marine Insurance Guru, V. K. Bhandari, and got our agency and technical department to douse the fire by sacrificing a substantial volume of jute cargo.

There was a London-based average adjuster for the owners, and by the immediate declaration of the general average from the owner's side in consultation with the adjusters, we started discharging the entire jute cargo from the vessel under the Custom's supervision. Over 10–15% of jute cargo was fire-damaged, and debris was on the quayside yard to be auctioned and sold as scrap. Good cargo was of substantial value and was discharged in barges alongside. This fetched good value from sale to the parties by auction under customs supervision, despite handling losses through multiple agency handling. The vessel was old and had a few months to go for SS after a class extension. BSC had a very competent technical director, Mr. Rahman, with an efficient team. Mr. Bhandary got the vessel's P&I Club and Marine Insurance to deal with the insurable interest of Hull & Machinery and Cargo to structure a comprehensive recoverable PA, GA, and Cargo combined claim, which got the owners a fully classed liner vessel for another 4 years of operation with full cost recovery from insurance. For the total insurance consultancy, I billed BSC 30K and received very reasonable billing from Mr. Bhandari. BSC GM Afzal Khan was always a bit tight-fisted and negotiation-prone in settling bills, and I was called to Dacca to discuss settlement. He wanted to strike a bargain with me to get the bill reduced by USD 10K against BSC appointing us as their Indian agent for all ports and services. I wanted to discuss this matter with CMD Capt. Safi, and we went together to the chairman's office. Afzal was trying to impress the chairman by stating his reasons for a fair settlement while I was quietly listening. Capt. Safi went eloquent in praise and appreciation of a fabulous job done and requested that I give my reaction to the Afzal proposal. I politely stated that as a shipping professional, I did my job with sincerity and commitment to perfection, and I would accept BSC Agency for India only if BSC was fully satisfied with my credibility, competence, and integrity. If BSC considered my billing to be unreasonably high, they would have full freedom to deduct, and I would consider that my intellectual integrity was failing me in my assessment of reasonableness. Capt. Safi asked Afzal openly in my presence, 'I thought we had taken a quotation from a London consultant who quoted over USD 100K for this job, and Mr. Mitra should be given at least 50% of this. Afzal got defensive and said that would raise an audit objection, and the best he could do was to pay Himalaya's bill without any deduction.

We also scrapped Gourishankar in 1978 by selling her to the ship-breakers by auction. There was an understanding among the ship-breakers to form cartels to get a price advantage. Despite this, there was hidden competition. In the first auction, they were way out of my reserve price of Rs. 40 lacs. Before going for the second auction, I made a side deal with one of the lead breakers to bid the reserve price by convincing others in the cartel to offer incentives. Finally, we could secure a net of Rs. 38 lacs. It was painful to part with this dear old lady who had brought substantial wealth to the Himalayas at the time of our fund crisis, but the inevitable end of a life cycle had to be accepted with grace. This was in keeping with our plan for replacing our old ladies with new building acquisitions from the early 1980s. Since our West Asia Gulf service needed maintenance of call frequency for client servicing, we decided to purchase another old liner vessel from Scindia Steam Navigation, 'Jala Dhruv,' which had a little over three-year trading period before her next SS. This vessel was bought through Samir Dasgupta of Sinclairs as a broker for a negotiated price of less than Rs. 70 lacs, which was more or less the scrap value of the vessel. She was larger than Gouri Shankar and almost the same size as Kedarnath, with a higher LDT. I was already checking the scrap market value for the Kedarnath sale in mid-1979 when her SS was due. This meant some cash out from our reserve as we bought this vessel with only a working capital facility from UIB, who were very happy with our 'Kedarnath' loan servicing, where we had substantial cash build-up with all instalments paid to Great Eastern by early 1979. I was calculating the replenishment of this cash from the sale of Kedarnath in the 2nd and 3rd quarters of 1979. I was dead on target to build a reserve of Rs. 1.5 crore for capitalization to go for Rs. 4.5 crore public issues with Grindlays Bank Merchant Banking underwriting the issue. We secured the Govt. of India SDFC approval in the last quarter of 1978 to provide up to a Rs. 36 crore ship acquisition loan based on our enhanced paid-up capital of Rs. 6 crore through a public issue. In fact, based on a little less than Rs. 1 crore of reserve and Rs. 18 lacs of paid-up capital in our balance sheet, SDFC financed our Sri Kailash purchase in 1977, with SBI providing us the foreign currency loan for the purchase price at the ruling LIBOR plus a 6-month fluctuating rate.

With the Iran and Iraq conflict and tension escalating, I was visualizing a change in our West Asia Gulf service pattern, and it was almost written on the wall that container vessels would take over the break-bulk vessel business in the 1980s. I thought we would continue with 'Sri Kailash' and 'Jala Dhruv' up to 80/81 and then two feeder container vessels and 2/3 Panamax bulkers during the next decade and pursue innovative ship, port, and IWT integration projects linking for effective integration of transport supply chain servicing through ocean, river, rail, and road. Himalaya Shipping moved on a charted path with divine direction despite many initial hiccups and internal human failings.

I was focusing on the BSC Agency business on a pan-India basis, using Himalaya's agents in Madras, Cochin, Gujarat Ports, etc. I always had the confidence and complete trust of BSC Chairman

Capt. Safi. He appreciated my project paper on container vessel introductions in their 2/3 liner service routes through tie-ups with large main lines. I was visualizing the creation of a powerful container feeder service network for servicing the container traffic flow of East Coast India and West Coast India ports through mainline call ports like Singapore, Colombo, Dubai, and Jedda by introducing 10/12 custom-built container vessels of different sizes.

I knew the efficacy of container shipping was to be focused on round-the-world Panamax and post-Panama-size ships servicing clockwise and anti-clockwise global ocean routes, as this alone can achieve substantial cost savings per unit through multiple slot utilization during one round voyage of the vessel. Export and import container traffic from each of the large mainline vessels would get a big boost in the spread and long-term scaling with a 2–3 day call frequency. Round-trip direct and indirect costs of the vessel would remain the same for any volume of container carriage, and port CY cost would have a separate cost-saving equation through large container terminal operations and door-to-door transport supply chain management. The 'would be' development prospect of land bridge system which was emerging in the USA, India, China, Australia, etc. with the potential of extension of this system between nation-states with small and large land masses was of huge benefit for the trade and shipping. More than 4/5 consortiums of large, big-ticket ship owners around the world were to optimize both the capex and opex of such a round-the-world container service operation successfully. Similarly, feeder container service consortiums, land bridges, and other multimodal transport service consortiums were required to make an impact on international commodity and consumer trade sustainability.

After this little reflection on my vision for the industry, let me land back on the ground for the 1979 Himalaya Shipping storyline. In the 2nd quarter of 79 SNR, Shiva and Capt. Barve left us as an outcome of Dada not agreeing to give a stake in Samal Harand to the SNR and team. Dada brought in M. K. Sircar in place of SNR, who was looking after both the Himalaya Engineering division as well as Samal Harand. Repair bills started shooting up almost immediately. A few bills from Samal Harand were held up, and Gopal Da wanted me to take action by speaking to Dada and Kaka Babu if required and deal with the situation in the same way as I did with ECB earlier. I frankly talked to Dada and advised him that with SNR leaving us due to the SH dispute, there was a setback for our ship management division development plan. M. Sarkar, as part of the SNR team, was serving SH with stake expectations. If he has stayed back to serve both the Himalayas and SH, then there is a very potential conflict of interest. Gopal Da was receiving pressure from Tutu to bring back ECB on the stevedoring and chipping painting jobs. Dada knew of my earlier intervention with ECB stevedoring bills and Gopal Da's consent to bring in other stevedore at a competitive rate in the interest of the company.

Dada's angry reaction was adverse and furiously violent. He blamed me for taking unilateral actions on operational and administration matters. SNR according to him was unduly pampered by me and Ashis Mitra was creating problem for M Sarkar at my indulgence. He went to the extent of exposing his hidden agenda to oppose my decision to sell Kedarnath to the breakers in last quarter 1979. He had a report from a third-party consultant secured by M. Sarkar, who opined that Kedarnath SS should not cost the company more than 25/30 lacs with a maximum 30-day lay-up. Since the vessel was free of any debt, she could generate substantial cash for the company for the next 3–4 years. There was also resentment expressed about my investment decision in a new office of 10,000 square feet at Middleton Row. I tried to calm him down by explaining our expansion plan with the new building container feeder service and the public issue, along with the expansion of our agency division. He was still in a rage to say that although the board cleared my expansion plan with fleet modernization, he was not happy about the public issue and the high investment in fleet modernization. Regarding SH bills, he simply said they were cleared by M. Sarkar, based on which he had released payment. I had to call Gopal Da in Dada's chamber to announce my decision to quit the company if there was any backtracking on our expansion plan and public issue. I lost my cool to say that a non-shipping person without any in-depth knowledge and vision of the global shipping market would bring ruin to a shipping venture meticulously planned for phase-wise development and growth. Dada had false notion that' Kedarnath,' which had given us a high cash yield for the last 4 years even after paying our deferred payment instalments, would continue giving us a handsome cash yield free of debt instalments. I explained to him that this size of over 20-year-old tween decker vessel would have no demand in the liner market from 1980 onwards with the start of the container vessel regime.

Gopal Da was trying to mediate by stating that no decision would be taken without consulting me, which infuriated Dada to say that I must not expect the company to run under my unilateral decisions only. I left the meeting stating that my decision to resign was final. After about one hour, Gopal Da came to my chamber and requested that I give him one more year to resolve matters with Dada so that none of my expansion plans were hindered by our internal disputes. I must not take any hasty decisions in the meantime.

Next morning, as I was coming down the stairs to start for my office, Kaka Babu called me to our ground-floor hall, where he was sitting with Dada by his side. He said emotionally that I must not resign and allow Gopal Da to create rifts in our family. Gopal Da, according to Dada, was using my resignation threat to pressurize Dada to withdraw Samal Harand as Himalaya's marine repair engineering contractor and make room for me to be MD by removing him from the management team. SH's investment in the Marine Engineering Division was based entirely on exclusive servicing of Himalayan vessels, and in view of Dada's full-time involvement with the Himalayas, SH's original electrical engineering work was not generating expected revenue. I narrated Dada's breaching of agreement with SNR and Engineering Team and explained that it was at SNR's recommendation and initiative that we introduced ECB, SH, and Capstan Ship Chandling as contractors on a competitive basis to have effective cost control. While ECB and Capstan were working for other shipping lines like Everet, ISS, Ratnakar, SCI, South East Asia, etc., the SH Marine Engineering division was created by SNR and team to build a base for Himalaya's vessel repair work on competitive terms and then scale up to secure other clients' orders and be a part of Himalaya's Ship Management Service Division long-term. Dada could not contradict me but feebly complained about SNR being too ambitious and exploiting my giving him undue importance in the management. Dada also stated that Gopal Da was using Tutu as his remote handle to take management control, always keeping a good front face with me. I knew very well that Tutu was an intelligent, competent, and ambitious young person with his own style of entrepreneurial flair, which did not match my style, and unlike Partha, he was capable of taking control of ECB to scale heights in port and shipping projects. I had hidden affection in my mind for his uncanny dexterity and quick reflexes. I told Kaka Babu that I had neither interest nor time to dissect internal conflicts or get involved with anybody in any ego issues. My focus was on the growth and development of the company phase-wise as per the long-term plan for three decades that I had presented to the company's board and moving forward as per board approval. If there was any backtracking, be it from Dada or Gopal Da's side, I would be compelled to quit, as, in my opinion, in terms of success measures, we had done more than our expectations during the first decade with frugal capital and old vessels. For the next decade, without the replacement of the old tonnages by custom-built new buildings through raising the capital base to Rs. 6 crore, all the good results we have achieved so far would go to waste, and the company would be facing serious problems. Kaka Babu, without giving Dada any chance to speak, assured me that from Dada's side there would be no interference in the implementation of my plans. He repeated his insistence on taking me on board in his place and advised Dada to remain a director only so that he could give more time to SH management and make room for me to be MD by the 3rd quarter of

1980. Dada was silently sulking, and I gave my consent to Kaka Babu by clarifying that I was not against Dada continuing to be part of the management, but I was genuinely concerned about the company's survival without fleet modernization through a public issue.

When I advised Gopal Da about my decision to continue till the 3rd quarter of 1980 at Kaka Babu's request and Dada agreeing to quit his JT MD position by then making room for me to be MD and Gopal Da becoming Chairman, Gopal Da was sceptical about Dada's keeping this commitment.

We unfortunately lost our dear lady Nanda Devi towards the end of 1979 when she sank near Karachi while returning to Bombay from Dubai in Ballast. By Thakur's grace, the entire crew of the vessels were safely rescued. The vessel was debt-free and fully insured. We could recover Rs. 50 lacs from insurance against our TLO claim. Although this vessel was included in my list of replacements for fleet modernization, I felt sad to lose our inaugural peak going down in the ocean.

Our new building container vessels were due for delivery by the last quarter of 1980, and I was discussing this with SDFC at the Ministry level and also with SBI, which had already tied up with SDFC for loan financing of Sri Kailash. Koyo Shipyard and Mitsui's notice for delivery was already received, indicating a 3-month span between December 1980 and February 1981. Although between Bula Da, Prasanta, and me, we had in-principle clearance from the Grindlays Bank merchant banking division for underwriting our IPO for Rs. 4.5 crore with Rs. 1.5 crore promoters holding in our Rs. 6 crore capitalization plan, SBI was also trying to introduce their merchant banking division in our public issue and capitalization plan. We were expecting over Rs. 2 crore in reserve building out of profit in our 1979–1980 financial year, including a Rs. 50 lakh insurance claim cheque expected to be received within February 1980. Therefore, it was smooth sailing for the company to step into our next-decade fleet modernization plan. The Kedarnath special survey was due in December 1979, and I already had a demolition price offer of nearly Rs. 80 lacs for delivery of the vessel to the breakers in January 1980.

Our new office of over 10,000 square feet at Middleton Row had interior décor where we planned a separate agency division, a ship management division, a port and shipping project consultancy division, and a ship chartering outfit. Our prime Himalaya Shipping's vessel operation was kept in an exclusive 3000-square-foot separate block with the directors and CEO's secretariats and marketing division. Repair and maintenance of vessels, port servicing, agency, and ship management were consolidated under our own ship management division, which occupied a spacious area of nearly 6,000 square feet. Just over 1,000 square feet were designated for port and shipping development projects, research and development, and consultancy, including a proficient chartering outfit. Towards the end of 1979, my Indian port and shipping industry development dreams were almost at the threshold of their phase-wise fruition over the next decades.

Kedarnath was sent on her last West Asia Gulf voyage, which included Khorramshahr and Basra cargo, and was expected to be back by the end of January or early February 1980 for delivery to the breakers. In early January 1980, I got somewhat busy with my table tennis engagement for the conduct of the National TT Championship at Durgapur. Although the tournament was held in the 3rd week of January, I was committed to frequent travel and stayed in Durgapur for almost a fortnight along with my BTTA colleagues. A new indoor stadium in Durgapur was built during this time, and Chief Minister Jyoti Basu was to inaugurate the National Championship and the stadium. Unforeseen organization commitments for the 5th Asian TT Championship also came to BTTA at the TTFI AGM at Durgapur, held at the end of January. At the end of all this, when I returned to business in the Himalaya office, Gopal Da and Bodhon Da advised me that Dada had taken a decision to undertake a special survey of Kedarnath instead of selling her to the breakers based on a 3rd party report secured by

Mr. Sarkar, Engineer Superintendent, where a 3-week layup time and a cost estimate of Rs. 25 lacs were indicated. They were waiting for my return to have a meeting on this. We had an emergency board meeting where I strongly spoke against this decision, as the demolition sale of this vessel was planned when she was purchased before her next SS was due, and accordingly, we did not undertake any major expenses on repair during her over-4-year service tenure. I emphasized that special survey expenses and lay-up period would not be less than Rs. 50 lacs and 2 months. Dada explained that Mr. Sarkar and his team in Samal Harand had gone into details in working out a cost estimate and timeline for work completion, and we should go by such concrete technical assessment and not by emotions alone. I bluntly asked what would be her deployment for the next 3/4 years as the West Asia Gulf market would be fully containerized within the next couple of years. Iran and Iraq were also on the horizon, and it would be unwise to count on our freight revenue from Khorramshahr and Basra ports. Mr. Sarkar was called in the meeting, and I bluntly asked him what had made him change his opinion on Kedarnath expressed with SNR and Rakshit when we purchased the vessel. He was somewhat fumbling when I further asked whether he would guarantee to keep the SS cost within his estimate and timeline. He was uncomfortable to say that it was difficult for him to guarantee, but surely we could take a few other repairers' quotations to verify the authenticity of his estimate and timeline. When Sarkar left the meeting, Dada, in an agitated voice, declared that he would like to stick to his decision, which we all found very unreasonable. Gopal Da, for the first time, went to the extent of stating that Mr. Sarkar's dual role as Himalayan engineer super and Samal Harand MIC would be causing a serious conflict of interest.

Gopal Da sat in my chamber after the meeting and advised me that Tutu, Partha, and Dada had teamed up to take the decision to go for Kedarnath SS. He felt things were not going in the right direction for the company. I predicted to him that our mega expansion plan, for which we made an investment in the big new office, might get seriously impaired by such a silly decision, as we could easily manage our trade commitments through vessels we chartered from ISS and the cash yield I was expecting from the sale of Kedarnath to the breakers of around Rs. 80 lacs. This will serve our promoter's contribution requirement for the public issue. Kedarnath was sure to become a liability for us even after spending Rs. 50 lacs plus for SS and 2/3 months idle time for the vessel to deplete our cash reserve. Gopal Da felt I should talk to "Kaka Babu" about Dada's working full time for Samal Harand and making room for me to become MD in the restructured board, where he agreed to have three each from both families with Gopal Da as Chairman.

I had a long talk with 'Kakababu' and explained to him about my concern on Dada's decision for Kedarnath to go for SS. This was going to be a major catastrophe for the company, and will be affecting my plan for capitalizing the company in our major expansion drive. I also briefed him about Gopal Da's board restructuring plan to save the company and from further conflict of interest between Himalaya Shipping and SH due to Dada's sense of insecurity about protecting SH's interests only. Kakababu advised me to allow Dada to promote interest in SH, which was his own engineering enterprise created with hard work and struggle. Dada was 12 years older than me, and Kakababu very candidly stated that there was discomfort in Dada's mind to accept me as the decision-making leader of our shipping venture. He felt Gopal Da was trying to create a rift between me and Dada to take control of the company. Tutu was used by Gopal Da as the frontman in the entire plan. He was concerned about Dada's mental health, as Dada was feeling lonely and cornered by the Bose group without any support from me. I could not agree with him but at the same time felt concerned about a rift in our happy joint family, which was still held tight by Ma after Babi's demise. I had to talk to Ma about my concern. Ma knew that Dada was egocentric and not spiritually splurged like me with faith and surrender to Thakur. She had already advised Dada many times to refine his ego and trust me, as Thakur was holding my hand. She advised me to always follow Thakur's direction in combating adversities, even if this meant making apparently unpleasant decisions. She also advised me to talk to Maharaj (Swami Lokeswarananda) to seek his wisdom in any conflict situation. 'Kakababu' after talking to Dada confirmed to me that Dada was agreeable to keep his commitment to quit and make room for me to join the board as MD, but he would like to be Joint Chairman with Gopal Da. Alternatively, 'Kakababu' was to be the chairman, which was not acceptable to 'Kakababu' as he wanted Sejda Malay to join our board in his place to represent the Mitra family group.

I got extremely busy from March until May 1980 with the 5th Asian TT, as organizing this massive international event in three months was a tall task. Capt. Ronie Ghose, our Marine Super in place of Capt. Barve, was a very experienced and competent Master Mariner, much senior to me in age and experience and known to me from his ISS days, as I narrated earlier. He was having serious altercations with Mr. M. Sarkar directly and Dada indirectly on Kedarnath SS repair jobs. I expressed my helplessness to Gopal Da and requested that he intervene. During 1975 World TT, I could manage Shipping and Table Tennis with equal passion at a time of extreme financial crisis and adverse situation of the company, but in 1980 I was out of breath for handling Kedarnath crisis by getting into confrontation with Dada. The cost of repair exceeded Rs. 60 lakh, and it took over two months for the vessel to be back in operation. Through Sinclairs, I fixed her on a 6-months charter with a Far Eastern ship owner at a reasonably good rate for delivery in Singapore. Vessel sailed out for Singapore in early May to meet her end May' Lay Can' dates in chartering terms.

The 5th Asian TT was over by mid-May, and it took me and the BTTA team a few more days to wrap up the event. We planned a family holiday to North Bengal between me, Purnima, Soma, Gopi, Monica, Chandak, Sarojda, Boudi, Asim, and my sister-in-law Sumitra, Arindam, and Kabu. In the middle of our holiday when we were in Darjeeling, I got a message and call in my hotel from Dada that Kedarnath climbed a rock near Andaman and became a constructive total loss. I was required to immediately fly back to Calcutta to handle the complicated insurance claim and investigation of the cause of the accident. When I reached home, Ma expressed her relief and told me that despite her advice to Dada to surrender to Thakur, Dada was feeling helpless and restless, and she was very concerned. I assured Ma that with her blessings and Thakur holding our hand, we should be able to come out of this calamity. It was Thakur's divine design to fortify us with our mental strength to face such adversities. Ma assured me that total faith and surrender to Thakur would always give me light in the divine direction. I contacted my insurance Guru and friend, Mr. V K Bhandari, and arranged an independent survey and investigation of the vessel log and the watch-keeping officers, particularly the master of the vessel, by MMD surveyors. The Independent Class Surveyor's report was also essential to establish that the vessel was beyond recovery and salvage, and she would break her back to come out of the rock even by deploying a powerful tug. Fortunately, the vessel was in ballast condition, and there was no cargo interest involved. Although there was no crew casualty, we informed and involved our P&I Club to deal with crew-related medical claims.

It was revealed that the newly appointed captain was drunk while on watch, and the chief and second officer had to face the wrath of the master's irresponsible behavior. VKB guided us to submit our final CTLO claim for a total insurance value of Rs. 1.5 crore with very sound documentation to the Oriental Fire & General Insurance Company, who had their head office in Madras, and we were asked to submit our claim to their Bombay branch. Their GM, Mr. Bantwal in Madras, was a very knowledgeable and straight-forward officer who became a very close and personal friend of mine through the VKB connection. The Bombay office claim processing officer did not like my pushing him through Mr. Bantwal; I had feedback from Kelekar that this Bombay officer was expecting some speed money. It took us until the end of July to prepare and finalize our claim submission.

During June and July 1980, I was very actively pursuing a container feeder service networking between BSC and the Himalayas, with the initial placement of two vessels each by both parties on the Calcutta-Madras-Singapore route and the Calcutta-Madras-Clombo route. I was also interacting with Ceylon Shipping Corp. and their subsidiary Ceylon Shipping Line for opening up West-Asia-Gulf-Ports container service and Red Sea Ports on Service/Through B/L arrangements using strong market support from Himalaya and BSC in West Asia Gulf, Red Sea, UKC, and USA East Coast Liner service. I was also negotiating with emerging Main Line operators like Maersk, P&O, and APL to collaborate in servicing these markets with MLO 'through' B/L and our consortium's feeder service B/L. I was extensively traveling West Asia—Gulf-Dubai-Emirates, Iran, Iraq, and Kuwait—with Kelekar and also with Gopal Da, Purnima, and Meera Boudi, who accompanied us on a few trips. Gopal Da and I planned a pre-puja trip to Europe, UK, Greece, and Scandinavia to develop our agency business and MLO container service tie-ups. On my Bangladesh and Sri Lanka trips, Dada often accompanied me, particularly on Dacca trips. With three dear ladies, 'Gouri Shankar,' 'Nanda Devi,' and 'Kedarnath,' making their exit from Himalaya's fleet, we were left with 'Nilkantha,' 'Sri Kailash,' and 'Jala Dhruv' for servicing our West Asia Gulf trade route, while container vessels were waiting on the fringe, about to take over. Also, the Iran-Iraq conflict situation was taking a somewhat ugly turn, and we were feeling sceptical about our revenue flow from Khoramshahr and Basra traffic. With 'Kedarnath' exit after very heavy cash outflow for her two-month SS drill without any revenue generation, we had to face an adverse cash flow situation as our operation team count expanded and investment in our new office, coupled with the skeleton running of our old office (keeping an eye on our future expansion plans), impacted our cash-flow with increased overhead expenses. For the 31st March 1980 financial year closing, we had booked Rs. 1.8 crore net profit with Rs. 2 crore plus in our reserve. The 'Gourisankar' demolition sale and recovery of 'Nanda Devi' TLO insurance claim recovery gave us some cash surplus even after the cash purchase of 'Jala Dhruv' in late 1979. Stoppage of revenue flow from three vessels and debt servicing of' Nilkantha' and 'Sri Kailash' needed working capital support from both SBI and UIB. It was important for us to keep in mind our promoters' contribution requirement of Rs. 1.5 crore for the impending IPO.

To mitigate the cash flow crunch, I decided to place all three vessels for Khoramshahr and Basra one by one, starting with 'Nilkantha' in the second half of July, followed by 'Sri Kailash' in the first half of August, and 'Jala Dhruv' in the second half of August. There was a heavy accumulation of high-valued tea cargo of shippers like Macneil Magor, Iran Tea, James Warren, James Finlay (later to become Tata Tea), Harris & Crossfield, etc. All the vessels earned good freight for us, and we had to charter another small vessel from Hauer Line from my friend Mr. Narsimhan to load the left-over cargo for September.

In the midst of all this turbulence and tornadoes, a terrible blow came to my life when Ma left for her heavenly abode on August 19, 1980. She was my source of spiritual power and a lighthouse for me in the ocean of Thakur, Ma, Swamiji's spiritual bliss. I returned from Dacca sometime in July and found Arijit at the portico to tell me as I was coming out of the car, 'Didu had a fall in the bathroom in the morning and was having a breathing problem.' I went straight to Ma's bedroom on the 2nd floor and found Mejdi, Chordi, my sisters, and Boudi, Purnima, and Mandrita in the room. Ma always had acute asthma, and due to the fall and chest congestion, it got aggravated and needed immediate aggressive treatment. We were six siblings, which always created decision-making problems concerning Ma's treatment. Dr. Prasanto Banerjee, a renowned homeopath, was our close family friend, and on the previous occasion of Ma's illness, when Babi, my father, was alive, we could get Babi's friend and our family physician, Dr. Rabi Mukherji, to intervene after over 7 days of distress under homeopathic treatment to get relief through aggressive allopathic treatment. I wanted to consult Dr. Rabi Mukherji and Dr. Sunil Sen, but Dada had already called Dr. Chadha after consulting Dr. Prasanto Banerjee. After 4–5 days of suffering without much relief, I personally brought Dr. Mukherjee and Dr. Sunil Sen, and they prescribed aggressive treatment with 'Nursing Home arrangements' at home to start immediately. Dada and Chordi did not want to upset Dr. Chadha, who was literally making a mess with the treatment, and we lost Ma. It took a lot of time for me to come to terms with Ma's demise until I received a divine gift from Thakur to have her subtle presence in the depths of my being forever.

During the second half of September, I went on a seven-day tour of Europe, Scandinavia, and the UK with Gopal Da and Boudi. We got confirmation before our departure that 'Nilkantha' was to complete her discharge at Khorramshahr within the next 2–3 days and proceed to Basra for discharge of the balance cargo. Dada was to take care of RBI formalities for ensuring the remittance of Basra port disbursements for the vessel to sail out immediately after she completed discharge. Unlike other ports in the West Asia Gulf, government-controlled Basra agents were not permitted to release vessels from the port without receiving remittances of port disbursements from the owners. 'Sri Kailash' had already sailed out of the port of Calcutta, and 'Jala Dhruv' was to sail out of Kolkata within the next two days after our departure. Our 6,000 DWT chartered vessel from Hauer Line was already delivered to us and berthed in the port to commence loading. We had Subrata Bose as our operation manager, who replaced Mr. Shiva, and Capt. Ghosh was looking after the loading and stowage of the vessels. If my memory serves right, there was a Bangladesh vessel 'Banglar Maan' loading carpet backing and jute cuttings for east-coast USA ports, and booking and handling were looked after by Ranjan Mukherjee and my nephew Amit, along with Mr. B. K. Banerjee and S. Chakraborty looking after cargo documentation and port handling, respectively.

In our seven-day hectic travel plan, we had scheduled meetings with A. P. Moller in Copenhagen, Clarksons, David Bruce, and John Okeffee in London, Louis Dreyfus in Paris, and a number of Greek shipowners in Piraus and Athens. We had an optional plan to visit Bremen, but ultimately we could not manage this due to time constraints. I invited Gustav Drohse to meet us in Copenhagen to follow up on our 'Becket' lash barge project, which I was discussing with Frederikshavn Shipyard. This project was filling up a very innovative part of my port and shipping project consultancy area, covering the linking of rivers and oceans through mobile virtual port development at a deep-sea location at the mouth of Calcutta port. I had primarily discussed this concept through big and small barge carrier vessels. While Gustav and Frederikshavn were specializing in the dumb barge lash concept, with the carrier vessel providing the power with ocean-going class and navigation capabilities, I was also discussing with Capt. Olsen of Scandimar, Sweden, a bigger-size barge carrier cum transloader for plug-in, plug-out self-propelled barges of over 20k ton DWT with a broad beam to carry and discharge full-load bulk cargo in Haldia port. I was also discussing with Clarkson and Louis Dreyfus a different concept of transloading, which was only at the conceptual relation-building stage in 1980. Meeting with A. P. Moller and Maersk was also very constructive and educational for me, particularly on the container shipping part, as Maersk, P&O, and APL were having major R&D desks for the total container logistic planning globally in the early days. Gobal Da was always a keen observer in such meetings, but his post-meeting comments and inputs were both very motivating and useful for me. In London, Bubai was working as an intern with David Bruce under the parental care of my friend James Felton. Both Gopal Da and Boudi were very happy to find Bubai comfortably engaged and making satisfactory progress in professional shipping. He was enrolled with The Institute of Charter Shipbrokers—both me and James were Fellows of this august professional shipping institute. James invited us for dinner at his home in honor of Bubai's parents, and we spent a very enjoyable evening with James and his family. I was told by James that my chartering guru, Louise Hoare, just retired and was coming to the City of London once or twice a week only. I could only speak to Louis over the phone when he promised to meet my nephew Bubai by talking to James during one of his city visits.

James gave us an introduction to 4/5 Greek owners to meet in Piraus. Our visit to Athens and Piraus was the last leg of our trip when we could secure a few important agencies of Greek ship owners regularly calling E-C Indian ports, including Haldia and Kolkata, as part of their Transchart CP terms.

While in Greece, we got news of the war confrontation between Iran and Iraq and the closure of Khorramshahr and Basra ports to commercial shipping trade. I immediately called Dada to inquire about 'Nilkantha' in Basra Port and our other three vessels that were en route. Dada reported Nilkantha had already completed discharge two days ago, but agents were not giving port clearance to sail out due to an RBI clearance delay in the remittance of port disbursements. Dada also diverted 'Sri Kailash' to W C India Gujrat port with full cargo and was waiting to talk to me about discussing similar action on 'Jala Dhruv' and other chartered vessels. I requested that Dada immediately ask all three vessels to go to Dubai, where I was going to ask our Dubai agent, Mr. Shivaswami, to discharge the cargo and retain it under our custody in rented custom-bonded warehouses. Dada advised that Sri Kailash was already in Indian port and shippers/their cargo interest insurance was already informed. I requested that he give instructions to other vessels to proceed to Dubai. I contacted Mr. Mustafa in Kuwait and Shivaswami in Dubai immediately. Mustafa mentioned that Nilkantha is trapped within the war zone in the Shat-El-Arab River, and we needed to arrange for the crew of the vessel to be repatriated to Calcutta via Kuwait, which he was trying to coordinate. Shivaswami endorsed my decision to unload all Iran and Iraq cargo in Dubai and keep it in a bonded warehouse for future delivery to the consignees or shippers after they pay the cost and charges. He was to give me a total estimate in due course. It was indeed a very messy situation that needed calm and skilled handling.

After our return to Calcutta 10–12 days before Durga Puja, I had my hands full dealing with cargo insurance, war risk insurance, anxious calls from the shippers and the ship brokers, and fund demands from Dubai and Kuwait. There was also Bombay office funding for Sri Kailash requirements.

I was expecting cash inflow from the settlement and release of the Kedarnath CTLO insurance claim of Rs. 1.5 crore by January 1981, but for the last six months of 1980, I was compelled to take the risk of servicing the urgent needs of the shippers in loading Iran and Iraq cargo by three of our own and chartered vessels to mitigate our liquidity crunch. All the shipper's clients appreciated our predicament and endorsed my decision to discharge and store cargo in Dubai, giving them the opportunity to negotiate with their consignees and even nominating buyers on default to take delivery of the cargo after paying us our costs and charges. Sri Kailash cargo at Indian Gujarat port became a problem both for the shippers and the ship-owner as customs, port, and government red tapes were not allowing us to make similar arrangements as Dubai. Substantial expenses on Nilkantha at Basra and Kuwait and Dubai Port expenses had to be recovered by us from the cargo stored in Dubai before their release. The Hauer Line Charter vessel was redelivered to the owners in Dubai. Jala Dhruv was fixed for a trip TC to AHR Europe through David Bruce with delivery sailing Dubai.

The Durga Puja celebration of our family in 1980 at our Bishnupur ancestral heritage house was the first time without Ma giving me Ma Durga's blessings and Ma's hand holding in her subtle presence to face and combat the massive misfortunes in Himalaya's history. Within November, we could meet our huge expenses burden at the Dubai, Kuwait, and Bombay offices for Sri Kailash disbursements at Gujarat port from collection of our charges against Dubai warehouse cargo release.

I made only one visit to Dubai with Kelekar, and between Mustafa, Shivaswami, and Kelekar, everything was managed with efficient dexterity. As usual, I received total support from my insurance Guru, VKB of Crow Boda, and his associated London P&I Club in handling and structuring our Nilkantha CTLO claim in the war zone, backed up by war risk trapping and seizure claims. Our London Average Adjusters firm, Richard & Hogg, also made a substantial contribution in handling of our Sri Kailash GA claim with VKB, ensuring cooperation between the P&I club and Average Adjusters. I could submit a cast iron claim document for near Rs. 2 crore to the Hull Committee and the Finance Ministry for war risk insurance through our upfront insurance company within February 1981. The insurance claim of Sri Kailash for her long period of waiting with Cargo on board, incurring full operating costs, was difficult and complex, but this was also progressing towards a happy solution within March or April 1981.

In November/December 1980, I was consciously planning our container feeder service to launch in July/August 1981 after taking delivery of our two NB container vessels from Koyo Shipyard and a commitment from BSC to join us as a consortium partner by chartering two equivalent-size geared container vessels. Ceylon Shipping Corporation was also very eager to provide container service linkage between Colombo-West Asia Gulf Ports, Red Sea Ports, and UKC both ways. I had a virtual container service consultancy assignment from the Sri Lanka Shipping Ministry, and I was confident of securing their agency. I was targeting the commencement of our container service between Calcutta-Haldia-Chennai-Singapore and Calcutta-Haldia-Chennai-Colombo by placing two vessels in each route—one Himalaya and one BSC in each. I was already having ready West Asia Gulf Market, USA EC Market, and UKC Market to support us on' Through' B/L and 'Service' B/L arrangements between Himalaya, BSC, and CSC. Major MLOs like Maersk, P&O,NYK, APL, etc. in the early days of containerization were fully exploiting the changeover inexperience of the trade and shippers from break bulk to containers. Advanced countries like the USA, UKC, and Far East were almost ready with infrastructures like the Land-bridge – rail and road container haul network, TEU and FEU container manufacturing, and stock building by the shipping lines and container leasing companies. In the West Asia Gulf, many small container vessels and container barges were getting engaged in intra-port transportation services within the West Asia Gulf. It was a very challenging and interesting door-to-door transportation supply chain management logistic operation for Himalaya's future growth. It was also a tall task to make the Indian Port and Shipping Industry conscious of their matching role to cope with the sea change taking place in the global port and shipping industry and its necessary fallout demands on the port infrastructure and shipping fleet modernization requirements for transport supply chain logistics management, both for containers and bulk cargo handling, with technical equipment and trained human resources support. When port and ship management internationally were getting modernized with strong R&D support on technology innovation and their rapid project-centric implementation, corrupt Indian politicians and bureaucratic red tape were in league to inculcate in the system a decadent logistic of live and let live through innovative intrigues of window dressing balance sheets of the organizations both in the public and private sectors. In the port sector, IAS officers were serving major port trusts as chairman and deputy chairman for 4–5 year terms after getting their postings through political lobbies, making room for new incumbents even before grasping the nuances of port infrastructure and business model based on departmental needs for running as independent profit centers.

The scenario was not much different between the public and private shipping lines. Old and historically established shipping lines like Scindia and ISS, who were prominent players in UKC Conference liner service, practically collapsed with the advent of containerization. SCI, as a PSU, was also oblivious to the containerization need in the initial years of containerization. As I stated earlier, SCI was also led by admirals and Navy personnel for many years, and the behemoth grew horizontally fat under the umbrella of government patronage, with conventional operation planning and corruption tainting their balance sheet like the major port trusts. Apart from Great Eastern Shipping and a few family-owned smaller ship owners like Dhanjibhoy and Dr. Tolani, the Indian shipping industry was lacking the dreams, visions, and character to face international competition. Himalaya's phenomenally aggressive growth on a long-term plan canvas with frugal start-up capital was viewed with envy by less-performing industry players.

BSC and CSC of neighbouring nations appreciated my enterprise and expertise, particularly because of BSC Chairman Capt. Safi's trust and confidence in me and Mr. Wikramsinghe in the Sri Lanka Ministry of Shipping getting close to me for the development and planning of CSC container service.

Coming back to Himalaya's finance planning in December 1980, I was finding reserves depleting fast with revenue drying up due to Sri Kailash stuck in Gujarat Port and Nilkantha trapped in Basra. The debt servicing of Sri Kailash and the last two instalments of Nilkantha also caused further cash outflows. I was banking on the recovery of the Kedarnath CTLO insurance claim by January to keep our promoters equity commitment for the IPO through SBI within March to pay Shipyard for the delivery of two NB Container vessels in July. Although our Nilkantha CTLO cum War risk trapping and seizure claim for Rs. 1.75 crore was submitted with an appropriate breakup of Rs. 1.25 crore for CTLO and Rs. 50 crore for war risk, the Hull Committee and Insurance Company forwarded the same to the Finance Ministry War risk insurance division as they considered this a clear case of a war risk insurance claim. It was in the knowledge of INSOA and the entire shipping fraternity and Hull committee that the war risk insurance premium collected by the finance ministry was substantial from the Indian ship owners, and for over 15 years there was no war risk insurance claim. Despite this, the joint secretary in charge at the FM was haggling with me, offering an immediate settlement of Rs. 1.25 crore. I consulted VKB, and he advised me we were legally entitled to receive the full claim amount and I should discuss the matter with INSOA to put pressure on the Ministry. A strong letter went from INSOA to the FM, and I decided not to yield to FM pressure.

Jala Dhruv was the only vessel on operation, and I was regretting our wrong decision to bring Sri Kailash back to India with Cargo, which happened due to Dada's inexperience in my absence. VKB was helping me to finalize a claim between P&I Club and GA Adjusters to get the vessel free of cargo and part recovery of vessel idle time and port expenses.

Our agency and projects division were in a good direction for long-term scaling. I am narrating all the above in detail for my readers to understand that the apparent adversities of the company happening one after another were ultimately proving to be Thakur's blessings for our good as modernization of our fleet was going to happen with optimum yield through disposal of our old overage vessels after they played their role in building the very solid foundation of our start-up shipping venture. In those days, I had a Baul Singer friend in Sanatan Das and his son Biswanath, who used to sing one of my favorite songs, "Sarpa haiya dangsa Prabhu, Ojha haiya jharo.."

In December 1980, as a deviation from my intense activities and complex skill demand on my innovative detached self to combat adversities, I got busy preparing and directing a play Parashuram's 'Bhushandir Math' by all the children of our family. I always enjoyed playing with our children and engaging them in competitive sports, painting and poetry writing competitions, recitation, singing, dancing, play acting with rehearsals, and all kinds of creative activities. Our Elgin Road heritage house, with its large lawn and garden, generously offered the space and ambience for such activities, with a large gathering of our joint family and extended family members. When I was traveling with Gopal Da and Boudi in Europe, I got letters from Soma and my nephew Ronti expressing in sweet words their expectation of my organizing something big for the children on my return. Maharaj (Swami Lokeswarananda) always encouraged the children and me to attend such creative cultural events and used to come to our house with other junior monks and Brahmacharins to attend such events. My Ma, Babi, and all in the joint family had cultural inclinations. I used to consciously announce the names of producers and directors as Ma, Baba, Kaka, Kaki, Mama, Mami, Pisi, and Pisey for these children. In Bhushandir Math to create atmosphere at the start, the hall was made totally dark with Ghanashyam Pyne, the brilliant 'sound man' creating the music and sound of the 'Ghosts Abode.' All the children performed brilliantly, and Maharaj was full of praise for them.

This family bonding and joy of the children gave me tremendous spiritual bliss in the midst of the mental turmoil I was going through with Dada's awkward, complex-ridden mind, creating hurdles for Himalaya's management and growth.

I was almost sure that our 'Kedarnath' CTLO Claim Settlement would happen within December, and we should get our Rs. 1.5 crore cheque by the first week of January 1981. There were resentments and exchanges of letters from Tutu, Bodhon Da, Gopal Da, and me about funds going out to Samal Harand from Dada's desk unilaterally without allowing Capt. Ghose and our management team to scrutinize the bills. I spoke to Kakababu and passed on these letters to him, clearly advising that Dada was not only breaching his agreement to quit and restructure Himalaya Board but also creating an unhealthy condition of mistrust and confronting situations with the Gopal Da and Bose groups. Kaka Babu talked to Dada, but he was naive in his own simple way to sincerely request that I do not get into any quarrel with Dada at Gopal Da's instigation, and Tutu had advised Dada confidentially that he had written the letter as per Gopal Da's advice. Tutu was satisfied with Samal Harand Billing after talking to Dada at length. Gopal Da clearly advised me that Tutu was in league with Dada to ruin the company, and things were getting out of his hands as Partha was behaving foolishly to toe Tutu's line. I was noticing thereafter that funds were flowing out of the Himalaya's coffer without the knowledge of Prashanta or me. Dilip Roychoudhury was Dada's front man and aid. There were ECB bills suddenly appearing in the surface for substantial chipping painting work done by them for Kedarnath SS in the past, which was getting paid simultaneously with SH bills at the detriment of cash flow and reserve drying up. While Bodhon Da and Capt. Ghose were lamenting, Gopal Da requested that I explain the situation to Partha at his residence. Partha argued with Gopal Da and me that I was going to expand the company through an IPO, going beyond our means, and that after the IPO, the company would be out of our management control. He voiced Dada's view that our big new office investment had become a white elephant for the company. He also said, according to Tutu, our IPO was designed by me to take full control of the company as the professional front man, and all other directors would be dwarfed as insignificant. He also complained (taking Tutu's name) that I did not stop SH siphoning out money from the company and took advantage of Gopal Da's cooperation to deprive ECB of their rightful business share.

Gopal Da told me later that Tutu from his Elgin Road 'Roy Mansion' flat was regularly in touch with Dada, and Partha was his blind follower. He asked me to push for the restructuring of the board as was discussed and agreed upon earlier with Kakababu's knowledge. I was smelling disaster for the company through the blocking of the IPO and the Container Vessels NB acquisition. I discreetly discussed the matter with UIB CMD J. N. Biswas and Mr. Kundra, the then GM of SBI, without divulging to them our internal issues. Both of them were convinced that without an IPO and fleet modernization, our company was heading towards a serious existential crisis. They got alerted to protect the bank's exposure to our company. I advised them for their comfort that our receivable insurance claims of Rs. 1.5 crore for Kedarnath and Rs. 1.75 crore for Nilkantha have an early recovery time. I requested that JNB hold Kedarnath's claim money in a one-year FD on receipt within January 1981 and allow us to make an equivalent promoter's equity contribution to our IPO.

Mr. Kundra, SBI, after consulting his CGM, advised me to submit a 10-year project financial plan focusing on container feeder service and Panamax NB bulk carrier acquisition and deployment, linking our earlier board-approved 3-decade DPR to the company's long-term business model. With Prasanta's help, I managed to submit this to SBI by December 1980.

I had to spend the last week of December in Bangalore for the TT Nationals and the TTFI AGM, where Ranga had to end his long innings with TTFI to the Bagla/M.C. Chowhan group. VKB advised me before I left for Bangalore that our Kedarnath CTLO claim was cleared by the Oriental Fire and General Insurance Company board in Madras, and their Bombay office was advised to release our settlement payment. I felt much relieved and advised JNB at UIB and our management.

In 1980, the Ramakrishna Mission International Convention was held at Calcutta on a grand scale under Maharaj Swami Lokeswarananda's leadership. The last time such a convention took place was in 1926, when Swami Sivananda – 'Mahapurush Maharaj' was President. There was a very soul-enriching seminar for three days at Netaji Stadium, where RKM monks from all over the world and Indian centers of RKM participated as eminent speakers and also as part of the audience. There were also other erudite speakers invited by Maharaj to speak in different sessions on selected topics to expose the wisdom of Vedanta philosophy and human architecture for detached karma through service and renunciation as emanated from the Holy Trinity. Maharaj gave me the privilege to manage the Netaji Stadium event, and this was the first time I got the opportunity to work on a mega RKM project under Maharaj's guidance and blessings. I involved Gopi and a few of my BTTA colleagues in the team, and it was a first-time experience for all of them. Maharaj had stalwarts like legendary painter Ramananda Bandapadhya, Sanjiv Maharaj, and other monks and brahmacharins/karmis of RKMIC to provide support, and it was a seven-day festival of detached karma and learning experiences of divine delivery.

Ramananda Babu created a Dias with flower decoration on the press block side of the stadium. A life-size portrait of Thakur Ramakrishna was hoisted in the middle of the press gallery, and arrangements were made for the monks to sit at Thakur's feet with artistic flower decoration. Ma and Swamiji were on the Dias on the left and right sides of Thakur. With the depth of the Dias converging up to the first row height of the press gallery, a gorgeous art work emerged, giving the look of Thakur with the monks at his feet, presenting the event on the Dias. An artistic floor-sitting arrangement with a mix of chairs and a floor sitting on the carpet was created by Ramananda Babu with simple flower arrangements of different colorful, giving the floor a look of alpana when viewed from the galleries. There were no tickets but only cards for delegates, monks, and invitees, apart from registered devotees. The numbers were well above the capacity of the stadium galleries and floor accommodations combined. VIP Block was reserved for senior monks of the order and special invitees. With Maharaj's guidance, RKM's brand discipline, and my experience of World TT with Gopi and BTTA teams by my side, I could ensure smooth delivery of the event with the Holy Trinity's blessings. It was a soul-fulfilling experience for me. I will narrate an incident of embarrassment for me on the opening day, which Thakur helped me to skilfully negotiate. Almost one hour before the start, a group of monks came and occupied the total VIP Block seats. I was finding it very awkward to tell them to shift. Ultimately, I could gather the courage to go up and request with all humility that we have made arrangements for them to be seated at the feet of Thakur in the opposite press block behind the Dias. Within 15 minutes, Revered Monks shifted themselves to the press block in their brand RKM discipline.

I had a busy few days in Bangalore with my TT commitments. I remember at the extreme end of the TTFI AGM, just after the election results were announced, ending Ranga's long and eventful innings at the helm of TTFI, I had to come out of the meeting to take an urgent call from Dada and was advised that the Kedarnath Insurance claim cheque had been sent back by the Bombay UIFGI office to their Madras HO. Dada requested that I immediately fly out to Madras and meet my friend, Mr. Bantwal, in their HO, as advised by VKB. I went back to the meeting to inform them of my decision to leave Bangalore next morning, explaining a business emergency.

Although I supported S. P. Bagla when he promised to support my TT Academy dream with his influence in the Sports Ministry, I felt sorry for Ranga, remembering his sterling contribution to TTFI and table tennis for over three decades with passion and dedication. Ranga emotionally expressed in the meeting how soul-fulfilling his experience was in the conduct of the 33rd World TT in Calcutta working with 'Probir and Gopinath on a professional corporate sports management culture introduced by the BTTA team.' I was emotionally moved, and at the request of Bagla, I gave an emotional farewell tribute to Ranga before leaving the meeting.

I had to make a few important phone calls to Mr. Bantwal to fix my meeting time with him the next day in the early afternoon and informed our Madras Agent, V. K Sharma about my Madras visit. While waiting at the Bangalore Airport to catch the early morning flight to Madras, I was reading a compilation of lectures and articles in the publication brought out by RKM on the 1926 convention. Articles and talks by Thakur's direct disciples appeared in the publication, which was very soul-inspiring. After boarding the plane, I dosed off for 10–15 minutes when a glimpse of hope filled my mind with blissful faith that something good would happen in Madras. After checking in at the hotel about noontime, I had lunch with VK Sharma, our Madras agent, and then went with him for the 2 p.m. meeting with Mr Bantwal, Mr. Bantwal explained that some queries were raised on our claim, which caused their Bombay office to send the file back with the cheque to HO, and it would take some time to deal with the file and send the same back to Bombay with their appropriate release order.

I explained to him our urgency for this cheque as our banker would issue a certificate of promoter holding in the IPO under process with SBI for financing our USD 10 million loan for the two container vessels NB, which were ready for delivery in June 1981. I requested him to expedite the process so that we could secure payment within the first week of January from Madras without the file going back to Bombay and then potential further delays in the Bombay office. Mr. Bantwal asked me to wait and went to his boss to discuss. He returned after half an hour to inform me with a lot of genuine disappointment that it was not technically possible. I appreciated his efforts and sympathetic concern, and after a half-hour spiritual discussion on the RKM convention, I got up to leave. He held me back as I was approaching the door, requested that I wait a little longer, and went back to his boss. He came back after about twenty minutes with satisfying relief in his face and handed over to me the Cheque for RS 1.5 cr with greetings to say 'Mr Mitra, your unwavering faith in Ramakrishna helped me to convince my boss to bend rules considering your urgency.' I was speechless in spiritual bliss and only could utter in choked voice 'Mr Bantwal, you are His chosen instrument.'

I spoke to UIB CMD J. N. Biswas in Calcutta. JNB gave me the address of the only UIB branch in Madras and the name of their manager. He advised me to deposit the cheque there for transfer to our Calcutta account. He agreed to create one-year FD to earn interest. He promised to issue the promoter's holding certificate to SBI whenever required for the IPO.

I returned to Calcutta the next morning and was jubilantly greeted by all my colleagues. Gopal Da and Bodhon Da came to my chamber to congratulate me. Dada was sulking a bit over my placing the money in FD. He mentioned his intervention through his IAS friend Arindrajit Da with the insurance boss. I advised Dada, Gopal Da, and Bodhon Da that even then, nothing was possible without Thakur's intervention. I explained my reason for blocking the money for one-year FD to protect the promoter's contribution to our impending IPO. Dada was expressing his concern about the company's cash flow crisis due to practically no earnings from our vessel operation and substantial payment obligations for meeting Kedarnath repair bills for SS. I tried to convince him that without an IPO and the delivery of the NB Container vessels for the start of the feeder service jointly with BSC, the company would be on the verge of closure. BSC liner service to USA EC was to dry up without container service introduction.

We needed to defer payment to our creditors for a few months pending the recovery of our Nilkantha Insurance claim of Rs. 1.75 crore. It was unfortunate that in spite of substantial profit booking in our audited accounts for the year ending March 31, 1980, we were facing a cash flow crisis due to wrong decision-making and a lack of financial discipline. These exchanges were between four of us—Gopal Da, Dada, Bodhon Da, and me—in Gopal Da's chamber. Dada kept on harping against my arbitrary decision to go for NB orders with high investment, and the purchase of 10–12-year-old second-hand vessels would have been far more prudent, even if this meant higher repair and maintenance costs. Bodhon Da commented that Dada was only trying to create an opportunity for Samal Harand to drain money out of the company. He further added that the cash flow crisis of the company was purely due to Dada's continuously taking out the company's funds to pay inflated SH invoices without the knowledge of any other directors. This made Dada furious, and he reacted by saying that, as joint MD, he was not obliged to get clearance from other directors, including me, to pay the bills of repairers already passed by the Engineer superintendent. Bodhon Da bluntly questioned M Sircar's integrity when he was placed by Dada from the SH side to promote SH interest by getting rid of S N Roy. He went on to say that Dada was hell-bent on killing a golden goose out of his ego and jealousy, with the only objective of scuttling 'Probir's professionally designed growth plan' for the company. He was blunt in stating that even the SS of Kedarnath was undertaken against Probir's advice to serve SH's interests. Dada retorted to say that after SS, debt-free Kedarnath would have been very profitable for the company but for the unfortunate accident. I chipped in to say that in real terms, the accident was a divine boon, as this overage vessel was neither a bulk carrier nor a competent substitute for container liner service. I never expected the realization of more than Rs. 70 lacs from the sale of the vessel, and the Rs. 1.5 crore insurance claim realization was double this amount.

For 'Nanda Devi' after she had served us for 7/8 years profitably, it was not expected to give us a yield of more than Rs. 10 lacs from the scrap market as against the Rs. 50 lacs we realized from insurance.

Nilkantha was also not expected to give us more than a Rs. 25 lakh yield from the scrap market. While I already had an offer from the Finance Ministry War Risk Insurance Wing for Indian Ships to close our Rs. 1.75 crore claim at Rs. 1.25 crore, Gopal Da asked why I was not accepting this to generate immediate cash for the company. I explained that we had framed the claim for war risk trapping and seizure after consultation with VKB and the London Consultant, and we were sure to recover the entire amount. From 1965 onwards, the Finance Ministry was collecting war risk insurance premiums from the Indian ship owners. This was the first time war risk claims from a few ships had emerged, and INSOA had taken up the matter strongly with the government on behalf of the Indian shipping industry. Bodhon Da made the comment that if this money had come in quickly, it would have also been drained out by SH. Dada left the room in anger.

Gopal Da mentioned after Dada left that Tutu and Partha were continuously in touch with Dada and scheming to scuttle our IPO and new building purchase. Tutu was indeed living in Elgin Road's 'Roy Mansion' opposite our Elgin Road house. I explained to Gopal Da that if this happened, I would not have any option but to resign, as the company would come to a dead end without container orientation and fleet modernization. A huge opportunity for phenomenal growth for the company would be lost. I told him that a container feeder service network through a consortium with BSC would help us to retain our market share in the USA, UKC, and West Asia Gulf and secure the agency of Ceylon Shipping Corporation, which had already acquired container vessels for servicing the West Asia Gulf, Red Sea, and UKC markets, and I was interacting with them on the Himalaya's proposal for a 'through B/L' linking with CSC Service

B/L arrangement for West Asia Gulf cargo, where they were fully aware of our market hold. APL USA was also keen to collaborate with BSC for USA cargo by forming a consortium for the benefit of both parties market share. By using our feeder service, there were multiple opportunities opening up, and our turnover volume would have an 8–10-fold rise. Agency, project R&D, consultancy, and ship management divisions would all become high-yielding independent profit centers. With the raising of promoters equity to Rs. 1.5 crore for Rs. 6 crores, IPO capitalization, Himalaya Share will jump at least six times within the next two years. Our 25% Promoters holding was much higher than all big industrialists holding 12/15% of their open market subscribed share capital. As against this, we would be left with two break-bulk vessels, Sri Kailash and Jala Dhruv—one of them stuck with cargo on board at Port Okha without any earnings, and the other one was to be scrapped in another 18–24 months. We would lose BSC Agency without the feeder service consortium, as break bulk USA traffic would dry up for them. BSC would be compelled to team up with APL agents if we did not team up to generate common interest. ECB were APL stevedores, and Gopal Da was aware of their containerization in a big way. Bodhon Da insisted on Gopal Da talking to Partha and Tutu in the presence of Bodhon Da and me to stop them from supporting Dada to scuttle the IPO and new building acquisitions. Gopal Da frankly stated that, unlike Bubai, Partha did not have a rational, analytic mind, and he was vulnerable to brainwashing.

However, Gopal Da did arrange an evening meeting at his residence for me and Bodhon Da to convince Partha. I explained Himalaya's future expansion plan to become a leading corporation in the Indian shipping industry, how ECB's future as a stevedoring house was linked with Himalaya's future and the major role ECB was to play in future port infrastructure development projects as part of Himalaya's R&D and project consultancy division. Bodhon Da also bluntly advised him to build trust in my expertise and wisdom without getting influenced by Tutu, and this would protect his and ECB's interests long-term. Partha was motivated but was somewhat defensive about Tutu. He said Tutu had big plans for expanding ECB business, and both he and Tutu had respect for my shipping knowledge and innovative development dreams, but Tutu felt that by taking the IPO route, ECB stakes in the Himalayas would get marginalized and management control would go out of hand. I explained to him that I liked Tutu as a young entrepreneur with an extremely sharp reflex, business sense, and his brand style of winning over politicians and bureaucrats, which would take him a long way in his entrepreneurial journey independently. But his style was significantly different from mine, which was building of a value-based team of quality human beings with 'Truth and Integrity' as the password to my portal. Gopal Da intervened to advise Partha that Tutu's agenda was to take control of ECB after Gopal Da's lifetime, where Partha would be side-lined. I did not quite agree with this and stated that Tutu was an ambitious young entrepreneur, and he would never remain within the narrow precinct of the ECB family business and would be inclined to build his own empire. As far as I remember, Bubai was still in London at that time; otherwise, for some reason, Gopal Da did not involve him in these discussions.

At home, Kakababu expressed to me his concern and anguish about Bodhon Da insulting Dada in my presence and my lack of trust in Dada to honor his commitment to board restructuring. He was sure Dada would not hesitate to allow me to take the position of MD and pursue the growth path of the company as planned through an IPO. Kakababu was not prepared to accept that there was any conflict of interest between Samal Harand working as a repairer for the Himalayas and that there could be any siphoning of funds by SH. I requested that Kakababu attend a board meeting for the restructuring of the company's board and clearing the IPO and NB container vessel acquisition as already ordered and ready for delivery. Kakababu did not want to attend the meeting, as he wanted me to be inducted into the board in his place. I expressed to Kakababu my apprehension that Dada, in his effort to scuttle the IPO and NB acquisition deal, was doubtful to allow me any voting space, and if he could do this successfully, then this would end Himalaya's dream journey, bringing substantial damage to my own visions and dreams. Kakababu assured me that Dada would not breach his commitments, but I was expected to protect his SH interests and not quarrel with him at the instigation of Gopal Da and Bodhon Da. I could see Kakababu was talking for Dada based on his information feed. I told him that I would not be able to support Dada's siphoning out money for SH at the cost of Himalaya's interest. I did not resign from the Himalayas a few years ago at Kakababu's request to protect Dada's SH interest when Dada agreed to shift back to SH, allowing me to run the company as MD by board restructuring within 1979, but Dada did not keep his commitment. Kakababu was uncomfortable and had embarrassed frustration. I closed the discussion by stating that another breach would compel me to resign this time.

I was under pressure from the shipyards to send a technical team to the shipyard to start the delivery process, and I was planning to send Capt. Ghose and Debangsu Rakhshit in March for this purpose.

In the midst of all the internal rumblings, I was kept extremely busy pursuing two insurance claims: one for Nilkantha with the Finance Ministry, and the other was a Sri Kailash cargo GA claim with average adjusters and P&I Club, who were interacting with cargo insurance companies. While the Nilkantha claim was fairly straightforward, the Sri Kailash claim was extremely complicated, and VKB was guiding me to navigate multiple agencies. The third task was establishing collaboration with BSC for the container feeder service consortium. Progress on all three fronts was in a positive direction, and I was expecting happy closure within May–June 1981.

I was also in close touch with Mr. Kundra, GM, SBI, for following up on the IPO, and SDFC for container new building loan financing, which assumed urgent priority for taking delivery of the vessels in July 1981. When Mr. Kundra requested that I provide SBI with a board resolution, I requested that Gopal Da hold the board meeting for board restructuring and the formal passing of the IPO and new building vessel purchase resolution.

This board meeting was held sometime in mid-March 1981. To my surprise, I found Tutu in the meeting, who came at Dada's invitation. Tutu had the indulgence of Dada, Partha, and even Gopal Da, who was chairing the meeting, to speak out of turn at length after my moving the IPO and vessel acquisition resolution. Tutu spoke in Bengali as an outsider to protect the interests of all stakeholders. He said, "Probir Kaka is taking the IPO route as a shipping expert to make other directors 'thunto Jagannath' (insignificant) and take full control of the company." I felt insulted and requested that the Chairman note that our board had already approved a long-term expansion plan for the company, which included an IPO and fleet modernization, and I had gone ahead to finalize two new 500 TEU capacity container vessel acquisition contracts with Mitsui-nominated Koyo shipyard with full knowledge and consent of the board in 1979 for delivery now. Our loan applications with SBI and SDFC have also been processed. We were under notice from the shipyard to take delivery in July, and this kind of insulting statement from an outsider in the board meeting was most derogatory. Without naming Dada, I also stated that if any director had invited Tutu to insult me in the meeting with the intention of changing the board decision, then this would be disastrous for the company's future. Bodhon Da was emotionally vocal. He said because of SH and Dada, we lost experienced and committed officers, and it was our good luck that we could get an experienced senior person like Capt. Ghose as Marine Super, who has repeatedly warned us about SH's inflated repair bills and the requirement for fleet modernization. It was more than a miracle that the company had achieved such a reserve building with frugal capital. All this the company achieved through one man's shipping knowledge, long-term planning, and team-building capacity. Had Dada not taken the wrong decision of ordering Sri Kailash to sail back to India instead of going to Dubai like the other two vessels, we would have seen more cash in the company and the vessel operating and earning for us like Jala Dhruv. We were handling two complicated insurance claims involving a nearly Rs. 3 crore claim amount, which he told Tutu and Partha, 'We are dependent on your Probir Kaka for recovery.' Bodhon Da further stated, 'Agency business, particularly BSC, was thriving because of Probir, but for him, I would have been sitting in Bhowanipore Motors and Salil in Samal Harand. Therefore, do not try to kill the Golden Goose.' I had never imagined Bodhon Da could be so forthright and blunt. Tutu said he had a lot of respect for me, my shipping knowledge, and my international connections, but even as an outsider, he was to protect the interests of ECB as a stakeholder. Dada expressed his view against the IPO and was not in favor of any board restructuring until our internal management differences were addressed and resolved. I was expecting Gopal Da to give a conclusive decision for the resolutions to be carried, but Gopal Da wanted to know from me whether we could secure two months of extension from the shipyard for delivery. I said we only had paid a token deposit with the Shipyard at the time of contract signing, and as per the price prevailing in 1981, such NB Container vessels would secure a minimum of USD 8.5 million each against our contract value of USD 5 million each. Even if we wanted to "resell' the vessels after acquisitions, the company would make a clear trading profit of USD 7 million. I further explained that SBI would need board resolution to move fast forward to meet our dates. For some reason, Gopal Da postponed the decision by a few days to reach a consensus. I stated with decisive clarity before ending the meeting that if there was a U-turn by the board on a decision already approved earlier, I would be compelled to put it in my paper, as this would not only bring disrepute to the company in the international shipping market but would also tarnish my own personal and professional image. I repeated that despite a healthy financial condition, without an IPO and fleet modernization, the company would close down within the next 18–24 months.

After the meeting, Gopal Da confessed to Bodhon Da and me that he was under tremendous pressure from Partha and Tutu, and I should ask Kakababu to attend the next meeting to sort out this. He also advised me to speak to SBI to move forward based on our earlier board resolution, as Dada had brainwashed Partha adequately through Tutu and it would be difficult to resolve this early. I explained to Gopalda that the company was in very sound financial health with BSC Agency revenue and reasonably good cargo storage and release fees collected from two vessels carrying Iranian cargo to meet our expenses in Gulf ports and office overhead. We were also expecting a recovery of over Rs. 2.5 crore from Nilkantha and Sri Kailash insurance claims. Only the last installment of Nilkantha's loan payment of less than Rs. 20 lacs was due to SBI, apart from Sri Kailash debt servicing of Rs. 3 crore loan, which had SDFC refinancing at a low-interest rate of 3% with a two-year moratorium. I stated to Gopal Da in the presence of Bodhonda that there was a floodgate opened for cash going out of the company to Samal Harand and ECB without any consideration for the company's future, and I was very disappointed that, as Jt Managing Director, Gopal Da was allowing this unholy nexus between Dada, Partha, and Tutu to continue. The design was crystal clear, but Gopal Da, like Dhritarastra, was succumbing to the dumb pressure of Partha at home. I was not prepared to accept that Partha was doing this at Tutu's instigation only, as I had respect for Tutu's intelligence and business sense. When Gopal Da was fumbling, I bluntly pointed out that Gopal Da was consciously aware that Bubai's active presence in Himalayas was developing some complex in Partha's naive mind like Dada's complex against me.

I predicted that if this IPO was scuttled and I quit Himalya's life span would not be more than two years at the outer limit. Gopal Da requested that I did not take any hasty decisions. Bodhon Da implored Gopal Da not to kill the golden goose.

I briefed Kakababu at home in detail about the whole episode, including what I told Gopal Da. I reminded him about what Dada promised about restructuring the board and his going back to SH, which was conveyed to me by Kakababu in Dada's presence four years ago. On this basis, I agreed to continue with the company. By not attending the board meeting, Kakababu was supporting Dada's breach of trust. He was not prepared to believe that SH was siphoning out money and that Dada, Partha, and Tutu nexus was behind this drainage He was not prepared to continue on the Himalaya board and had been insisting on my induction in his place. I mentioned that Dada did not report this to the board and opposed any restructuring, with Partha and Tutu backing him. Kakababu was defending Dada without any conviction in his mind when I quietly said I made a terrible mistake by not listening to Babi when he advised me not to take Dada in Himalayas at the start when Kakababu fought with Babi to convince me. He angrily told me that he did that for the sake of family harmony.

I was desperately concerned about saving the company and pursuing my long-term shipping industry dream. I had to take Mr. Kundra, GM SBI, into confidence and narrate our internal conflict. As per Gopal Da's suggestion, I requested that he get the IPO and NB acquisition loan cleared based on our earlier board resolution. I also explained to him the mess we got into due to Sri Kailas being stuck in Port Okha and complicated GA and cargo claims, which were taking time to process and recover without any earnings coming from the vessel. We were pushing for the recovery of Manning and the daily running expenses of the vessel through GA and the P&I Club. Without the IPO and the start of container service with BSC as a consortium partner, the company's future was doomed. I requested him to insist the management to go for the IPO and fleet modernization to protect the banks near Rs. 3 crore loan and interest exposure on Sri Kailas. Mr. Kundra knew from our earlier presentations that we placed an order for two NB container vessels at a very low market, and the shipyard would gain substantially through the cancellation of our order and the resale of these ready NBs in the present market. He was astonished at the ineptness of the unprofessional board members, who were so naive in not realizing that a shipping company with Rs. 18 lacs in paid-up capital could hardly expect survival in the competitive and ever-evolving international shipping industry scenario. He was exuberant in his praise for the competent and committed professional management team under my leadership for building such a solid foundation for the company, which would be a unique shipping industry growth model story in the history of the Indian shipping industry. He added that the vulnerability of the corporate professional at the hands of unprofessional control-seeking promoters with meager holdings would also surface in the corporate history of the industry. Mr. Kundra promised to take up the matter with higher management but warned me that SBI, as the lead nationalized bank of India and a behemoth, was bound within the precincts of rigid rules and conventions where internal management conflicts would be viewed with serious concern.

Mr. Kundra suggested that I should seek the intervention of the Govt. of West Bengal at the CM level to take equity in the company to save the company by supporting me and the professional management team. If I could convince the CM to advise WBIDC and the Director of Industry to invite me and one or two of our team members to make a presentation in the presence of SBI and UIB, then banks could lend support to my cause.

I could meet CM Jyoti Basu within the next few days, and he gave me a very patient and sympathetic hearing. I strongly played on the 'only Bengali shipping company' in the Indian Shipping Industry card. CM pampered me with high compliments for my entrepreneurial drive and introduced me to Mr. Manomoy Bhattacharya, Director of Industries, to take the matter forward by arranging a presentation as I requested. This was the start of my very valuable intimate relationship with Manomoy Bhattacharya, who was a delightful positive personality for the development of industry in Bengal.

I made the presentation with Prashanta Ghose by my side, Mr. Kundra and one other from SBI and Mr. J. N Biswas UIB CMD, personally, with one of his GMs actively supporting me to add credibility and full banking support for the project. I could get a letter issued from Mr. Manomoy Bhattacharya committing 10% equity in the project from WBIDC. Miraculously, all these happened within a span of 3 weeks, and I requested that Gopal Da and Bodhon Da hold a board meeting to get the resolution cleared, not only to save the company but also to protect the vulnerability of the director's personal guarantees against their personal property assets. I was already under notice to start the delivery process of the two NBs from the shipyard by April 15, 1981, failing which they would treat our order as canceled. I clearly advised Gopal Da that I had taken the bank into confidence as per Gopal Da's advice, and both SBI and UIB provided me with strong support but warned me that they should not be officially advised about any internal management conflict. I confessed to Gopal Da that I could not confront Dada earlier to the extent required for restructuring the board due to Kakababu's request. Kakababu genuinely believed that Dada would keep his promise to move out of Himalaya's management, which was made in Kakababu's presence. At that juncture, I confronted Kakababu to save the company, but Kakababu was not prepared to attend the board meeting. I insisted Gopal Da take a firm stand in the board meeting to get the restructuring and IPO resolution cleared, even if this meant confrontation with Partha for his own good. Bodhon Da also implored Gopal Da to be firm on this, as an alternative would be disastrous for ECB and their personal property assets. Bodhon Da asked bluntly: What would be the fate of our Nilkantha and Srikailash insurance claim recoveries? 'Is Salil capable of running the company if Probir leaves?' I said even I would have no capacity to save the company without an IPO and fleet modernization, and our high image in the Indian and international shipping markets would reach the point of no return. Gopal Da said he would speak in support of the resolutions on the board, but Kakababu must chair the meeting. Gopal Da was hesitant to cast his vote against Partha, as that would cause fireworks in his family. Finally, Kakababu did not attend the meeting as Dada advised him that he would be insulted by the Bose Group, which was not in favor of board restructuring and IPOs, and Dada was not allowed to quit by the Bose Group.

The board meeting was held at the end of March 1981. I reported to the board about the West Bengal government's commitment to take a 10% stake in the IPO, which had given much comfort to SBI.

I also emphasized the urgency of starting the delivery process of the NB Container vessels before April 15th to refrain yards from cancelling our contract and resale the vessels at a substantially higher price. Gopal Da did speak to convince others strongly. When Dada expressed his anguish over my unilateral initiatives with the Bankers and West Bengal Govt without consulting the directors, Gopal Da backed me to state that I consulted him. However, Gopal Da ended the meeting naively, stating that the board could not come to any consensus and that I should advise SBI to move as per our earlier board approval authorizing me to sign a contract with Shipyard and make a loan application with SBI and SDFC. Dada protested and left the meeting fuming. Partha went to Dada's chamber to calm him down. Gopal Da explained that it was the best he could do under the circumstances, and I should not resign. He was expecting me to pursue the project and start the delivery process, taking SBI in confidence. I was not at all happy and was anticipating irresponsible vindictive action from Dada.

I discussed with Kakababu the outcome of the board meeting and advised him clearly that Gopal Da and Bodhon Da wanted Kakababu to attend and chair the meeting so that both board restructuring and the IPO/new building container vessel acquisition would have been passed. Dada, with Partha on his side, fought against the resolutions, and having a fifth member present was necessary to avoid a stalemate. I was very upset with Dada's destructive attitude to scuttle the IPO and board restructuring that he had earlier committed in Kakababu's presence, and I did not resign at Kakababu's request at that time. I could find Kakababu uncomfortable and avoiding the main issue; he was asking me to make up with Dada and save the company and our own family harmony. I firmly advised Kakababu that, as per Gopal Da's advice, I would try my best to convince SBI to process the IPO and vessel acquisition loan based on our earlier board resolution. SBI GM advised me that in view of my securing West Bengal Govt support, the bank would have no problem doing this but warned me that if internal disputes among the board members surface officially at the bank, then it would be difficult for him to take our project forward. I requested Kakababu to advise Dada to refrain from bringing any internal disputes to the bank's knowledge. Kakababu was expressing concern about Dada's lonely mental condition and worry about Samal Harand's financial health. Dada briefed him about the huge losses SH incurred due to backstabbing by SNR and engineers in the Marine Division. I found no point in discussing it further.

I was making arrangements for Capt. Ghose and Debangsu Rakshit proceeded to start working with the Koyo Shipyard in Kobe, Japan, for the delivery of the vessels, and I advised Hugh Maccoy to interact with the shipyard and finalize the delivery date in June 1981. My plan was to send Capt. Ghose and his team two weeks before delivery. I was discussing with Wallem Shipping Hong Kong for their appointment as ship manager for the first year, taking delivery of the vessels at a very reasonable cost and managing two NB vessels. Capt. Ghose was recommending this as our own ship management division was not fully functional. Based on Dada's strange attitude of negativity, I was not sure about the immediate return of SNR to the company. With Gopal Da's consent, I invited Mr. Kundra of SBI and Mr. Manomoy Bhattacharya to accompany Gopal Da and me to Japan to attend the delivery ceremony.

I reported to Gopal Da and Bodhon Da about my discussion with Kakababu, who was advised by Dada not to attend the last board meeting due to differences and apprehension that he would be insulted by the Bose group. I was expecting that after Kakababu talked to Dada, he would not communicate with SBI to discuss the IPO and Vessels acquisition loan. We decided to have a joint meeting with Dada to advise him about our decision to go ahead with the IPO and vessel acquisitions, as despite a stalemate in the last board meeting, it was clear that Gopal Da, Chairman of the meeting, was in favor of the resolution, which tantamount to his casting vote. I was pretty sure that Dada would insist on another board meeting, and Gopal Da must be prepared to give his casting vote in that meeting. Gopal agreed under pressure but suggested I arrange a meeting for him with Kakababu, and he would personally request Kakababu's intervention to save the company if necessary by holding the board meeting at our residence. I clearly advised Gopal Da that Kakababu would not agree, as he was fully brainwashed by Dada. Bodhonda implored Gopal Da to be unhesitantly firm in his stand to save the company, even if this meant going against Partha. We had a long discussion with Dada. I bluntly asked him why he was so adamant about closing the company, which was going to make both SH and ECB suffer badly. Dada was in favor of running the company within our limited means instead of going for grandiose expansion with the risk of promoters getting marginalized. I repeated like a parrot that the company had no chance of surviving with Rs. 18 lacs or even Rs. 1 crore of paid-up capital and would be facing an inevitable shutdown. Dada added that I was blackmailing the management by threatening resignation after investing in this large office to pursue my utopian dream projects. He mentioned that the company could have comfortably run from the Brabourne Road office with much lower overhead by acquiring 2/3 old vessels like Jala Dhruv and BSC Agency, which supports us with good revenue. With a shipping professional of lesser ambition than me as CEO, the management could have run the company more comfortably within the means and financial capacity of the promoters. Gopal Da protested to say that 'I invested in the company, fully trusting in Probir's shipping expertise and planning, and the company had done better than what was projected. Had Dada not created mistrust and misunderstanding between the two groups, Partha and Tutu would not have appeared on the Himalaya stage.' He blamed Dada for repeatedly breaching his words and made promises to allow restructuring of the board with my induction into the board as MD and having equal representatives of both groups in a six-member board. The board had fully supported my long-term expansion plan, which he was convinced was essential for the company's survival. Samal Harand had no investment in the company and was only taking out money through inflated bills in the absence of SNR. As against this, the ECB invested in the company, and Gopal Da went to the extent of handing over the

Stevedoring contract to the TPRC in the interest of the Himalayas. Bodhon Da added that SNR revived SH by creating the Marine Division, and we lost him because of Dada's greed and arrogant refusal to honor pre-agreed terms. We were killing a golden goose due to totally insane attitude of Dada with single focus on Samal Harand. He suggested we should meet Kakababu jointly and ask for his intervention to bring sanity in Dada's mind to save the Company. Dada became emotional after finding the going tough to say 'Probir is my own brother 12 year younger, I have no complex or jealousy but Probir's mind has been poisoned by Gopal Da to make him my adversary. Probir dreams big and too much dependent on his faith driven spiritual surrender on Divinity. This had paid dividend in the past but this had emboldened Probir to be Utopian in thinking which was dangerous for the company.'

I advised Dada that 'I am continuously moving on a pre-planned expansion plan for the company by presenting 3 decades forward projections to the board earlier in consultation with Bula Da and Prasanta. I explained the financial model to you in **London**. By going public Promoters shares at face value will get a quantum jump of 10 times. I am confident share valuation in two years-time will be 10 times more in addition to further capitalization of reserve after paying dividends. SH is a private engineering company with totally different mind-set for growth and expansion. Himalaya Shipping is bringing revolutionary and innovative thinking in Indian Shipping industry. Closing of the Company will no doubt cause a roadblock on my meticulously planned Shipping Industry dream but this will also hit all the promoter directors individually and collectively. With NB acquisitions I was planning cost control through-out sourcing ship management and obviously SH Ship repairing opportunities will get marginalized but 25% promoters equity in a thriving shipping company will more than adequately compensate such small time loss of business. I have love and affection for you as my elder brother and went against Babi's advice to bring you in the company despite your non shipping background. I am totally shocked to know from

Kakababu that you asked him not to attend the board meeting as there was risk of Kakababu getting insulted.'

Dada flatly denied this and when Gopal Da said this could be verified when we were meeting Kakababu jointly, Dada said that Kakababu would never agree to meet all jointly. Gopal Da insisted Dada to make this joint meeting with Kakababu possible as otherwise it would prove that Dada was not allowing Kakababu to attend board meeting. Dada said he was concerned about Kakabu's health getting impaired by participating in our internal differences. Before leaving the meeting I told Dada that 'if any damage is done from your side to scuttle the IPO and NB acquisitions, I would immediately resign and leave the company and it would be your responsibility to look after the shareholders responsibility and Director's personal Guarantee.' I requested Gopal Da and Bodhon Da to discuss between the directors to protect company's interest.

We were coming to year-closing in March 1981. Both Bula Da and Prasanta were busy with our accounts. I had my personal salary dues of Rs. 25 lacs as my salary enhancements with other perquisites cleared by the board almost 3 years ago could not be given effect until receiving statutory clearance from the government, which finally came in the last quarter of 1980. Dada was withholding payment as an excuse for my blocking of Kedarnath CTLO Claim Recovery in Fixed Deposit with UIB for IPO. The constant drainage of cash in paying inflated SH bills and the later addition of ECB bills in January 1981 were draining out our liquidity to a critical level. Capstan Enterprises ship supply bills for over one year were deliberately not paid due to a liquidity problem, and they were managing through bill discounting facilities from Indian Bank against cleared bills, obviously at a cost. There was constant pressure from the shipyards and Hugh Maccoy to confirm the delivery date of the NB Container vessels. Bula Da was keen to get audited accounts for the 31st March 1981 year closing within June 1981 but was finding it hard to get the auditor's comments on the conflict of interest on Samal Harand bills satisfactorily answered. Nilkantha War Risk Claims and Sri Kailash

GA/P & I Claims were intellectually complicated and required physical and mental energy for pursuing their early recovery. In the midst of all these intense activities, I was dealing with Dada's unexplained vendetta gathering speed in its ferocity and fierceness. I was feeling both frustrated and distressed and was constantly seeking Thakur's blessings and guidance to resist negative thoughts. I was critically doing self-introspection and trying to find the reason for such a sea change in Dada's behavior and attitude after the first four to five years of excellent teamwork during our building days, when we faced a severe and acute existential crisis. Babi and Ma were both strong pillars for us at home until 1976, when Babi had his first heart attack, requiring pacemaker support. I remembered the sleepless nights we three brothers spent in the Calcutta Hospital, frankly exchanging feelings, emotions, and concerns for Babi's health and family harmony. Dada often expressed his concern about my aggressive expansion drive and excessive dependence on divine intervention from Thakur, Ma, and Swamiji. Sejda (Malay) always used to chip in that every time during crisis hours, Dada gave him an indication of company closure, but when he asked me, he got an all-well message without any trace of concern. Dada always used to say that was his main concern, as miracles do not happen every time. Hearing this, I always quoted Ma as saying, If your faith and surrender to Thakur are total, positive, and truth-based He will always hold your hand. Ma was the most powerful guide for both Dada and me. Babi was always very curious to know about the company's progress, and I was always feeding him important milestones and events in the company. When we won the historic court case against the Govt. of India, Babi took me to his friend Sankardas Banerjee, and he always loved narrating to friends how he replied to Sankardas when he was scolding me for going against the Order of Government. I used to keep quiet, but Dada always corrected Babi by saying we won the case on merit. Babi loved talking about my achievements in shipping and also table tennis among friends and relatives, and on many occasions, I had to accompany him to his para friend's house, who wanted to meet me after hearing about me from Babi, much to my embarrassment. There was a Bengali article published in the Bengali daily 'Jugantar' under the title 'Bangalee Shilpanayak' by Biswakarma, a very senior freelance journalist and writer and father of Shakuntala of TT fame. This also created some undesirable jealousy, which I consciously realized. Pampering from my seniors in the industry, which I enjoyed, and the continuous dependence of Gopal Da on me in any major decision-making were also building up complexities in Dada's mind. Dada's own dear friends like Bula Da and Bodhon Da were always speaking in support of my vision, and criticizing Dada for his narrow vision. This was also not sweet to his ears. Kutu Kaka (Ajit Mitra) Solicitor and our legal advisor loved Dada and me like his own sons and always advised Dada to be positive in his thinking and maintain harmony and rhythm in the management. Many such past moments and incidents were crowding in my mind to find an explanation for Dada's mental degradation to the level of jealousy and complex and destructive egocentric vendetta against me, particularly after Babi and Ma's demise. After Ma's passing, Kakababu lacked genuine mental support and sound advice. In his attempt to maintain family harmony, he unwittingly became a pawn in Dada's hands, inadvertently contributing to the tragic closure of Himalaya. When I mentioned Gopal Da's desire for a joint meeting, Kakababu vehemently refused, stating he had no interest in being involved in our internal conflicts. He believed the meeting was designed to corner Dada. I tried to explain that by abstaining from the joint meeting, he was essentially endorsing Dada's breach of commitment to board restructuring, a decision I trusted because it was made at Kakababu's request and in his presence. I also added that if he was supporting Dada to bring about Himalaya's closure, then the director's personal guarantee backed by property assets would be at risk. I also reminded him that he was compelled to resign as Basanti Cotton Mill MD when he found the company cash trapped due to his cousins taking money out of the BCM coffer. In this case, Dada was doing the same through SH. Kakababu was uncomfortably angry, as he had no credible answer.

I advised Gopal Da that the only option open to him for saving the company was to sign the minutes of the last board meeting passing the resolution by recording his casting vote as chairman, as after talking to Kakababu, I was sure that Dada would write a damaging letter to SBI in his capacity as Joint MD. If a resolution is passed to restructure the board, I could formally write to SBI as MD with confirmation of Gopal Da as Chairman to proceed with the IPO and NB acquisition loan as per the board resolution. Bodhon Da also requested Gopal Da and agreed with me that Dada would take some vindictive action unless Gopal Da took action as suggested quickly. Gopal Da was still reluctant, as Partha was backing Dada, and such action from his side would cause serious family problems for him. I explained to him with absolute clarity that there was a loan outstanding with SBI of a little over Rs. 3 crore and cash credit from UIB of around Rs. 80 crore, and we had only Rs. 1.5 crore of FD with UIB out of our book reserve. Our Nilkantha claim of Rs. 1.75 crore was being pursued, and Dada was not happy with my decision not to accept the war risk claim settlement offer of Rs. 1.25 crore from the Finance Ministry to close this. There was a GA cargo claim of Sri Kailash being pursued with P&I Club and average adjuster. This was to be handled by Subrata Bose in my absence. Jaladhruv and Sri Kailash were the two ships left in our fleet, and Jaldhruv would have to be scrapped in the next year. Outstanding creditors in the books were for nearly Rs. 1 crore. Creditors payments made during these years (from January 1981) were only to SH and ECB.

The personal guarantees of the directors to the banks would expose their properties and assets to the risk of attachment. Gopal Da felt concerned and promised to talk to Partha.

Capt. Ghose reported to me about the penalty claim raised by Customs for not reporting cargo sales on Barges of Banglar Maitree. I knew Subrata Bose was handling this and reporting to Dada. I had to ask Subrata Bose to update me on the details. He advised me that a few barges of cargo were sold on an urgent basis with knowledge of Dada and Gopal Da. Customs Officers were creating problems to squeeze money. He was to meet the Customs Commissioner to sort things out. I personally went to meet the commissioner, and he called the relevant officers, and a list of documents was handed over to Subrata Bose to provide within the next seven days for a penalty waiver. Subrata Bose committed to do so without any argument.

After a few days, Mr. Kundra had a meeting with me when he advised me with a sad face that Dada had sent him a letter advising SBI not to deal with me on the IPO and NB loan as I was not authorized by the board to interact on this with SBI. I briefed him in detail about our board meeting and about the very sound financial health of the company, and I highlighted the grim future without the IPO and NB Container vessel acquisitions. I appraised him about the Nilkantha War risk insurance claim status and the potential recovery of Rs. 70 lacs plus from Sri Kailash GA and P&I cargo claims. I assured him that even if I resigned from the company, I would help with the processing and recovery of both claims. He deeply appreciated my passion and professional ethics and asked me why I was thinking of resigning. I explained to him with lucid clarity that without fleet modernization and capital infusion through an IPO, the company had no chance of survival for more than two years at the most. I expressed concern about our fully furnished, over ten thousand-square-foot Middleton Row office, where we invested nearly Rs. 10 lakh. SBI had a requirement for such a big office, and Mr. Kundra got the office inspected by a couple of his junior officers. He offered me Rs. 10 lacs in full payback and Rs. 5 lacs for facilitating the deal as I was leaving the company. I politely requested to him to pay the entire Rs. 15 lacs to the company as I would not stain my hands while parting company with Himalaya Shipping, which had been built on the foundation of an incessant flow of divine blessings and was like my own child. He was emotionally moved and said, 'Mr. Mitra, I do not think I can convince SBI higher management to help you by taking a strong stand against the Himalaya Board, which would have been right and appropriate in SBI's interest, but I would be your admirer and well-wisher all my life.' I said, 'I treat this as a manifestation of Thakur's blessings.'

I confronted Gopal Da immediately in the presence of Bodhon Da and advised him about my decision to quit. I bluntly told him that Dada could not have sent such a letter without his and Partha's knowledge. He admitted that he was under pressure from Partha. Bodhon Da repeated that Gopal Da was to be blamed for killing the Golden Goose. When Gopal Da asked for extra time to handle his family issues, Bodhon Da responded angrily, "You have no right to ask Probir for anything." Much later, when Tutu advised me that it was not only Dada but Gopal Da who also used him as a goon against my IPO plan, I tended to believe him. However, I told Gopal Da then that when the company would not survive for more than two years, where was the time? I told him that I would give six months' notice and, during this period, pursue insurance claim recovery for Nilkantha and Sri Kailash. Since there would be no necessity to keep such a big office for running two vessels, and Jala Dhruv would be going to the breakers in 1982. The company office should go back to the Brabourne Road PNB building immediately. Gopal Da asked me what would happen to the investment in this big office infrastructure when I disclosed to him that SBI would buy over the fully furnished office for Rs. 15 lacs, which would be Rs. 5 lacs plus on our investment. Bodhon Da informed Gopal Da that Salil might resort to blocking Probir's outstanding dues, which could lead to the withholding of payment for Capstan Enterprise's outstanding stores and provision supply bills, which were discounted with Indian Bank by Purnima. 'Mejda, I am not sure if you will join hands with Salil in this under pressure from Partha.' Bodhon Da was genuinely upset; he said there was no point in his coming to the office anymore and requested that I ensure with the bankers to get the loan dues cleared out of Kedarnath FD with UIB and insurance claim recovery money of Nilkantha and Sri Kailash claims for SBI loans so that directors did not get impacted on their personal guarantee. I had to tell him that Dada had written to the banks as joint MD not to entertain any communication from me. Bodhon Da angrily told Gopal Da, *"Mejda, chotolokmir ekta seema ache, tumi Shib hoye bosey esab dekhcho. Tumi ki bhabcho Bangladesh Agency ar thakbe*

Probir chere dile?' This translates to English, "There is a limit to meanness, and you are digesting this without protest. Do you think BSC will be there if Probir leaves?' I told Gopal da, 'By blindly yielding to Partha's immature pressure, you are not doing justice to Bubai, and ECB will not survive under Partha's stewardship.' Tutu was far more competent as a businessman in his own right, and if Partha did not allow Tutu to run and manage ECB, the company would not survive. By listening to Partha, he was totally blocking Bubai's growth path in the Himalayas as a future industry leader.

I formally put in my resignation on March 31st 1981, giving six months' notice, but before that, Dada made a drama by coming to my chamber to confidentially advise me that he was compelled to take a resignation letter from Subrato Bose as there was major fraud detected by Customs on the auction sale of GA Jute cargo, and I should forget all internal squabbles and strongly take hold of the management to rescue the company and re-invent the company's operation plan in my own way. I told him firmly that my decision to quit was irreversible, as it was clearly beyond my capacity to make this company survive without fleet modernization through an IPO. I also made it plain that without the connivance of Dada and Gopal Da, such a huge under-invoiced sale with cash involvement could not have happened. Dada lost his guard to tell me that it was only ECB handling the cargo sale with Subrata Bose on the front line, and he had no hand in it. It was clear to me that Subrata Bose was made a scape goat to settle the issue with Customs on mutually agreed terms. It also became clear to me why Gopal Da yielded to Dada and Partha's pressure to refrain from giving his casting vote. I only advised Dada that, on this issue, Himalaya might lose BSC Agency. I clearly stated I could consider turning around the company on my terms only if the majority holding min the company was transferred to me. If this was not acceptable, then the company should shift back to the old office and focus on clearing all bank loans from Kedarnath, claim money fixed deposit, Nilkantha/Sri Kailash insurance claim recovery, and demolition sale proceeds from Jala Dhruv. Dada said no one was indispensable, and he would run the company by hiring a suitable CEO. I did not contradict and requested him to clear my dues and other creditors dues by suspending further payments to SH and ECB. He was upset and left my room.

Officers and staff of all departments, barring a few, were asking me about my next plan and eagerly waiting for my next move.

I was getting advice from my friends in the shipping circle and a few of our marine officers and engineers to jointly move against the Himalaya board with the West Bengal government and the Marine Officers Union for blocking the IPO and cancelling vessel acquisition order by default without any intention to infuse the requisite private capital for the company's survival. I was going through turbulence in my mind and continuously seeking direction from Thakur and Ma Swamiji for appropriate guidance, which Thakur considered best for me and to give me power to control my ego and impulse.

I had been visiting RKMIC Golpark frequently for words of wisdom from my mentor, Swami Lokeswaranandaji. Maharaj, after patiently hearing from me the entire story of my broken dreams in the Himalaya Shipping and Indian shipping industries, advised me not to spend negative energy on legal and emotional issues to retain management control for the revival of the company. He said if my faith and surrender to Thakur were total, then my mind would identify some positives in the adverse predicament I was facing with my own brother on a complex mental issue of 'competence' against 'insecurity of the inferior mind complex.' This complexity will grow in proportion day by day, causing a roadblock for my positive mind to dream and deliver by following my natural growth path in life's mission. Maharaj quoted Swamiji's lines: 'Change not thy nature, gentle bloom, thou violet sweet and pure; but ever pour thy sweet perfume unasked, unstinted sure.' Maharaj's words of wisdom in his inimitable presentation of love and empathy made a deep impression on me when he said, 'Spiritually splurged human beings enjoying the blessings of Thakur are like painters painting their art of life on the large canvass of eternity. They sit before life's canvas with easel and brush in hand, aiming to "tone down the line so sharp and make smooth what roughness seems," as Swamiji said. He advised me to make a course correction by concluding this chapter with Himalaya, even if it seemed painful, and to pursue something creative and positive. Like roses, the path of truth, with Thakur's blessings, is always strewn with thorns.

After tendering my resignation on April 1, 1981, it took me another 40–45 days to make my final decision to start another new venture with frugal capital to pursue my dreams and vision for the Indian port and shipping industry. Capstan Enterprises (which was a partnership firm with Purnima, my father-in-law, as a major shareholder and two other close friends token contribution) was registered under the name of Capstan Shipping & Estates Pvt Ltd, with ship-owning, ship-management, shipping agency, port and shipping project consultancy, and real estate development in its object clause in the MOA sometime in the second-quarter of 1981.

Meanwhile, the Himalaya Shipping Office was shifted back to its old office in the PNB building on Brabourne Road, and the large, furnished Middleton Row office was taken over by SBI at a price of Rs. 15 lacs, fully furnished. I earlier inducted my table tennis senior friend Dilip Roychowdhury in the Himalayas as company secretary when he came back from London with his family. After the first couple of years of his joining, he got thickly involved with Dada to share intrigues and anxieties relating to Samal Harand vis-à-vis the Himalayas. He had a habit of having unhealthy back chats not only with the directors but also with many of the dedicated officers, which often created undesirable misunderstandings in the harmonious Himalaya management team. After my last chat with Dada and my clear refusal to continue in Himalayas, Dilip Roychowdhury was always filling Dada in with information on my next steps and the general feelings of the officers and staff of the company about my resignation. He was literally working as a spy and was not popular in the office. As a direct outcome, many of the officers and staff who had been closely working with me for years got a letter of termination notice from Dada. After I shared my decision to start a new company, the majority of the officers and staff wanted to join me in the new venture, and I was very embarrassed to tell them that in a new venture, it would be difficult to afford a big salary overhead during the initial years of business development. I was emotionally moved to hear from them that they would be prepared to share my burden with a low salary or even without drawing for the first 6–9 months. A few of them, like Prasanta Ghose, Ashis Mitra, Sudhis Bose (my secretary), and Swamy (the telex operator), started looking for a suitable office for the new company, and ultimately I could finalize our first-floor office in the Harrington Mansion in front of the American Consulate in Harrington Street, later Ho Chi Min Sarani.

Dada was communicating with me through Gopal Da and Dilip Roychowdhury. Bodhon Da's chamber in the old office was next to my chamber, and he was often coming to me and lamenting over Himalaya's fate. He informed me that it was a priority from Dada's side to clear Samal Harand and ECB bills and put all other creditors, including Capstan Enterprises's outstanding bills, on hold. Since SBI was not extending further cash credit facilities, UIB CC facilities of Rs. 80 lacs were almost exhausted by June 1981, and Kedarnath FD of Rs. 1.5 crore on maturity was the next target for drain. Bodhon Da was concerned about his personal guarantee and property risk and requested that I talk to SBI about blocking 'Nilkantha' insurance claim money when received for mitigating loan exposure on 'Sri Kailash.' I knew that SBI could block money to the extent of recovery of loan instalments when due but could not block the entire money until there was any default in payment of any loan instalments. However, I gave Mr. Kundra at SBI the total picture of the 'Nilkantha' war risk insurance claim of Rs. 1.75 crore from the war risk insurance department in the Finance Ministry, where I refused to take Rs. 1.25 crore in total settlement without considering the war risk seizure and blockade claim, which was legally payable by them and being fought by INSOA on behalf of all Indian ship owners. I also briefed him about Sri Kailash GA and P&I cargo claims for over Rs. 50 lacs, which I was pursuing so far with an insurance consultant, and I thought in my absence Mr. Subrata Bose would be able to follow up with the insurance consultant. However, after Subrata Bose left the company, I was trying to get the matter settled by 1981, even after leaving the company. But for this, SBI should talk to the Himalaya's Board to ensure recovery. Mr. Kundra was very sorry about the gloomy future of the Himalayas, in spite of a very promising and rapid growth path if pursued as per plan, but expressed his helplessness to trigger bank intervention. He explained that as the largest nationalized bank in India, SBI is a behemoth with frequent changes of officers in the management system through posting at different levels, and everybody would stick to the laid-out rules without taking the risk of any out-of-the-box decision-making.

After shifting back of the office to the PNB building, I attended office during my notice period, particularly pursuing recovery of insurance claims and ensuring payment of creditors' dues at par with SH and ECB through Gopal Da's intervention. I had already informed BSC that the consortium with the Himalayas for container feeder service operation as planned was not materializing due to my differences with the Himalaya's board on the major IPO issue and the cancellation of the order for new container vessels, and I had tendered my resignation. Capt. Safi, CMD, as far as I remember, was completing his term in 12–18 months, and BSC was not ready to invest in container vessels and start container feeder service on their own. Ethically, I did not want BSC to shift their agency to me from the Himalayas. In the absence of Subrata Bose, Dilip Roychowdhury was sent to VKB to get updated on the insurance claims, and VKB advised him to get guidance and updates from me even if I had resigned to suitably follow up on the process. He also reminded DRC that there was substantial payment outstanding on his company's bills, for which he had already requested that I ensure payment before leaving the company. After failing to get any positive intervention from Gopal Da, I advised other creditors to take legal recourse for recovery. When DRC came to my chamber with feedback from VKB, I handed over all the insurance files with proper advice and clearly explained that INSOA had intervened with the war risk insurance division in the Ministry on behalf of all Indian ship-owners and he should ask Dada to pursue recovery through INSOA with the Ministry for the total Rs. 1.75 crore claim instead of falling into the trap of immediate payment of Rs. 1.25 crore offer of the Ministry. DRC offered me elder brotherly advice, recalling my TT playing days when he was JT Secretary of the BTTA, to withdraw my resignation and save the company. He thanked me for creating an opportunity for him to come back from London by taking him to the Himalayas. He had been watching Gopal Da and the ECB group, creating a rift between me and Dada. He said that I should not expect others to have an equal level of spiritual faith and surrender, which had made me fearless and dynamic. Dada was always carrying a sense of insecurity about SH but was always appreciative of my entrepreneurial initiative in promoting Himalaya Shipping, which had given him space for his disturbed mind to escape at a crisis point. However, he needed some more importance and soft ego massaging by me instead of allowing him to be isolated and side-lined. As a non-shipping man, Dada was falling short of my aggressive speed and velocity in taking Himalaya forward, and Gopal Da's constant mentions of Dada's wrong decision to call Sri Kailash back to Indan port instead of discharging the cargo at Dubai as I did for other vessels, the delay in sending Basra remittance to the agents, the Kedarnath SS decision, and top of all SNR episodes were all generating a feeling of discomfort in his subconscious for years. He needed soft and sympathetic treatment of his egocentric overtures from me instead of confronting him at Gopal Da's instigation. It was very late in the day, and although I did not fully agree with DRC's analysis of the situation, I appreciated his genuine concern as a part of the Mitra family, which he identified as his own. DRC was in his late 40s and a rather weak-hearted person who was feeling extremely unsure about his future. He identified himself with Dada, fully knowing that without a job in Himalaya Shipping, he had a very bleak future. Similarly, Capt. Ghose, who was in his mid-fifties and a widower with a school-going daughter close to his heart, was not prepared to go out to sea if Himalaya Shipping closed down. He was expecting Gopal Da to support me in taking our expansion plan forward and was deeply hurt by my decision to quit. It was a pall of gloom in the office, with uncertainty and insecurity looming large.

Capstan Enterprises had to move the court for the recovery of payment for the discounted bills, making Indian Bank the confirming party. My personal salary dues of Rs. 25 lacs were deliberately held back.

Bula Da advised me that after Prasanta's removal from the company, there was no genuine effort to complete the audit of accounts for the year ending March 31, 1981. I sat down with Gopal Da and Bodhon Da to tell them that if it were their intention to close down the company by pumping out substantial reserves by SH and ECB without providing for the settlement of bank dues, all the director's properties would be at risk. I asked Gopal Da why they turned down my proposal for their transfer of 60% of their holding to me if their intention was to close down the company. Gopal Da was only lamenting that we were killing a "golden goose," and he was helplessly witnessing the planned destruction of the company by Dada, Partha, and Tutu, which had gathered speed and momentum after my resignation. Gopal Da also confidentially informed me that Dada was contemplating legal action against me for antitrust activities during my notice period to hold back payment of my salary dues. I advised Gopal Da and Bodhon Da to speak to the auditors and appoint an agency to complete the updated accounts duly audited. Bank dues of Rs. 3 crore of SBI and Rs. 70 crore of UIB with recurring interest needed to be secured properly against the Nilkantha war risk insurance claim, Sri Kailash GA/P&I cargo claim, and the balance remaining out of the Kedarnath FD of Rs. 1.5 crore encashment. Even if the company had eventually gone into liquidation, the priority payment of a secured bank loan would save the director's properties charged against their personal guarantee.

Afzal Khan visited Kolkata and clearly advised me that even if I did not take BSC Agency on ethical grounds, the management decision was to appoint a new agent and not to continue with Himalayas. He had communicated this to Dada and Gopal Da when he was invited to lunch with them at Bengal Club. I explained to him that without container vessels, BSC liner service to the USA, EC, and UKC had no future. I advised him that I was already negotiating with the Agency of Ceylon Shipping for their logistics planning to establish main-line container services to UKC, Red Sea, and Arabian Gulf ports, linking with the introduction of a container feeder service to link traffic from Calcutta and Madras.

Ashis Mitra, Sudhis Bose, S Chakravarty, B K Banerji, Pinaki Ghose, Amit Mitra, Swami, Sankar Narayan, and a few others got busy under Prasanta and Purnima to set up the Capstan Shipping Estates Harrington Mansion office, and up until September, I was attending the Himalaya office in the first half and the Capstan office in the second half.

During one of my visits to the Himalaya Shipping Office, DRC came to my chamber and hesitantly served me a notice from Himalaya's lawyer, Subir Majumdar of Bose and Mitra, with a copy of the complaint for the case filed against me alleging breach of trust in corresponding directly with the banks without knowledge of the management. There was also an allegation that I attended the office during the notice period after tendering my resignation with the purpose of creating disharmony and misunderstanding among the directors. DRC stated he was painfully complying with management's direction and immediately left my office with some emotional drama.

Bodhon Da was not on speaking terms with Dada. He came to my chamber bursting in rage and asked me to contact my own legal friends to take appropriate action. He earlier requested that I use my contacts with the bankers to save his properties by getting him out of the personal guarantee; he apologized for that and asked me not to come to the office anymore and let the directors stew in their own juice. He was also going to resign and stop coming to the office. I bid adieu to my nursing quarter for my dream child that day, never to return again.

After my raging mind came under control through Thakur's grace, I was sadly reflecting on the efforts, emotions, and continuous flow of divine grace that had gone behind the creation of the edifice of a spiritually splurged corporate art piece that was internationally acclaimed. As SNR always told me, in the Himalayas, I had been able to transmit a rare brand of selfless corporate culture among the entire Marine team, both onshore and offshore, with a spirit of ownership and the aspiration to fly high in the open sky. Then what had gone wrong with my own brother, 12 years older than me, who had marvelled at my faith and surrender to Thakur and always came to me for peace and solace during the crisis time of our journey? I was praying to Thakur Ma Swamiji for course correction if I had erred anywhere, and I was always seeking strength and power to stay positive. How much I wished that Ma was there. Purnima was a constant source of patience, purity, and love. She silently suffered but always maintained her balanced love, empathy, and concern for the entire family. She had the gift of intellect and intuition to spiritually absorb and deal with many adverse situations in the joint family with grace and poise. She was sharing my pain with feelings and emotions but always offered positive thoughts, sometimes very critically, to help me stay focused on my path towards truth and perfection, even at the cost of much suffering and discomfort.

I consulted my senior legal friends Sidhartha Sankar Ray and Dipankar Gupta for strongly dealing with the Capstan Enterprise case for recovery of dues and Himalaya's suit against me for breach of trust. My friend Arun Mandal of Fox & Mandal, as a solicitor, came to my assistance. They were genuinely sympathetic and too considerate financially, much to my embarrassment. I was no doubt very stressed financially at that point of time. Eminent Barrister Sidhartha Sankar Ray gave special attention to me in spite of his many political commitments, along with the relatively junior lawyer of Indian Bank and my solicitor friend Arun Mandal, and the HC order on the Himalayas to pay Capstan Enterprises and Indian Bank dues within 15 days or face liquidation was secured. Paralelly, Dipankar Gupta was defending me in Himalaya's breach of trust case against me, and a counterclaim for recovery of my salary dues with interest was lodged. This case came up for a final hearing and order on the bench of Justice Bhaskar Basu.

I could feel Dada finding himself on uncomfortable ground when Kaka Babu spoke to me at home and asked me why I was fighting with my own Dada at HC, engaging heavyweight Brristers like S. S. Ray and Dipankar Gupta even after resigning from the Himalayas. My answer did not satisfy him, as he was always championing Dada's cause. As the last resort, Dada approached Somnath Chatterji. On the day of hearing, Somnath Da and Dipankar Da called me at the Bar Library. Somnath Da told me with much concern and pain that he was very unhappy about this situation with the Himalayas, and he was always praising my youthful drive and initiative in promoting the only Bengali shipping company to friends at all levels. He accepted Dada's brief with the condition to mediate an amicable out-of-court settlement by calling both parties to his residence chamber with their respective lawyers, as this quarrel between two brothers must not be allowed to escalate further. Dipankar Da appreciated Somnath Da's sentiment, and it was agreed that Somnath Da would seek time from the court for mediating settlement with Dipankar Da's consent.

Somnath Da emotionally pleaded in court as a friend of the family, seeking time to mediate the settlement of this unfortunate family fight, which the court gladly granted.

Within a few days after that, Somnath Da fixed a meeting of both parties at his residence after having a chat with me to hear from me the root cause of Himalaya Shipping's abrupt fall from its phenomenal growth trajectory and the principal cause of my dispute with Dada, who was his school friend. He thought that Dada was always very appreciative of my courage and faith.

Somnath Da personally fought for me and the Himalayas earlier against the government of India. He gave me a very patient hearing when I could narrate the entire saga of the Himalayas. He wished I had informed him about this earlier for timely intervention. Chandi Da was also his childhood friend, and he respected Gopal Da as his elder brother and mature businessman. Somnath Da felt that instead of confronting Dada and Kakababu, I should have insisted on Gopal Da and the Bose group to directly intervene.

In the meeting at Somnath Da's chamber, I went with Dipankar Da and Arun Mandal. Dada and Gopal Da came with Subir Majumdar of Bose and Mitra. Somnath Da allowed both parties to state their cases. After hearing both sides, Somnath Da stated that there was no room left for any emotional conciliation to save the company from the predicament it was facing. 'Probir's courage and drive in promoting the growth of this phenomenal Bengali shipping venture always had the support and acknowledgement of Salil and Gopal Babu, and the timely intervention of the Bose Group was needed to avoid this very unfortunate conflict between the two brothers.' He mentioned that it was good that my position in the company was in an executive capacity only and not as director. After my resignation, I should cut off all my connections with the Himalaya's administration, as the directors did not like it. As far as my salary dues, which were undisputed, he requested that Dada and Gopal Da pay the same without delay and requested that I drop my interest claim. There was a court order for payment of Capstan-Indian Bank discounted bills, which should be complied with in the company's own interest. Dada said that the company would need some time to pay the entire Rs. 35 lacs due to a liquidity problem. While Rs. 10 lacs Capstan would be paid to comply with the court order, they would require 18 months to pay salary dues in quarterly instalments. I mentioned that the Rs. 1.5 crore FD for one year had already matured with Rs. 12 lacs interest, and the company also received Rs. 15 lacs from SBI against the sale or lease transfer of a fully furnished Middleton Row office, apart from the Rs. 70 lacs CC facility from UIB. Dada defended his stand by stating there were other creditors and substantial loan instalment dues for Sri Kailas. Understanding the position, Somnath Da intervened to say that in the case of quarterly instalment payments, Himalaya should pay interest at the bank FD rate to me and provide a bank guarantee.

Dada finally agreed to pay my salary dues with interest in four quarterly instalments and secure installment payments by BG from UIB. Capstan/Indian Bank dues would be paid immediately, as per court order. Dipankar Da suggested that Somnath Da record the amicable settlement in a minute form to be signed by the parties and their respective lawyers. Somnath Da immediately dictated the settlement terms in record note form, which was brought to the table for the parties' signature. Dada stated he would require Board authorization to sign the settlement terms. Somnath Da expressed his displeasure that two joint MDs had come to this amicable settlement meeting on leave from court without Board authorization. He insisted on all attendees signing the record note by adding a line that the Himalaya board resolution authorizing two JT MDs to sign the amicable settlement document would be provided within the next five days and Subir Majumdar would draw up the document to be signed by the parties for filing in court. He asked me and Subir to come to the bar library on the 7th day to sign the final document after the other side had signed it.

On the appointed day, I went and met Somnath Da at the HC Bar Library. Somnath Da was in pain and rages to tell me that Subir Majumdar came and informed him that 'Salil is not prepared to sign the settlement document. Somnath Da could not imagine such meanness from his friend belonging to the illustrious family of Sir Ramesh Mitter and legendary predecessors like Sir B.C. and Sir P.C. Mitter. He was misled to believe that I was resisting their plan and efforts to run the company by hired professionals. He could clearly see that they had no intention of running the company and gave me appropriate legal advice to protect my dues with the Official Liquidator as the company was heading towards closure. He was visibly pained at this family-breaking outcome between two brothers and only hoped that time would mend my deep wounds. He knew CM Jyoti Basu wanted this only Bengali shipping company to flourish under my leadership and offered state government support, and he wondered why Dada did not allow this to happen instead of closing the company. I enjoyed Somnath da's love and affection as my elder brother almost lifelong, until it was unfortunately interrupted at the very end of his life through a minor table tennis dispute with his son-in-law.

Within the next year, Himalaya Shipping, with its strong asset base of two ships and a 1600-square-foot flat at the prime Nariman Point location in Bombay, went into liquidation, causing suffering and problems for secured and unsecured creditors, including SBI, UIB, officers and staff of the company, and a number of unsecured creditors. I was later advised by my friend J. N. Biswas, CMD UIB, that no administrative support came from the directors for recovery of dues from insurance, selling of the assets, daily maintenance of the ships with limited manpower, etc., even with banks offering to meet the cost.

We formally started the Capstan Shipping & Estates operation at the Harrington Mansion Office on October 24, 1981, with a couple of telephone lines and our wonderful, simple, but spiritually elevated soul, Swamy, the telex operator, toiling and traveling between the Capstan office and my dear friend Raman's Geat Eastern Chartering office, using his telex facility until we secured our own. Again, we started with a frugal capital of Rs. 10 lacs, with 75% coming from me, Purnima, and my father-in-law and the rest from Prasanta, Saroj Ghose, and friends in bits. 10/12 of my close, dedicated workers from the Himalayas joined me, and there were another 7/8 of Capstan Enterprises staff who were absorbed into the team. The office space was nearly 2500 square feet, fairly large, and we got it appropriately furnished as a shipping office with primary focus on agency and project consultancy. I was working with Ceylon Shipping Corpoation and their Ministry on Container Project Consultancy on both main line service to UKC and West Asia Gulf and also container feeder service between Calcutta-Madras-Colombo for some time while in the Himalayas, and after a trip to Colombo in November, I could secure the agency of CSC for container liner service to UKC and West Asia Gulf/Red Sea ports. A separate agency for Ceylon Shipping Lines to operate a feeder service between Calcutta, Haldia, and Colombo with a small 300 TEU capacity ship under CSL period charter was also offered to us. Capstan Shipping became the pioneer to introduce the first container feeder service in Calcutta port, initially with an Indian container vessel under CSL charter, from a start-up single-ship-owning company belonging to Mr. Jhunjhunwala, where my friend S. N. Roy was Chief Executive. SNR advised me frankly that this vessel was to go for SS after 4–6 months, and its condition was not ideal for a smooth service before extensive repair, and we should look for a better-geared container vessel within the next few months. This geared container vessel, Panch Ratna, was a prompt vessel that could start CSL feeder service in December. SNR, from my Himalayan experience, had a special capacity to run old SS-due vessels.

In the Calcutta Port, Mr. Tarun Dutta just took over as Chairman, and he had my old friend from table tennis playing days, Pranab Sen, as his OSD. I developed strong bonding with Tarun Da as a shipping professional, particularly on my pioneering initiative for starting the first container feeder service in Kolkata port. P&O started the Calcutta-Singapore container feeder service a few months later. NSD Berths 4 and 5 were dedicated container berths for the port. Only geared vessels could be handled, as the Berths had no crane. The container stacking yard at the back had no digital tracking system, and Stevedores were deploying their equipment for stacking, de-stacking, and shifting of containers, resulting in slow feeding at the quay side for loading and unloading. The port had very limited handling resources. The connection between NSD Berths 4, 5, and 6 and Berth D, later to be called Berth 7, was totally blocked by debris and scraps, and officers had been debating methods to clean this up and establish more space and connectivity between the berths. The result was ominous for the port users, particularly after container service introduction, where separate loaded and empty container stacking space was required, including space adjacent to the sheds and warehouses for offering stuffing and de-stuffing facilities to the shippers and consignees, who were still in the process of creating their own in-house facilities in the works and mills for total door-to-door handling system logistics. Tarun Da was an extremely intelligent and competent administrator with a positive and aggressive mind-set for no-nonsense delivery. He appreciated and understood the messy scene after a few evening sittings with me. The root cause of the abysmally low productivity, Dock labour board issues, and officers'/Stevedore's nexus to thrive financially at the cost of systems and efficiency were all identified with clarity. He requested that I give a brief report on a container terminal development in NSD, covering all berths and warehouse sheds, and a model container freight station at the adjacent Garden Reach Jetty, which had been lying idle for years. I gave him a brief note outlining my ideas on the introduction of high-end container handling equipment, both for on-shore handling as well as vessel loading, and a digital Port-net system for tracking and feeding of containers with compatible linking with the calling vessel cargo loading and discharging plan. I recommended his appointing a reputed container port terminal operator from Singapore, the UK, or Europe as a consultant to prepare a detailed report with estimates for time-bound delivery phase by phase without disturbing the limited operation of the container feeder services of CSL and P&O. I explained to Tarun Da that, as a port user, I was not qualified to officially act as a port consultant except by providing innovative ideas unofficially.

My friend Pranab Sen, as OSD, was Tarun Da's 'Man Friday' and he advised me that Tarun Da was planning to lead a port delegation to Singapore Port and Felixstowe Port, UK to identify and appoint a container terminal operator consultant soon. Tarun Da personally advised me that he was waiting for ministry clearance before scheduling dates. Meanwhile, he wanted to clean up the debris and scraps between NSD berths and requested that I attend his site meeting with all the relevant officers of the port to initiate action. I knew many of these officers personally, and by speaking to Pranab, I could see that he had already influenced Tarun Da's mind against many of the good officers who were not involved in his coterie to trade favors with contractors, stevedores, and port agents. I attended the meeting at the site and observed with amazement and amusement Tarun Da's assertive administrative style. He opened the meeting by asking the officers collectively why the debris and scraps were not cleared for so long, creating an operation problem in the port. There was fumbling and an exchange of blame between the officers—different HODs—and Tarun Da identified Chief Engineer as the implementing HOD. He asked CE, 'How long will this take to clear the mess?' CE gave a long list of processing formalities that would take a few months to select a contractor through tender and then about a month to complete the job from the date work commencement. Tarun Da asked CE to call two or three Kalwar scrap dealers to offer the best price for buying the entire debris or scrap materials and clear the mess within 7 days. CE looked puzzled and feebly uttered that there would be an audit query. Tarun Da wanted three parties to bid in his office within the next three days for the opening and finalization. Within the next fortnight, the entire mess was swept away.

I had a difference of opinion with my friend Pranab when, at the end of the delegation visit, Tarun Da appointed Felixstowe UK as consultant instead of PSA Singapore, which was slightly more expensive but covered Haldia container terminal and CFS at GR Jetty in their report. Tarun Da went by his man Friday's advice that Haldia was meant for bulk carrier traffic only and that creating a container barge handling facility at GRJ was premature. P. C. Mitra was deputy chairman of Haldia at that time, and a few of the outstanding senior officers, like Suniti Bhose, Pama Roy, and S. Chakravarty, were in Haldia, and they all agreed with my view, including Mr. Tikku Calcutta Traffic Manager. But Pranab and his coterie's views prevailed with Tarun Da. As I said earlier, there was a strong contractor-stevedores-port officer's nexus prevailing, and it was far too important for me to keep my good relations with Tarun Da and Pranab at the starting point of my new venture. Suniti Da was a very close friend of Tarunda, and Pranab Sen also worked under him in the coal docks in the mid-sixties, but he also failed to change the situation. Despite this, Tarun Da was always paying serious attention to many of my innovative project promotion ideas for the port.

Tarun Da led a cargo marketing delegation to North East India, North India, and neighbouring states for Calcutta-Haldia ports, in which Suniti Da was a very prominent member. Tutu got very close to Tarun Da and Suniti Da, and both of them were very impressed with his intelligent relationship-building capacity with two major steel plants, SAIL and Tata, and his substantial volume of import coal traffic to Haldia. Laxman Seth, in those days, was a militant labour leader in Haldia. He was a terror for the port officers operating as young CPM Turks in the Eastern Midnapur area with Haldia Base. Tutu tamed him down with sops, much to the relief of the port officers. Port Officers were looking for smooth-working and Tutu handsomely looked after the welfare of the port officers and their families. Tarun Da considered Tutu a benevolent well-wisher for the port. Tarun Da was very close to CM Jyoti Basu and knew about CM's help offer to me for the survival of the Himalayas. When he heard from me in detail about the rise and fall of the Himalayas, ending my courageous entrepreneurial journey, he was not willing to believe that Tutu played a major role in the closure of the Himalayas knowingly. Tarun Da corrected his opinion almost after a year when he confidentially advised me that Tutu badmouthed me to CM in his presence when he told him a completely different story regarding the Himalayas exit from the Indian shipping industry. Tarun Da also added that perhaps Tutu, as an outsider, was not aware of the full Himalaya history and CM's personal liking and respect for me. CM later expressed his displeasure to Tarun Da separately. I expressed my appreciation for Tutu's uncanny PR skill to handle bureaucrats and politicians, but it was totally different from my style of detached karma for building enterprises.

I predicted to him that Tutu would amass cash fortune but was to look for spiritual solace at the end for mental peace and bliss. Tarun Da agreed but misinterpreted Swamiji in stating 'Vivekananda was prepared to tolerate lies from a person with enterprise and aggressive delivery.'

Capstan's start with the CSC agency was reasonably promising with market support. The first few months with Panch Ratna gave us trying times coupled with the messy situation at the NSD container berths, which was deftly managed by SNR and TPRC as our stevedores. Between S. Chackravarty, B. K. Banerjee, Pinaki Ghose, and Amit Mitra, our operations and marketing team were strong.

Within the first-quarter of 1982, we could develop good market support for CSC, UKC, and West Asia Gulf container liner services. Bombay-based Seahorse Shipping was CSC's container leasing agency, representing a few international container leasing companies. Capt. S. Majumder was their Calcutta office head, partnering Capt. Batra and Capt. Katre in their Bombay Central office. They were frequently visiting our office and servicing our various shippers' container requirements and handling the logistics of empty container handling for the import consignees. In the first-quarter of 1982, CSL feeder vessel Panch Ratna was changed by the chartering of a more modern vessel with more efficient handling gears. Even then, we were feeling the need for a second feeder vessel to meet the frequency requirements of the trade, particularly for the UKC service. The turn-around of the vessel was always extended due to deficient port infrastructure and the vessel's call schedule at Madras. I was frequently traveling to Colombo to interact with CSC management and their Shipping Ministry for improvement of their service logistics in the areas of call frequency and container logistics handling, particularly with the leasing companies. Unlike BSC, under the strong leadership of Capt. Safi, the CSC management team was more scattered, and there was a lack of cohesive initiatives on the marketing front, particularly with their UKC agents and also agents in West Asia Gulf Ports. There were expectations of personal favors at all levels of management.

With the presence of 3/4 major main line operators like P&O, Maersk, Hapag Lloyd, APL, etc., UKC, West Asia Gulf, and Red Sea services were highly competitive, and all these lines were servicing multiple routes with aggressive marketing and a very competent agency network. For Himalaya and BSC services, I was the principal marketing strategist and was giving 24/7 client servicing attention with prompt decision-making, which was the main cause of the huge market support I was enjoying during the break bulk service days. CSC was not consciously caring about the marketing strategies I was suggesting and was reacting very slowly. Young officers visiting port agents had different priorities for their perverse personal favors. I was not very optimistic about the long-term sustainability of the service. As part of my business strategy, I pursued and secured Maldives' Line Agency for log carrier vessels that were regularly bringing timber cargo for Calcutta Shippers. I also secured owners agency for a few Greek owners importing coal with bulk carriers, generating marginal revenue. I also personally engaged myself in providing chartering and consulting services to ISS and Ratnakar Shipping for revenue augmentation.

CSL's one vessel feeder service was primarily linked to CSC Main Line services to UKC, West Asia Gulf ports, and Red Sea ports and was generating cargo support at discounted freight from my West Asia Gulf support base, mainly with a limited number of tea and jute shippers supporting our UKC service. Most of the MLOs were more Singapore-centric, particularly for UKC and Far Eastern traffic, but CSL, as a subsidiary of CSC, was not allowed to place a second vessel for the Singapore feeder, where there was more demand for feeder container cargo. Return leg traffic was insignificant, and that too had more Madras cargo than Calcutta. Both loaded and empty containers logistics handling was also far below the desired level. Unlike the Himalayas, where after a couple of years we became the preferred service providers for the shippers and the trade, for CSC, our marketing team had to do substantial leg work with the shippers to secure their support. My nephew (Sister's son) Aveek Ghose joined as an intern, and I took Chand Ghose after he lost his EPI job more as a gesture of friendship, allowing emotion to get the better of the professional competence. Chand was a good PR man but always suffered for his drinking and other lower attributes of sensual pleasures. He had a Dr. Jekil and Hide personality, and my continuous counselling had some impact on his temporary productive and civil life style, but this did not last long. He was effective in handling the perverted CSC officers during their visit to Calcutta.

From 1982 to 1987, Capstan had a very trying time in its relentless struggle to build a sustainable business structure. By nature, I was always having a multi-tasking bent of mind with passionate commitment to the development of table tennis as an academy-centric intellectual sports discipline and simultaneously pursuing establishment of the Indian port and shipping industry on a multi-modal transport chain logistic management role model. For the international commodity trade, raw material sourcing, transportation by custom-built trade-specific vessels and innovative port, ocean, and river cargo terminals were necessary. This was important for impacting the global economy with real-time wealth creation and its distribution through the creation of multiple MSMEs as support industries. I knew it was a tall task and needed human resource development and spiritually splurged skill training for building human architecture as per Thakur, Ma, and Swamiji's concept of integrated body-mind-soul. This was practiced on the ground by RKM under Holy Trinity's subtle leadership and active hand holding. Maharaj (Swami Lokeswarananda) always encouraged me in my quest for balancing Spirit with Matter by giving me some precious moments in his RKMIC room in the monk's quarter. Stories of his inspiring life experiences and supreme faith in Thakur for the delivery of myriads of detached karma like the building of RKM, Narendrapur, Ashrama as an international showpiece of man-making education, rural community development through

Lok Shikha Parishad, Blind Boys Academy, multiple skill training, Rambagan slum dwellers total physical and mental rehabilitation, RKMIC policy of cultural reorientation of human mind through international intellectual exchanges of spiritual science of Vedanta as the future unification link for all religions. I got a mortal glimpse of Swamiji in Maharaj's personality and wisdom. Like Swamiji, Maharaj's love and empathy made him a personified manifestation of truth in its glorified beauty.

I was still struggling to heal my deep wound in the mind at the sudden suicidal death of my shipping dream child—the Himalaya Shipping at its second decades take-off point in its flight towards a path-breaking destination of dream realization. The CSC Container Services Development Project consultancy with the Sri Lanka Ministry was started from my Himalaya-BSC-CSC consortium model, originally with a strong feeder service network with MLO tie-ups to service multiple container liner service routes. With Himalaya's closure, my entire vision for round-the-world container service with multiple stakeholders got obliterated. I used to sometime forget my agency role in dealing with CSC's young, inexperienced officers who were serving their assigned duty with a casual mind-set without any sense of ownership. We could continue with CSC Agency for less than two years. Sea Horse offered them a container logistic management package and took over their agency. We continued with CSL Feeder Service Agency for about three years before we had a rather unpleasant situation with accumulated port disbursement dues of over Rs. 15 lacs. We were making monthly remittances of freight collected on their behalf as a routine exercise and never adjusted their dues to us from the freight collection. We remitted a little over Rs. 20 lakh to them on their assurance that our total dues would be cleared before the next call of their feeder vessel. Unfortunately, they didn't settle our dues and advised us to adjust a part from the voyage freight collection and wait for the balance settlement before the next call of the vessel. Voyage freight collection was rather small, and we heard from the master of the vessel that the owners were having some disputes with the charterers on timely charter hire payments and considering withdrawal of the vessel from the charter. I could read the writing on the wall and insisted on full remittance of our dues before the vessel's departure from the port. CSL appointed a new agent to take port clearance by terminating our agency to retaliate. We had to take legal action at Calcutta High Court to protect our dues, and as per court order, CSL provided a bank guarantee for the entire outstanding amount for securing port clearance of the vessel by their new agent. This court case dragged on for nearly 6 months before we could recover our dues, incurring substantial legal costs.

The period 1984–1988 was financially trying for Capstan, and with frugal income from shipping consultancy, chartering, Maldives, and one or two other Greek vessel agencies, we could hardly meet our overhead. I was personally involved with a small consultancy assignment for preparing a confidential rehabilitation report for K. K. Birla and Ramesh Maheswari at India Steamship Company, where my friend Capt. J. C Anand was CEO. The company was continuously accumulating operating losses, and Capt. Anand's own Pentocean Shipping Company and ISS management were having some conflicts of interest. My assignment was to confidentially assess unproductive expenditures and unreasonable cash drainage in various departments and also recommend revenue augmentation through container orientation of their liner service and deployment of their reasonably large fleet in the international charter market for cutting down port expenses and delays they were incurring in their traditional UKC liner service. It was interesting for me, and I could finalize and submit an over 50-pages report to KKB and Ramesh Maheswari within 6–8 months. The report was positive and result-oriented, without any names mentioned as responsible for the identified ailments. After a few weeks, KKB requested that I see him in his ISS chairman office. I was pretty embarrassed to find Capt. Anand sitting in the chairman's office when KKB called me in. KKB handed over a copy of my report to Capt. Anand, stating that he and Maheswari studied my report in detail and identified serious lapses in the management of the company. He added that both Maheswari and he had long working experience with me as a knowledgeable shipping consultant, and the report had been prepared by me at their request. Capt. Anand was asked to study the report and discuss it with me, if necessary, for further interaction with the management.

Capt. J. C Anand was a highly respected person in the Indian shipping industry. I personally held him in very high esteem. He also respected and regarded me as his younger brother. When he was brought into ISS to take over from Chris Smart at the time of takeover of ISS from Khemka Group by Birlas, they had full knowledge about JC's ownership of Pentocean Shipping. PS was successfully running old wartime 'liberty' type vessels for coastal coal and salt carriage with very tight and competent technical management. ISS management was traditionally running primarily UK Liner service with a large fleet of excellent vessels under the protection of the conference pool system, where Scindia, ISS, and SCI (joining later) were sharing the lucrative trade and high freight yield with a small number of British and German liner shipping companies without much competition. Chris Smart efficiently created a network of British and European agents and kept the trade happy with multiple port calls for the vessels without much concern about the extended port stay of the vessels, compensated by a high freight yield. Having worked in their London and Bremen offices during my training days, I had some idea of the smart working style of Chris Smart. The vintage presence of personalities like Sir B P Singh Roy and Sir Ramaswamy Mudaliar at the helm of the board was the remnant of British Raj aristocracy to boost investors' confidence. Khemka Group's active representative in the management was J. N. Bhan, sitting in the ISS and Nicco offices as Director. In the sands of time, involution and evolution in organizations and industry are the universal laws of creation. Capt. Anand had a reasonably long tenure with ISS and Birlas and carried himself well in the luxury of the pool fence protection without confronting the agency network built by Mr. Smart. He was super smart and intelligent to understand the upcoming tide of containerization in the international liner trade, but as a techno-commercial entrepreneur, he had to keep his focus on his own shipping company and left the traditional high overhead management system in the massive 'India Steamship House' few floors to continue growing of moss in its horizontal management structure.

I spent a full day with him in the ISS office to clear up his misunderstanding of my report, and the picture became clear to both of us. I got a lot of useful insight on the conflict of interest issue raised by the group management and the compromise on conscience a CEO had to accommodate in working with the group, which had an adverse impact on the company's balance sheet. Captain Anand initially thought that with Himalaya's unfortunate abrupt ending, I was asked by the management to take his position in ISS, but after our long heart-to-heart talk, he understood and appreciated my entrepreneurial spirit and total reluctance to work for any private or public corporation. He offered his sincere good wishes for the fulfilment of my shipping industry dream. He respected Ramesh Maheswari and marvelled at his skill set to be KKB's 'Man Friday' without compromising his independent decision-making mind. I knew Ramesh Maheswari joined the KKB group with the condition of total freedom in decision-making. This has helped the group with his coming to KKB's rescue at all the crisis points of the group and building Texmaco with top efficiency as a state-of-the art engineering giant.

In a month's time, Capt. Anand left ISS, and up until 1987, two or three CEOs did their rounds in ISS without showing much visible improvement. I reported to Ramesh about newly appointed CEO Keshav Mathur's mental issue, which gave me much importance in his decision-making.

In Capstan, we were somehow managing with meagre revenue generation from the chartering and handling of agency vessels of Maldives Shipping and a couple of Greek ship owners. We were exploring the diversion of business to the export of CI goods and leather during this period. Manoj Bose joined our company as a metallurgist with good knowledge of the CI goods manufacturing industry, mainly in Howrah and Liluah. There was a sick engineering foundry, Banerjee & Chakraborty, in Liluah with their office in Fairly Place. They were nursed by the Industrial Rehabilitation Bank of India. IRBI, who deployed their management supervision by posting officers in their factory and city office to structure rehabilitation plan for funding and managing the company. This was necessary for servicing the reasonably good order book of the company, which needed both funds and efficient technical and labour management support for quality production augmentation and order servicing logistics handling. Skilled labour forces in the factory approached the West Bengal Govt Labour Ministry for support as owners declared closure after suffering a few years of continuous losses due to their banker SBI not supporting them with the requisite working capital. IRBI, at the request of the West Bengal government (from the CM level), agreed to lend support, and they were looking for good techno-commercial management support from selected corporate houses with export orders and technical management skills. I was introduced to IRBI by my friend Kirit Ghose, a very old college friend from St. Xavier's days. At IRBI request, I got Manoj Bose to make a full survey of their factory and made several visits with Manoj, Kirit, and Prasanta to their Liluah factory and city office to discuss with the labour union and a few old clerical staff in their office and factory to prepare a realistic rehabilitation plan. IRBI committed limited fund support for 1 year to restart production and finalize the requirement of funding support for technical reorientation and financial rehabilitation of this sick company. Within 3 months, we submitted our report with the capex and opex requirements to be financed by IRBI for the capex part and SBI for the opex working capital requirement. We consulted the erstwhile owners, particularly Mr. Banerjee, who was an engineer and technical expert and assisted Manoj in the preparation of the technical report, and also the labour union to assess the extension and reorientation requirements of the foundry and the workshop to maintain a steady stream of quality production lines for our export orders servicing. We found the foundry and the factory environment satisfactory, with a high potential to meet the quality of export products manufactured with capacity building. Our report and financing proposal were cleared by the IRBI Board and sent with a recommendation to SBI for fresh working capital support to restart the full-fledged operation of the company under new management with a clean balance sheet. Unfortunately, in spite of the CM personally taking up the matter with the highest level of SBI management, SBI made us run around for one year and did not clear the proposal. IRBI requested that we fund the working capital from our own resources, which we did not find prudent to do, and the project was abandoned. Even Maharaj, who was keeping a regular track, felt deeply disappointed, as, in his wisdom, Maharaj saw great potential in MSME initiatives for the development of the foundry industry in Howrah, Liluah, and Belur.

During these few years of struggle and hardship for Capstan Shipping in the decade of 1980, I was always going back to the robust container feeder service network plan of the Himalayas earlier made for its next two decades of expansion projection. Maharaj always mentored me to move forward and take lessons from the past for course correction. During this struggling time, Thakur, Ma, and Swamiji created opportunities and mental space for me to actively participate in four specific projects to keep alive my divine multitasking assignments and passionate love for sports and spirituality.

In the year 1982, the late Prime Minister, Mrs. Indira Gandhi, organized Asiad 82 in Delhi, 31 years after her late father organized Asiad in 1951. The Indian Olympic Association and all the affiliated sports federations were requested to put their best foot forward for efficient organization of their respective disciplines. After the conduct of Asian Table Tennis at Calcutta in 1980 by the BTTA, at the request of the Sports Ministry and TTFI, we shared our much-lauded 1975 World TT DPR, including my note on our herculean efforts to build Netaji Indoor Stadium in six months with active help from CM Siddhartha Ray, who was close to PM. Massive sports infrastructure building happened in Delhi in less than two years, which included the main Nehru Stadium, the Indra Prastha indoor stadium, the Asiad Village with self-contained duplex apartments and all road and bus services, the dining hall with multi-cuisine catering, etc. All existing facilities, like National Stadium, Talkotra, etc., were thoroughly renovated, including the Pragati Maidan complex, where the Hall of State was allocated as the venue for TT. TTFI was given well-furnished office accommodation for event organization preparation. Apart from being part of the organization as TTFI VP, I was made manager and in charge of the Indian table tennis team. For the last two months before the start of the event, I had to spend a lot of time in Delhi. I will not go into further details as narrated in my TT memoir.

I organized a 15-day Vivek Mela at Nazrul Mancha in the year 1983 as a 10-year program to work on Swamiji's Mission Man Making project pursuit for building Thakur Ma Swamiji's concept of human architecture. This event was organized before the 100-year completion of Swamiji's clarion call to the world for universal religion of non-sectarian sect at the Chicago Parliament of Religion, 1893. This was planned with the guidance and mentoring of RKM and particularly Swami Lokeswaranandaji. I was initially enthused by Asit Banerjee and his youth organization team of 'Vivek Barta' who exhibited youthful team spirit for taking the organization's responsibility under my leadership and support. I could involve my friends Tarun Dutta, Dipak Rudra, Amal Dutta, Sunil Mitra, Gopinnath Ghose, P. C. Goenka, Bimal Roy Choudhury of Modern Decorators, and a few others from my BTTA team in this project. They were all impressed with Asit Banerji's youthful spirit and commitment. However, Maharaj had experience working with Asit and discreetly expressed his personal concern about Asit's total integrity, and warned me to be careful. I pleaded about Asit's commitment to Swamiji's ideals and my intentions and efforts to convert Asit's mind from the realm of negativity to the kingdom of positivity through active participation in Swamiji's Mission Man-Making project. Maharaj did not discourage me but only asked me to keep Asit under watch and check.

The 15-day project was successfully conducted, starting with the inauguration by Swami Bireswarananda, the then President of the Ramakrishna Mission. We arranged transport for over 100 monks of RKM from Belur Math and other centers to attend the event. Eminent speakers, including Swami Lokeswarananda, created a heavenly atmosphere for the packed auditorium. Ramananda Bandopadhyay and Swami Purnatmananda gave me guidance and support for the colorful organization of this event. President Maharaj inspired all of us with his twenty-minute address when he gave his unstinted blessings for our ten years of community development and man-making project dreams on the advent of the centenary of Swamiji's Chicago address at the Parliament of Religion. We organized an exhibition of Swamiji's rare photos with Swami Purnatmananda and Ramananda Bandopadhyay's help, which attracted much attention from the devotees and visitors to the Mela. The large Dias in the Najrul Manch open auditorium were beautifully decorated by modern decorators under their chief, Bimal Roychowdhury's, supervision. Morning and evening sessions covered workshops, debates, and inspiring talks by eminent speakers like Swami Lokeswarananda, Swami Atmashtananda, Swami Gahanananda, Swami Ashaktananda, Swami Bandanananda, and others from RKM. Also, other eminent speakers like Prof. Nimai Sadhan Bose, Gobindo Gopal Mukhopadhyay, Shankari Prasad Basu, Amitava Chowdhury, Tarun Dutta, Deepak Rudra, Husenur Rahman, Ramananda Bandopadhyay etc. enthralled and inspired the audience in different sessions, debates, and workshops. There were cultural programs like plays by reputed groups, performances by CLT children, musical evenings, etc.

With adequate sponsorship support, the fortnight-long event ended with applause. More than 50 rare photos of Swamiji were acquired from Adwaita Ashram and nicely framed for the exhibition sponsored by P. C. Goenka personally. The pictures were planned to be given to RKMIC to be permanently exhibited in their art museum, and Ramananda Da, in charge, made all arrangements for their artistic display in the museum. Asit created a hurdle for smooth delivery by claiming the photos as Vivek Barta property. It caused embarrassment for me, and when I informed Maharaj, he rebuked me instantly by saying you deserve this in the presence of Sankar Maharaj and Ramananda Da. Ultimately, between Tarun Dutta, me, Ramananda Da, and Sankar Maharaj, we could salvage the photos from Asit with police help after Ramananda Da and me spent over two hours at the police station. Maharaj, in his ever affectionate way, contacted me next morning to say, 'I have heard everything from Sankar; you have won a spiritual battle with Thakur, Ma, and Swamiji's blessings, and he reminded me of his warning about Asit. Maharaj advised me not to go further forward on the 10-year project I was planning with Asit Banerjee and Vivek Barta.

My third project involvement was with the construction of Salt Lake Stadium. CM Jyoti Basu called me, Kamal Da (Basu) and Dodo Da (Snehangsu Acharya, Advocate General), to his office some-time in the 3rd quarter of 1983 and suggested the formation of a strong project finance planning committee with Dodo Da as Chairman, me as convenor, and Kamal Da as Secretary for expeditious completion of the project by making viable finance planning acceptable to a syndicate of banks for loan financing the project. K. K. Birla, Russy Mody, Jagdish Sapru, Jit Paul, Sudhir Jalan, and Raghu Modi and others were made members of this committee, and I took Gopinath Ghose into the committee to assist me.

I had involved my old friend and elder brother Sugata Das from London student days and his financial consultancy firm Conquest team, which included Debu Mukherji, another elderly friend from London days, for this stadium project. I knew about this project, which was first conceived during Sidhartha Sankar Ray's tenure as CM, almost within a few months of the completion of the 33rd World TT. The then PWD Chief Architect, Biswanath Banerjee, developed the architectural drawing after visiting Munich, Germany, on the Munich Stadium model. The West Bengal Govt, under Kamal Basu's leadership, appointed Hirak Sen, a young competent architect, as principal architect consultant for this project. He had Balerie

Thomsom & Mathews as his support architect firm for this turn-key project. I held a few meetings with Hirak person-to-person and also a joint meeting with the full technical team at the Balerie Thomson board room with Kamal Da presiding. As Bose Brothers was asked to provide at the start of the Netaji Stadium project construction, I requested Hirak to provide a start-to-finish CPM analysis chart with a realistic cost estimate with a maximum variance limit and phase-wise cash outflow on a determined timeline to maintain uninterrupted work progress. Kamal Da fully supported this, but Hirak avoided this by humorously stating that all of them were expecting me to help fund mobilization from bank loans and sponsorships and that I should not divert my energy and focus in the technical management of the project. Kamal Da supported me to advise Hirak that, for the preparation of a bankable DPR, the information I asked for was very essential. The BTM technical team did not find any difficulty in providing the information, but Hirak interrupted to state that they would require some internal discussions before committing.

Later, Kamal Da advised me confidentially not to rub Hirak on this anymore for some reason that he didn't divulge.

Finally, based on a project report covering revenue streams from a 5-star hotel project to be built on the stadium land and other revenue sources from corporate block sales in the stadium gallery, we could mobilize a bank loan through a six-bank syndicate against a West Bengal Govt guarantee for repayment. There was also fund-raising by the corporate heavyweights in the committee, and with the single herculean efforts of Kamal Da, the stadium construction progressed with satisfactory speed. The stadium was completed in little over one year with state-of-the-art international-standard facilities, high-standard hostel accommodations, an athletic track, lush green international-standard football ground with lighting, multiple meeting rooms, a central board room, restaurant, bar, catering facilities, etc. The stadium was inaugurated with a Nehru Cup Football match.

My fourth major deviation from shipping was my 39th World TT Organization involvement in 1986/87, which I have elaborately narrated in my TT memoir.

We were having a tightrope operation during this period with revenue from chartering, break bulk agencies, exports, and project consultancy. During 1985/86, Ramesh Maheswari requested that I find a dynamic CEO for ISS who was capable of turning the loss-making company into profit mode by following my report to KKB. He knew I would not accept this assignment of paid service. S. N. Roy was working for Essar at the time in Bombay, and he agreed to take up this ISS assignment after reading my report. He first asked me why I was not taking this assignment but appreciated my independent thinking for the Indian shipping industry and port infrastructure development, which might not be compatible with KKB Group's mind set on corporate business thinking.

SNR took charge of ISS as CEO during the last quarter of 1986 and took a number of revolutionary cost-saving actions apart from revenue augmentation through a focus on chartering out of their vessels for gainful deployment. Fortunately, I rediscovered Hugh Maccoy as Chairman of Clarksons, and Hugh introduced me to a super smart chartering broker, Ram Nair, who was efficient, aggressive, and had a very positive and pleasant client service personality. Charter Market was reasonably good, and with Ram's help, Capstan became almost the exclusive house broker for ISS. Promod Gopalan and R. C. Pareekh were very competently handling Ratnakar Shipping Chartering, and Capstan-Clakson became their preferred broking channel. Ramesh Maheswari always had professional respect and personal love for me as a friend from the highest management level of the KKB group. SNR always respected my shipping knowledge and innovative ideas from the Himalaya days, and we got engaged in developing various port infrastructure development initiatives and both bulk and container logistic projects for ISS.

KKB Group was planning a merger of Ratnakar Shipping with their bulk carrier fleet with ISS under a separate bulk and tanker division, and SNR was focusing on maintaining a steady revenue stream through the acquisition of modern second-hand vessels and the replacement of some of their overage vessels, incurring heavy repair and maintenance costs. Technical management was totally revamped. The company's spread-out overhead expenses for London, Bombay, and Madras offices were substantially curtailed. With cost curtailment and revenue augmentation, the ISS balance sheet started generating profit and surplus for consecutive years, almost after a decade of huge loss accumulation of few hundred crores. From the Himalaya's hay days, SNR and I always worked together for a real-time fleet expansion business model with a clean balance sheet and reserve building. I discussed with him my round-the-world container service concept through consortium formation with a few major Main Line Operators like P&O, Maersk, APL, Hapag Lloyd, and one or two far eastern MLOs. A strong and effective container feeder service network building with back-up port infrastructure for smooth transport supply chain logistics handling, linking rail road and river routes was the ultimate goal.

SNR from the ISS side gave Capstan consultancy assignment for preparing a comprehensive DPR covering all components of the round-the-world container service with a backup container feeder service network in India.

It took us almost nine months to complete this DPR, covering over 150 pages. Hugh Maccoy was always very appreciative of my concept and assured total support from Clarkson's side in developing this long-term container logistics project for ISS. We also got in touch with Ibrahim Saraf and D. K. Choudhury in Dubai about establishing a compatible container feeder service network for covering the West Asia Gulf market. DKC always remembered his old Himalaya link. DKC was instrumental in developing the agency network for Ibrahim Saraf. He also extensively travelled in Russia with Ibrahim for building strong connection with Russian Shipping / ship-owners / barge-owners in multiple areas of the agency for a very sizeable fleet of vessels. DKC and his Dubai and Indian teams visited Calcutta, and SNR hosted a few very constructive meetings in the ISS Board room, which I chaired at his request with DKC and his team. SNR was planning over a Rs. 500 crore revenue target for ISS, with Ratnakar merging over the next five years. We identified through Clarksons four sister multipurpose break bulk cum container vessels 6 years old at a block price of USD 15 million with a two-year period charter. ROI was lucrative, and SNR got KKB's clearance jointly with Ramesh Maheswari to go for the deal. I requested Clarkson secure the owner's formal offer for closing the deal through negotiation, as is customary in S&P business. Clarksons reverted, after two days of waiting, that owners are committed to Indian owners at a much higher price through another broking channel. When I informed SNR over the phone, he wanted to have a confidential meeting with me.

SNR advised me that Chairman KKB called and instructed him to meet Nigel Bell of Galbraith, another reputed London Broking House, who was in Calcutta, and close the block deal for the purchase of these four vessels at a substantially higher price already confirmed by KKB directly. SNR feebly argued that such a high price was not compatible with a two-year charter rate for the vessels to give a positive return. Nigel Bell opined that such a low charter rate was a reason for the owners to consider a lower price, and the vessels were capable of much higher revenue in spot market operation. SNR was highly embarrassed and upset and asked me to suitably explain to Hugh and Clarksons so that relationship did not get impaired. He also asked me to talk to Ramesh Maheswari. Ramesh was also equally surprised, but after some time, he advised me to digest this without rubbing further. When I discussed this with Hugh with a lot of embarrassment, he took the matter very seriously and thanked me for giving him useful insight on Galbraith's success in the Indian shipping S&P market. I could see SNR facing the impact of this deal on the ISS Balance Sheet, although the Indian Shipping Industry and the Shipping Ministry hailed Chairman KKB for the rapid turn-around of ISS and putting the company back in expansion mode.

SNR was a very mature and down-to-earth shipping professional with a very solid grounding in the Himalaya Shipping as my very close and trusted colleague to assist me during its build-up and development struggle with frugal capital. He did not take much time to accept this incident as a professional industrial hazard. Since the early 1990s, SNR has been actively supporting my two dream innovative projects, namely the round-the-world container service logistics building by forming consortiums with major MLOs at the macro level and the establishment of an Indian container feeder service network at the immediate micro level. For this top-priority container service project, I was requested to join many meetings with APL in Chennai, a few other Far Eastern MLOs in Singapore, and the DKC and Saraf group teams in Dubai. This highly potential long-term container logistics project was moving in the right direction. By this time, Dr. A. C Ray was Chairman of Kolkata Port, and Tarun Dutta was Chief Secretary of the Government of West Bengal. Apart from my own personal relationship with Tarun Da and Dr. Ray, SNR had the super PR skills to initiate a variety of innovative port infrastructure projects, both in the container and bulk cargo handling sectors, with Kolkata Port. SNR was always very upbeat about my Ocean-River-Rail-Road linking concept of bulk import of coal from source to destination Transport logistic chain management. We made a presentation to Dr. A. C Roy covering my friend Capt. Torsten Olsen's Scandimar Sweden's transloading project at Sandheads deep-drafted location involving high-technology transloaders with conveyor-loaders and unloaders that are reversible and have 4000 tons per hour of loading and unloading capacity. The equipment was horseshoe type with a plug-in/plug-out system for broad beam shallow-drafted 25000 dwt self-propelled barges that were powering the transhipper equipment with auxiliary engines support only for cargo operation. I backed this up with my other friend Gustav Drohse's Baket lash barges vessel design developed by Gustav with Faderiskhaven Shipyard, Denmark, for river operation. Dr. Roy and Tarun Da both appreciated the unique innovative concept to resolve the perennial draft limitation issue of Kolkata-Haldia for large volume traffic augmentation. Both SNR and I knew that such concept selling with high investment would take 4–5 years with end users steel plants and power plants and respective ministries. It was, however, very exciting and intellectually stimulating. Ramesh Maheswari, with his Eagle Eye, immediately saw potential for Texmaco's Rail Cars building in the logistic link.

Capstan, after 6–7 years of extreme struggle and hardship, reached some breather of stability by 1989/90. SNR and I were often discussing our Himalaya shipping days and dream expansion plans with our own build-up on frugal capital investment. I still remember SNR's very pertinent observation in one of our longish evening interludes at Calcutta Club, when he said that Dada's egocentric degradation of mind from constructive to destructive mode came from insecurity and fear of an unknown future, which he could not visualize due to his shipping industry inexperience. Both Dada and Gopal Da were sure to lick their wounds after the stormy consequences leading to the closure of the company and the killing of the Golden Goose. It was true that after the IPO, investors would have become totally dependent on the management team with strong leadership for share value to go up, but if I were allowed to continue the journey, a land mark would have been written in the history of the Indian shipping industry. In the case of ISS, he was apprehensive about the vanity and whims of the deep-pocketed private corporate owners who inherited wealth from their illustrious predecessors with little connection to their predecessor's dreams. He sadly reflected on his vessel purchase experience with KKB. SNR narrated KKB's matter-of-fact reaction when he mentioned to the Chairman the necessity of a clean balance sheet for ISS by writing off near Rs. 300 crore of accumulated losses (in the form of outstanding bank and mostly SDFC government loans). KKB was a Rajya Sabha MP in the early 1990s, if my memory serves right.

Kakababu passed away on January 9, 1988, after suffering from extreme mental depression and disorder for six to nine months before reaching 80. After the Shradh ceremony and all other rituals were over, we went to Mr. P. N. Mitter, a solicitor and Kakababu's close college friend. Mesomasai, as we addressed him, was like my mentor and guided me wisely in all my legal problems with affectionate parental care. In 1973, Kakababu executed a will and handed over one copy each to Dada, Sejda, and me after execution in the presence of Babi and our solicitor cousin Balai Da (S C Mitter), awarding all his estate properties equally to three of us and monthly stipends to our three sisters after his life. I went to Mesomasai with my copy of this will, expecting Dada and Sejda to do the same. When I presented my copy of the will to Mesomasai, requesting that Dada and Sejda do the same for processing probate applications, Dada presented a different registered will executed by Kakababu in 1982, which canceled the earlier will where Kakababu's entire estate was awarded to Dada's son Arijit 50% and Sejda's sons Ananjan 25% and Nilanjan 25%. I was specifically awarded two of his encumbered properties at Tollygunge Road and Deshpran Shasmal Road. Dada explained to Mesomasai that he was instructed by Kakababu to keep this will with him and not to disclose it to anybody during Kakababu's lifetime. Dada was upset when I openly advised Mesomasai that this was Dada's fraudulent manipulation in continuum with earlier manipulation of Himalaya's affairs, and this was the reason for Kakababu to lose his sanity during the last months of his life. Sejda kept silent and later told me that he knew from Dada of some change in the will without details. He tried to talk to Kakababu, who himself was feeling uncomfortable about this change. Will was executed at Dada's behest when he was taken to the Bose and Mitra Solicitors offices by Dada for execution and registration through commission. Kakababu had been talking to his friend P. N. Mitter about changing the will again as he was apprehending long-drawn litigation and a total break in family bonding after his lifetime. PNM requested that Kakababu give him the registered will, but Kakababu was told by Dada that the will was with the solicitor's office and kept defaulting for nearly 18–24 months before Kakababu's demise. Mesomasai later was very upset and fully endorsed my statement of fraudulent manupulation by Dada and the reason for Kakababu's mental discomfort expressed to him. He advised me to challenge the will and recommended a suitable lawyer practicing in Alipore Court. This matter caused litigation and a major disruption in family harmony, as anticipated by Kakababu. I had finally withdrawn and did not pursue this further by going to High Court. This I did at Dada's request for the restoration of our heritage family bonding. I will end this topic here without going further and come back to my shipping venture.

Soma was always excelling in her school in studies, sports, dancing, painting, and many creative activities, and both Purnima and I consciously encouraged her creative mind to be positive and intuitive and always tried to douse her anger and mental disturbance coming from injustice, and sometimes physical assaults at the hands of elder cousins in the joint family. Maharaj and Ramananda Babu greatly helped me in handling her 'Raja Guna' and intellectual talent to achieve big in life. She expressed her firm intention to pursue computer science at one of the Ivy League universities in the USA, with particular interest in MIT. I was not surprised when she secured admission in Smith College, USA, with a reasonable scholarship. There were eyebrows raised by family members and friends who advised us against her going to the USA at such an early age, particularly as she was our only child. We could keep our minds strong to let her dream fly high in pursuit of her own carrier excellence, and we saw her off at Bombay Airport for her destination, Smith College, in August 1989. We missed her every moment, waiting for the arrival of her weekly long letters to both of us independently and writing our prompt replies. Soma's Bhaiya, Diya, and Bakada grandparents from the maternal side were very depressed, as Soma was truly a cynosure in their eyes. Bania, my father-in-law, was hiding his emotional pain to console and control the pain and anguish of the two ladies in the house. Mani, my mother-in-law, was always talking loudly about our, particularly Purnima's, hard exterior for allowing their little Sombhai to fly out alone to a distant land far away from their love and care. Purnima was consoling herself in the garb of consoling me by humming great Atul Prasad's lines: 'Amay Rakhte jadi apan ghare, Biswa ghare petham na thai, dujon jadi hoto apan hoto na mor apan sabai' - If we had kept her within the precincts of our love and comfort at home and narrow nuclear family bonding, then she could never have made the entire universe her spacious home with creative work, love, and empathy for humanity. Smith College, on its sprawling campus, was breathing history and holding in its bosom over a hundred years of rich culture and creativity. Soma had to struggle hard in her hostel within the sprawling campus of the historic Smith College, the oldest of the five sisters women's colleges in New England. She was enjoying her multi-discipline graduation course with majors in economics and computer science. We were finding her bonding with new friends and professors and her alliance with the bounty of nature on the Smith College campus, reflecting her creativity to excel through her sensitive mind.

I made my first visit to her at Smith College in 1991 as a part of my business trip to New York and London. Due to a delayed flight from New York, I arrived at Smith College after midnight by taxi from the North Hampton Airport. Soma could arrange pizza for me at those unearthly hours. We chatted till 2 a.m. in her room, and then she took me to an apartment room she arranged for my stay. If I remember right, my visit was during her summer recess, and most of the hostel was vacant. During my brief stay on the Smith campus, she introduced me to many of her close friends and her French Computer Science professor, Dominique. She took me around the beautiful Smith College campus and showed me quite a few of her stand-alone beauty spots for painting and writing. I was very impressed with the indoor and outdoor sports facilities the college had, and I was glad that she was taking lessons in tennis. I visited her computer lab and spent some quality time with Prof. Dominique. He was very fond of narrating the story of Soma's encounter with 'Pig' on the Calcutta road with me teaching her driving. We hired a car for two days to explore the beauty of the Woods and Hills on the New England country side. We chanced upon a signboard in the woods directing us to the house of the great poet Robert Frost. He was the author of Jawahar Lal Nehru's often quoted lines, 'I have promises to keep.' We went inside, parking our car unknowingly on another gentleman's property. After a fulfilling visit to the poet's house, which was retained as a museum, we came back to our car and faced the wrath and fury of a disturbed mind from the owner of the property in the woods. After the fury was over, we exchanged civil, pleasant words and an apology from the gentleman for his anger. Another unpleasant incident, but an experience worth remembering, happened when one tire of our car got stuck in a roadside ditch. Both of us struggled and finally rescued ourselves with much relief. The scenic beauty of the New England countryside was heavenly.

On my way back, I was introduced by Ram Nair and Patrik O'neil to a deep-sea floating crane operation project of Louis Dreyfus in Paris and to a remarkable French man, Patrik Lescraign, who was the technical marine brain for the project and showed interest in bulk coal transportation contracts of steel plants and power plants with deep-sea transfer of cargo into specially designed barges from the large bulk carriers. They were already operating in Indonesia successfully. I was already discussing with SNR, Calcutta Port, and SAIL Capt. Orsten Olsen's transloading concept for such an operation, but I did not have a committed investor for the project. I invited Patrik Lescraign to visit Calcutta for the project presentation, as LD was a committed investor subject to a valid contract from the end-user as a counter-party.

After coming back to Calcutta, I was informed by SNR that KKB was considering the induction of Mr. Rajwar, who just retired as Chairman of SCI in ISS above SNR, and sounded him for his consent to lead ISS with full freedom under Rajwar, who was being brought in with some specific assignment for making the balance sheet clean by securing Govt approval for loan write-off. SNR was very upset, and when I asked whether he had given his consent, he said he had no option as asking for his consent on a decision already made was only a courtesan formality. SNR was almost sure that Mr.

Rajwar, with his SCI background, would have a totally conservative mind-set. He was not expected to let SNR lead and pursue long-term, innovative projects with independent authority. By this time, D. K. Chaudhury introduced me to Mr. Kleiman, his Russian friend from Vladivostok, for starting container feeder service between Calcutta and Singapore with small 225 TEU capacity newly built container vessels belonging to Shakhalin Shipping Co. The Russian shipping company was getting delivery of 12 such vessels in phases and had been looking for their profitable deployment. Capstan secured the agency of Shakhalin Shipping Co. through Mr. Kleiman's influence at a cost and started the service with the first vessel, 'Chekov,' which was joined by the second vessel, 'Tomari,' within two months. The vessels were ideally suitable for full-load operation within permissible Calcutta draft, and the vessels were plying with full-load cargo from both sides with a competent agent in Singapore introduced by my friend Mr. Peter Blumbach with DKC's approval from his own connections. SNR and I had an understanding with DKC for securing all 12 vessels over a period under ISS charter over the next year after adequate confidence building with Shakhalin Shipping by Capstan. The ISS agency for all the West Asia gulf ports was committed to DKC and the Saraf Group of Ibrahim Saraf.

It was just before the start of our container service sometime in 1989/90 that Mr. Bikram Sarkar joined as the Calcutta Port chairman and got into some legal battle with the then Shipping Minister, who was trying to remove him, as the Minister found Mr. Sarkar's strong management-oriented personality unbending to carry out his fund collection agenda for his political party. There were a group of port officers serving the minister on his ploy to remove Mr. Sarkar. Bikram Babu was a faith-driven devotee of Thakur Ramakrishna with total surrender, and he came out unscathed in the legal battle, fully exposing the minister and the group supporting him within one year. Bikrambabu and I were brought close and intimate by Thakur.

In a long session with him after he took firm hold on port management, I briefed him in detail on the mess at the NSD

Container Terminal handling and the unholy nexus and corruption prevailing between port officers and stevedores in container handling at the yard, causing delay and productivity losses to the vessels at heavy cost. By this time, Shakhalin Shipping Line had introduced four sister vessels in the Calcutta-Singapore feeder service, and we were successfully launched in our feeder service with both ends support from our MLO clients. All the port officers were consciously aware of the chairman's confidence in me as a shipping and port professional, and the Capstan dock team was successfully navigating our vessel call schedules comfortably against strong competition from two major Singapore-based feeder operators. At the chairman's request, I wrote to him a detailed, three-page letter on the container handling mess and the stevedore officer's nexus. The chairman instructed the traffic manager to immediately convene a meeting of the container operators, both feeders and MLOs, including the stevedores, to discuss my letter in detail and take steps for cleaning up the mess with short- and long-term measures. This meeting was well attended, and I sent my nephew Amit to represent Capstan in this meeting. I joined a bit late as I had another meeting with SNR at ISS that morning. When I entered the meeting room at the TM's office, the room was full, and TM was just reading out the unholy nexus portion of my letter to the Chairman with accented sarcasm. As I entered, there was a surprising lull, and TM's attitude took a 'U turn' when he got up and invited me to the top table. The entire audience was both surprised and amused to watch him. Gopal Da and Mahalingam from Stevedore's side were present in the meeting. My cousin Jayanta Mitter was senior rep from SCI. Everybody appreciated my constructive suggestions for the introduction of a digital port-net system by appointing Port of Singapore-PSA as a consultant and also terminal management with adequate container handling equipment support, including mobile handling cranes for handling gear-less container vessels for traffic augmentation.

As a constructive outcome of the discussions, Gopal Da proposed the formation of a special committee under my chairmanship to discuss and draw up a comprehensive report for the professional upliftment of the NSD Container Terminal. This was done with the chairman's approval. The committee is comprised of port officers, container operators, and stevedore members, with a specific assignment to hold regular weekly meetings and prepare a comprehensive report within three months for the chairman and the board of trustees' consideration. I had to work hard to complete this report within time through consultation with my international network, including PSA. Mr. Bikram Sarkar was very impressed and promised to ensure the implementation of the major parts of the report, if not all, before the end of his tenure.

On the ISS front, SNR was having differences with Mr. Rajwar on his forward-looking long-term growth plan for the company. SNR was bold and dynamic, with courage and conviction, to align himself with innovation and competition in the international port and shipping evolution as a professional and intellectual challenge. Mr. Rajwar, as retired Chairman of SCI, joined ISS with a single agenda and the conservative SCI culture of following international innovation leads after a few years of trial runs, even if that meant running behind in the competition. He was focused on cleaning the ISS balance sheet of accumulated old debts, primarily using his experience and contacts as a former PSU chairman with the government and nationalized banks. He was inclined to make use of the sick industry stigma of the company as a genuine cause for debt write-offs. He was not inclined to pursue and project long-term expansion with revenue generation potential for physical debt repayment over time instead of a relief write-off.

Mr. Rajwar found SNR's round-the-world container service initiative, as per my project report, with phase-wise build-up over years too ambitious in the Indian shipping industry. SNR confided to me his frustration and disappointment, and his sharp mind could easily realize that Mr. Rajwar's agenda was to engineer debt write-offs with the government and progressively work towards fleet and asset curtailment for the eventual closure of this historic shipping company. He was not finding space for adequate comfort in the organization, and he was thinking of quitting if this container project stalled. He requested that I talk to Ramesh Maheswari for a more clear assessment of the internal management policy. He compared my Himalaya story as a mini-ISS with Rs. 3 crore against Rs. 300 crore debt write-off.

I had a detailed discussion with Ramesh. I convinced SNR to join ISS at Ramesh's request, and the company was back to profitability for a few consecutive years. I re-emphasized my views earlier expressed to him about the totally different mind-set and philosophy of SNR and Rajwar and warned about the SNR decision to quit if this container project was blocked by Rajwar and wanted to know KKB's mind on this. He did not contradict the SNR assessment of Rajwar's agenda and suggested that Saroj Poddar, as an ISS board member, would be a better person to interact on this. When I mentioned to SP the Rajwar-SNR conflict, he simply told me that Rajwar had been inducted into the ISS by KKB with SNR consent, and there was no reason for my worry.

While the ISS crisis was getting serious, I had a call from DKC, who informed me that Kleiman came to Dubai and advised Ibrahim Saraf and DKC about the possibility of Sakhalyn Shipping giving out all their 12 sister vessels for deployment in the Indian Feeder Service network under Period TC to the Indian Shipping Company. They were exploring ISS and SNR status and stood on this while Kleiman was in Dubai. I briefed them about SNR differences with ISS management and recommended Ibrahim take the vessels on TC at a rate of USD 4000 daily within the next year in phases. I assured him that all these vessels could be very profitably deployed in Calcutta-Haldia – Singapore, Calcutta-Haldia – Colombo run and also in Madras-Singapore and Madras-Colombo run with an average TCY between USD 5K and 6K daily. I advised Ibrahim that over the last 18 months, the Shakhalyn Shipping team has made few visits to Calcutta and increased the number of vessels in the Calcutta-Singapore service from one to four. Market share had significantly increased, and all the vessels were performing at

90% of their capacity. All these vessels were giving over USD 6K TCY, and the owners were very happy. Ibrahim agreed to consider my suggestion. He also advised DKC to explore the possibility of SNR joining him in case he was thinking of leaving ISS. Later, DKC requested that I talk to SNR to find out his thoughts and expectations. He also advised me that Ibrahim had taken two British officers in the organization, Graham Norris and Howard James, along with a few other Indian officers who were giving wrong advice to Ibrahim behind DKC's back. Although DKC convinced Ibrahim to take Shakhalyn vessels on charter as per my suggestion, the British officer's team mooted the formation of the Integrated Container Feeder Service for Indian operations and took the Shakhalyn vessels under its management instead of taking the vessels on period TC. Kleiman was accordingly briefed with adequate financial support to manipulate Shakhalyn management. In 1992, Russia was in an economic mess and corruption was rampant, but I still told DKC and Ibrahim that such an arrangement was not going to be sustainable in the long run.

When I talked to SNR about Ibrahim's offer, he confided in me to tell me that he already had an Essar Shipping offer to join as MD of South India Shipping Corporation in Madras, which Ruia's were in the process of taking over at that time with Bunglow in their sprawling complex and terms matching with ISS. But he had an immediate requirement for substantial foreign currency income to meet the substantial fee requirement for his second son's education abroad. He asked for my advice as a trusted friend. I gave my clear view on DKC's position in the Saraf organization. DKC joined Ibrahim from the Himalayas at my recommendation in the mid-70s and then worked hard with Ibrahim almost as his trusted younger brother for traveling and building foreign agency business, particularly Russian connections. Ibrahim looked after DKC very lavishly, and with substantial expansion of the organization, DKC had been ruling the roost as the right-hand man of Ibrahim. He had built his personal fortune and a lifestyle with Indian and international contacts, causing envy in the senior British newcomers, particularly.

He had worked under SNR and me in the Himalayas and may feel somewhat insecure about SNR joining in a position above him. Even if SNR joined, it should be for a one-year trial contract to meet his immediate requirements, and he should keep his Essar option open with Ruias.

It took another few months for SNR to struggle in ISS in a last-ditch effort to get the container project approved, but finally KKB went by Rajwar's advice to decide against it. This was a major blow for SNR, and his decision to quit was final.

During these few months, there were some dramatic happenings between ICFS and Capstan. I was informed by DKC and Kleiman about the appointment of ICFS, Dubai, as the manager of Shakhalyn Shipping vessels. We were advised to report to ICFS, Dubai, on agency matters instead of direct communication with Shakhalyn. Capt. Philipov, the then MD of Shakhalyn Shipping, and his team, who were visiting Calcutta, always had reasonable marine demands from Capstan, which we were gladly meeting. They were not happy at all about this arrangement, and at Capt. Phillipov's request, I visited Shakhalyn Island to discuss the matter with their chairman. They gave me a warm reception at a time when Russia was going through a severe economic crisis after the breakup of the Soviet Union. I stayed in the best hotel they booked for me, as their own five-star hotel and guest house were still under construction. Room service was bad, and the heating arrangement was far from comfortable. There was a language problem, and the English-speaking retired lady officer helping me told me of her financial predicament with the pension she was getting in Roubles, which lost its value tremendously due to currency loss. High-breed shepherd dogs were let loose on the streets to fend for themselves. The picture of poverty outside Shakhalyn Shipping's office in the town was pathetic. I was really feeling guilt in my conscience about enjoying the guest reception privileges they were offering me. Anyway, during my short two-night and three-day interactions with Capt Phillipov and his team and a 45-minute meeting with their chairman, it was revealed that Kleiman had high-level contacts, and a three-year management contract was signed with ICFS with a clear understanding that all 12 new building sister container vessels under a contract with an European Shipyard (I am not remembering the name now) were to be taken on period TC at a reasonable rate compatible with the TCY the vessels would be generating during the period under ICFS management. I was advised to keep a full account of the TCY of the vessels to help owners determine a reasonable period TC rate at the end of three years.

Kleiman reported my visit to Ibrahim, DKC, and ICFS. British officers were aware of my domain knowledge and closeness to Shakhalyn Shipping and asked for my help to manage the show efficiently. Barely before two months of operation under ICFS, Capstan received an agency termination letter from ICFS, signed by one of the British officers, and was advised to hand over records and documents to their newly appointed Calcutta agent. It was a two-week intensive legal battle at the Calcutta High Court, with my solicitor, Uncle P. N. Mitter, guiding me and Barrister S. K. Kapur on the front battle line at the court, with Pradip Mitra as his junior. Capt. Phillipov from Shakhalyn Shipping helped me by giving me a strong letter of appreciation for our services to them prior to the appointment of ICFS as manager. Justice Ajit Sengupta's joint bench at the appeal court delivered judgment in our favor with directions on ICFS to restore our agency. Shakhalyn Shipping as Ship-owner was made a party. Ibrahim Saraf and DKC appeared on the scene, breaking their silence at this point, and I was invited to Dubai with the Capstan team to have a reconciliatory meeting with ICFS for the smooth running of the feeder service in close cooperation. These few months in 1993 were both eventful and turbulent, which was traumatic for me.

Purnima and I had been to Smith College to attend Soma's convocation after a prior visit to Rupa and family in Toronto, Canada, for a few days. Rupa has always been very dear to me and Purnima from her childhood days, and she was Soma's beloved Rupapisi.

Prasad was also our paraboy playing table tennis at our house and played for the Bengal Junior team during my peak playing days in the late fifties. We heard about little Raja from Soma when she visited her Rupapisi in Toronto earlier and met him for the first time to spend quality time with him at home. Rupa's delicious cooking pampered us throughout our stay with her. We visited Niagra Falls from Canada and did much sight-seeing and exploration between the five of us. Rupa connected me to Jahar (Dhiru) and family after a long twenty years. At Jahar's invitation, we spent a memorable evening at his house, where Jahar's two sweet daughters delighted us with their accented Bengali, asking questions on our memorable playing days. Jahar opened his well-preserved table tennis album with photos and press clippings from the 1959 Bengal State T-T Championship, where both of us had many sweet memories to share. The two beautiful young girls were sweetly asking their Baba whether I was the same Probir uncle who had defeated their Jethu and Baba and comparing our young athlete looks in the album with our present looks in accented Bengali. Our three families thoroughly enjoyed this T-T session of nostalgia. Prasad, (who was a junior Bengal team player in 1959) joined Jahar and me in sharing multiple old anecdotes. We were chit-chatting, forgetting the limitation of time. We ended the evening going up to late night with a sumptuous dinner with two young ladies pressing us to take more of the items cooked by them. Five of us came back from Jahar's house with soul-fulfilling bliss without knowing that Jahar and I were not to meet again as Jahar passed away after a few years.

We hired a car in my name for all five of us to drive down to Soma at Smith College and the car was to be returned to the rental company by Prasad. We reached Soma with a night halt. Rupa, Prasad and Raja went back after spending one night and we stayed back for Soma's convocation. This is a deep imprint in our memory and recorded in Purnima's travelogue.

Soma's convocation with many credit awards was also very memorable in its splendour in presentation. She was a favorite student of her French professor, Dominique, who was a very popular teacher with the students. Soma was emotional, remembering his treating her with lollipops for every meritorious achievement. Soma received her latest appreciation from her professor when she got her full scholarship letter from MIT to join her dream institute for her Masters. It was amazing to witness Alumni's in the wheel chair of this heritage educational institution and they joined the large number of former students in the Alumni parade before the convocation.

This was my third visit to Smith College during her four-year graduation course and Purnima's first. One year I visited her in Texas when she was serving as an intern at the Texas Instrument during her break. She did not come home that year.

We had met all her friends and spent some time driving in the beautiful New England countryside. The famous Margaret Mitchel author of "Gone with the Wind" was Smith Alumni. I also read about Swamiji lecturing at Smith College during his first USA visit after becoming famous at the Chicago Parliament of Religion in the book 'Reminiscences of Western Disciples.'

We had a very enjoyable three-night and four-day 'Grand Canyon' tour starting in Las Vegas and returning after a complete circle. We stayed at motels for economy, which was a very pleasant experience. Gambling at Las Vegas Casino was also an experience. I blew up a major portion of Soma's windfall jackpot dollar earnings in my effort to double it.

We flew down to Amsterdam from Las Vegas for our European holiday by Euro Rail to celebrate Soma's graduation. Visits to Van Gogh Museum, Rembrandt's house, river cruises, etc. were all beautifully recorded in Purnima's Travelogue. Soma was to follow this practice later in English in her extensive tours. Liliput town at the Hague and the International Court of Justice were on our tour itinerary. We spent over four days in my favorite city, Paris. We leisurely walked down the Seine river from Eiffel Tower to the 'Arch de Triumph' at Chassez liese through Plas du le Concord, taking relaxed sitting breaks at the riverside benches to chitchat on our cultural explorations, particularly the art pieces of the 'Louvre' and 'De Orsay.' We enjoyed our walking exploration of the lanes and bi-lanes of Momarte, watching artists paint at the feet of the Sacre de la Coure. We heartily laughed at the spontaneous expression of the French waiter at the Roadside Cafe when he slipped a chicken on the floor while serving us to say, 'I didn't know the chicken was alive.' We explored walking in the Latin Quarters and Sobourne University in the evening. One morning to late afternoon visit to Napolean's famous 'Tulier Garden' and Rodin Museum was soul-fulfilling. Post-lunch nostalgic visit to the famous Cemetery, where all Renaissance French masters like Victor Hugo, Balzac, Molière, Mount Passé, etc. were lying buried, including Oscar Wild, who died in Paris. This was one of the best of my many Paris visits.

We rolled out to Niece from Paris on our Euro Rail schedule for exploring the French Riviera. During my student days, I visited the Italian Riviera in a group with Chordi, Sejda, Gautam, Samir Da, Rotrout, etc., but this was my first exploration of the French side of the Riviera. Monaco, just opposite Monte Carlo on the Italian side, was equally reputable for casinos and tourist gambling meccas. There were beautiful beaches between Cannes (famous for the International Film Festival), Niece, and Monaco where topless young and middle-aged women were sunbathing and playing beach games totally uninhibited. This was a bit awkward for us on vacation with our 22-year-old daughter. Cannes was a major tourist attraction where we had taken a group boat tour for a visit to an island. We had spent time at the casinos in Monaco, and also at Niece. With the recommendation of one of my Clarksons friends, we visited the little wine-making village of Dentz on the mountain on the other side of Cannes, which was beautiful and endowed with the fragrance of the village away from the town. On the day we were to leave Niece, we packed our luggage in the hired car, which we were to return to the rental company near the railway station in the evening. We had a longish lunch and last round of casino gambling in the city, wrongly parking the car at a no-parking zone. When we came back to pick up the car, we found the car missing. It was a traumatic experience to recover the car from police custody after paying a hefty fine, and we could heartily recoil ourselves only when we were safely parked in our train compartment with our entire luggage.

After this heavenly holiday, we returned to Calcutta to confront a few unexpected unpleasant events at our Elgin Road joint family.

When Soma came back home with us for a longish stay until the start of her MIT session, I wanted to give her the privacy of her own bed and study room in my Babi's office room through some renovation, including the uplifting of the adjacent bathroom. My brothers filed a criminal case against her, and after lots of unpleasantness, through court order and police help, I could manage for Soma to stay in that room during her stay of a couple of months in Calcutta before joining MIT.

My legal drama with ICFS for Shakhalyn Shipping Agency, as narrated earlier, also happened during these few months, and ultimately, I had to visit Dubai with Amit for a few days during this time at Ibrahim and DKC's calling. There was another two-night, three-day business trip to Oman with DKC for a shipping consultancy assignment also during this period.

During this period, I had to legally force the delivery and shifting of Purnima's family back to the 5th, 2nd, and 1st floors of the Suryoday Building in the flats allocated to the owners with incomplete ground floor work by the developers.

Thakur, Ma, and Swamiji held my hands and trained my mind to retain poise and calm in the midst of the turbulent ocean of detached karma. A creative cultural relief came from Suniti Da (Bhose) when he read to us his script of Tagore's 'Gora' classic novel for Shruti Natak—a voice play on the stage by our family and friends at Gorki Sadan before Soma's departure for MIT. There was regular rehearsal at Mani's 171, S. P. Mukherji Road, 5th floor residence. Suniti da's 'Charyeari' theatre group friend and my TT senior from playing days Sitanath Da (Choudhury) was not only acting as Mahim in the play but was also assisting Suniti Da with his multi-talented personality of humour, acting, music, and the natural flow of useful tips. From our family, I was playing Pareshbabu, Purnima as Barada Sundari, Soma as Lalita, my sister-in-law Sumitra as Anandamoyee, Kakima as Harimohini, and our nephew Arijit Roychowdhury (Chotku) as Binay. Surojit, the son of my senior friend Dhruba Da (Sen), a famous architect and the then President of our Rotary Club of Calcutta Metro South, played the title role of Gora. Soma's friend, Amanita, played the role of Sucharita. Gopinath (Ghose) played the role of Krishna Mohon, apart from other friends participating. Despite Suniti Da getting sick during the last part of the rehearsal and his inability to attend the final show at Gorki Sadan, the show went off with tremendous success. Munia, Suniti Da's wife and Kanishka Sen famous stage lighting legend, looked after music, sound, lighting, and stage management.

Fortunately after my Dubai visit, ICFS- Capstan container feeder service got started for a very financially successful operation in 1993 with harmony and rhythm which gave me peaceful space in my mental corridor to express with poise and calm the Character of 'Paresh babu' in Gora and participate in a full team cultural party celebration evening at Suniti da's house in Hindusthan Park before Soma's departure. Suniti Da was already planning about our next presentation of his favorite not oft acted Tagore's play 'Bashonri' with Soma in mind for the title role. A real life drama between Gora and Sucharita got started during our rehearsals at the roof garden of Mani and Kakima's 5th floor flats in SPM Road which was unfolded to me after Soma's departure when Dhruba Da informed me with smiling face 'Probir, your eldest daughter visited our house last evening,' at a Rotary lunch party hosted by him to felicitate the international delegates visiting Calcutta to attend 100 years celebration convention of Swamiji's Chicago address at the Parliament of Religion organized by RKM under Maharaj -Swami Lokeswarananda' s leadership. My other Rotarian friend Satybrata (Dodo) Ghose told me in the same party that Dhruba Da was noticed emotionally sobbing watching Gora during the show. Later I had arranged a meeting between Dhruba Da and Amanita's father at Dhruba da's office for a wedding discussion which lasted for nearly 90 minutes for wedding finalization adda.

While our container feeder service in Calcutta, Singapore, was in full bloom with occasional Haldia calls for picking up export or dropping off import containers for client satisfaction, SNR joined Ibrahim Saraf for an intended trial one-year run, primarily to earn for his second son's education abroad. His eldest son was a doctor who settled in London with his beloved Gujrati doctor wife. SNR was deeply attached to his sons as a proud father. The second son got married to the famous election commissioner's daughter, and SNR hosted a mega wedding reception in Calcutta attended by ministers and MPs of the Center and State and captains of the shipping industry. I met both CM Jyoti Basu and former CM S.S. Ray at this party.

On the Capstan front, while the going was good on the ICFS-Shakhalyn shipping front, we were offered two old geared container vessels under the ICFS management of another Russian line, Fesco, for Calcutta-Haldia-Madras- Colombo service. By then, we had secured the agency of a few NVOCC firms in Dubai and Singapore. These were particularly focused on West Asia Gulf cargo and limited Singapore-based traffic for Singapore, Malaysia, Indonesia, and Thailand. We had to create a separate marketing division for NVOCC agency handling under experienced B.K. Banerjee, who had been with me since the Himalayas. I was requested by ICFS to set up an office in Madras, and I undertook a longish tour of Dubai, London, and Paris to discuss existing container feeder service consolidation with ICFS and a futuristic import coal bulk transloading project with Clarkson London and Louis Dreyfus Paris. This innovative transloading project, as narrated earlier, I had been pursuing since my Himalaya days and later with ISS under SNR when we made a presentation to Dr. A. C Ray and his team in Calcutta port. Louise Dreyfus had a successful high-seas specialized floating crane operation for coal handling with custom-built shallow-drafted coal barges under the very competent technical leadership of Patrick Lescraigne and his team, who had strong support from LD president, Phillip D'Orsay. I have been pursuing this with Ram Nair, Patrick Oneil of Clarkson, Patrick Lescraigne, and the LD team since early 1990, and LD has made several presentations to SAIL and RINL at their top management levels. LD made a presentation of the project, covering all technical logistic nuances, to Calcutta Port Trust and Vizag Port Management to convince steel plants and power plant end users about the technical efficacy of the operation at the deep-drafted ocean location for offering end users both cost and operation logistic benefits. My 1993 visit was to discuss SAIL tender participation by LD through the formation of a strong consortium between LDA-Paris and Maersk-Copenhagen as European shipowner investors and Capstan and J. M. Baxi for logistic consultancy and port terminal handling, including deep sea anchorage agency and cargo handling, respectively. SNR was already in Dubai for a few months, working for the Ibrahim and Saraf Group.

It was a hectic but constructive short trip for about 10 days. In Dubai meetings with Ibrahim, DKC, and SNR, I strongly expressed my apprehension that within the next two to three years, if ICFS did not take all 12 new container vessels of Shakhalyn Shipping on a long-term charter, there was a strong chance of ICFS losing the management contract. I explained that the vessels were earning TCY equivalent USD 6,000 daily in the Calcutta-Singapore run, which was very well known to the SASCO operation team, and any bribe culture to retain the ICFS Management contract would not be sustainable long-term. On the contrary, it would be prudent for Ibrahim to consider taking all the vessels on a bareboat charter cum purchase agreement over a period of five years to develop feeder service networks in Calcutta-Haldia-Singapore, Calcutta-Haldia-Colombo, Madras-Singapore, Madras-Clombo and Bombay-Dubai routes. This would open up an opportunity for Saraf Group to promote their own container liner service for the West Asia Gulf, and the Far East. SNR strongly supported me and even told Ibrahim and DKC that for 12 vessel fleets, a very competitive ship management rate can be secured from leading ship management firms. DKC was a little hesitant to fully support this and wanted to discuss further with the ICFS operation team, particularly Graham and Howard. I sensed a faint feeling of insecurity in DKC when Ibrahim was eloquent in his appreciation of SNR's experience and wisdom and remembered our good days in the Himalayas.

Later, when I spent an evening with SNR in his guest house, a kind of flat accommodation in Dubai, I found him cooking his own food and extremely lonely and uncomfortable. He narrated his over-four-month experience and DKC's mental discomfort and fear of losing prominence in the organization. Initially, SNR sensed a general feeling of undercurrent among the new senior officers of the organization in accepting DKC as second in command to Ibrahim in the organization. DKC's much higher drawings and lavish lifestyle with large house accommodations with swimming pools, etc. were viewed with discontent by others. They were plotting behind his back to poison Ibrahim. SNR tried to guide DKC as an old friend to be watchful. He also protected DKC's position with Ibrahim, using his position of respect for Ibrahim. He frankly advised DKC that he was not going to be in Dubai for very long and that DKC should not consider him as a threat to impair DKC's prominence. But DKC, even after appreciating the plotting of some senior officers against him in the organization, was sceptical about SNR, as a very senior shipping professional, getting close to Ibrahim. SNR requested that I counsel DKC appropriately, knowing DKC's deep respect and trust in me. DKC confided to me that he knew Ibrahim intimately well, helped him in the business building days with Russians and other foreign contacts, and earned his trust and confidence. Ibrahim had given him adequate freedom and liberty to manage the show, which had expanded to a formidable size in terms of revenue and business volume with the recruitment of many senior Indian and British officers. Management in the organization had become somewhat loose-ended, and when he was trying to consolidate and discipline the administration, some of the senior officers were reacting and trying to poison Ibrahim's ear against him. He thought SNR's joining in a very senior management position would help him in his management consolidation effort through SNR's mature wisdom and experience. DKC was disappointed to find SNR lending his ears to many of the officers plotting against DKC.

Although DKC was a few years older than me, he used to call me Dada from the Himalayas. He had deep respect, love, and loyalty for me and always valued my advice and guidance in his professional life. He introduced Kleiman and SASCO business to Capstan directly without Ibrahim's knowledge, initially with moderate commission to himself. Later, at my advice, he briefed Ibrahim about this business and our game plan for container service between ISS-SNR, SASCO, Capstan, and Saraf Dubai. When Kleiman visited Dubai later and discussed the period TC of SASCO vessels owned by the Indian ship-owner, the British officer's coterie misguided Ibrahim by telling him about the DKC-Capstan closeness, with Capstan securing a strong hold on SASCO. Initially, they were successful in creating some doubt in Ibrahim's mind and convincing him to go for a one-sided management tie-up with SASCO through Kleiman at a hefty price against the advice of me and DKC.

Later, when a termination of agency notice was served on Capstan by ICFS, Ibrahim ignored DKC's strong warning about its legal repercussions and long-term business building potential with my shipping knowledge and expertise. Ibrahim got furious with these officers after they lost the legal battle. Ibrahim was shown the strong support letter from SASCO to Capstan, which was produced in court.

DKC got back the trust and confidence of Ibrahim and could take credit for mending fences with Capstan by using his personal closeness with me. This also quickened the process of SNR joining Saraf, with Ibrahim meeting all his terms for a one-year renewable contract. DKC was in agreement with me about my bareboat charter cum purchase proposal to Ibrahim for the 12 SASCO new container vessels and the fragility of the one-sided management agreement for SASCO vessels. But he felt outsourcing the fleet management would be resisted by the officers, as this would potentially dry up their extra income sources. He was also apprehensive about Ibrahim agreeing to invest in creating a separate ship management division. I asked him bluntly whether he would also be a party to the officer's grievance mission against ship management's outsourcing proposal to SNR. He expressed his expectation of some commission arrangement with the ship management contractor, which SNR must confidentially consider. I advised DKC to have no misgivings about SNR's concern about DKC and his position with Ibrahim, but as far as I knew, SNR would not promote any extra commission arrangement behind Ibrahim's back. It was best for DKC to look after the health and comfort of SNR during his one-year stay in Dubai through his local contacts and influences and to take SNR's constructive advice and guidance in the consolidation of management and administration of the organization during his short stint with Saraf in Dubai. Ultimately, DKC should focus on running the organization as an efficient CEO when SNR is gone. For this, he was to strengthen his secretariat with adequate database of all departments and develop the core strengths of each HOD with full knowledge of their weaknesses. As a dear friend, I advised him to indulge in spiritual mind training and change his lifestyle and food habits completely for the safety of his own health and the health of his wife and only daughter, who were suffering from obesity and multiple health ailments. At his request, I had a session in his house with his wife and daughter.

Later, SNR, DKC, and I had a long session at the SNR flat, where DKC expressed very genuine apologies for misunderstandings and misgivings and sought his guidance and blessings for management consolidation before my departure from Dubai.

This particular Dubai trip gave me lots of insight into the SARAF organization and the vulnerable fragility of the SASCO management agreement with ICFS.

I had spent two days in London and another two days in Paris with Clarksons and Louis Dreyfus, respectively. I expressed my own personal views for the introduction of Capt. Orsten Olsen's Scandimar Transloading Technical Concept of Transloader and 21000 dwt Self-Propelled Barges at Permissible Haldia Draft to Ram and Patrick O'neil. Clarksons advised me that LDA had already tied up Maersk as a consortium partner based on the LDA floating cranes and self-propelled barge concept as already presented to SAIL, RINL, and Vizag-Calcutta port trusts. LDA would like to discuss with Capstan and Clarksons the logistics and costing of the project and finalize a week-long meeting date for all party discussions at their office on the SAIL tender. As far as I remember, Ram Nair and Patrick O'neil joined me in the Paris meeting with LDA.

In Paris, we had very detailed and constructive interactions with LDA President Phillip D'Orsay, Patrck Lescraign, and his team on the operation logistics both onshore and onshore at the ports of Vizag and Haldia. Equipment requirement with capability of handling both Panamax and Capesize Bulkers, cost benefits to the end users from the system, guaranteed discharge cadence for the charter party, investment assessment, etc. Both LDA and Maersk had adequate numbers of Panamax and Capes vessels under their ownership and control to service SAIL 6 mmt Coking Coal for the five-year period of the contract as per the SAIL tender. The mobility of the floating cranes between Vizag and Sandheads deep-sea anchorages was meticulously reviewed with detailed weather reports and wave heights done by experts under LDA assignment. I get nostalgic now in remembering the huge research work we had undertaken in the early 1990's for this dream innovative deep-sea transloading project concept, with so many bureaucratic, political, and vested interest lobbies working against its implementation without in-depth shipping knowledge and appreciation of the long-term benefits of all stakeholders. However, coming back to the historical past I am narrating, LDA proposed a meeting of all consortium members in their office one month before the tender submission date for 4–5 days of brainstorming and then tender document preparation and final submission meeting 3 days before the submission date at Capstan office in Calcutta.

After returning to Calcutta from Paris, I had to give attention to Capstan administration, as during our 5–6 month feeder service operation under ICFS management of SASCO vessels and their introduction of FESCO vessels in the Colombo service, we had created office infrastructure in Haldia and increased our staff layout considerably for port and customs operations. Cargo documentation, NVOCC handling, and complicated finance and accounts system management with SASCO vessels under ICFS management also needed discipline and control. There were senior and junior accountants working under Prashanta Ghose, and we also introduced computers and a digital EDP center in the office. Despite all these, I was blaming myself in my own mind for giving too many liberties to some of the senior officers, particularly my nephew Amit, who was doing well with marketing but totally lacked discipline and administrative experience. He was vulnerable to greed and vices and was corrupting junior officers working in the port with his drinking habits and trading favors with selected MLO clients. Container terminal operation at NSD was still going through the process of system consolidation through the introduction of port-net, digitization, and modern terminal handling equipment deployment. I was receiving complaints from the Port Container Terminal Manager's office about our SASCO vessels leaving Calcutta port by shutting out a large volume of overbooked containers. Amit and one of our port assistants are pressurising port officers to allow entry of overbooked containers after the expiration of the cut-off date by taking my name and good relations with the chairman. Many of our MLO clients were also complaining about the shutdown of their cargo, despite firm booking confirmation by Amit. Even internally in our office, B.K. Banerji was having continuous friction with Amit. Amit tried to defend himself by saying that to make our vessels full capacity utilization 10/15% over booking was necessary. About the port complaint, he denied using my name to pressurize or insult senior port officers but could not explain why container entry after the cut-off date was insisted on and call orders manipulated without following the port's first in, first out rule. His feeble explanation was to keep big MLO's volume support; bending of rules became necessary at times. I strongly chided him and reminded him of my own market image of Himalaya days, when all big and close clients were conscious about obeying port rules in cargo carting. I personally met the container terminal manager and traffic manager in the port office to apologized and advised them to insist on strict discipline to control the entry of overbooked cargo and communicate with me directly in case of any indiscipline from any of our officers, including Amit. Amar Dutta joined us from ISS, and he was looking after our chartering and demolition business after Udayan Sen left us. He was also to look after the limited general agency business. I put him in charge of monitoring booking containers and issuing carting orders within the discipline of the laid-out rules and procedures. This created some commotion and conflict between Amit and Amar. Purnima was attending office as director only after lunch, but her insightful inputs on Prashanta's too much dependence on Bhusan were very incisive. After discontinuing our C-I Goods export business, we retained Manoj Bose as manager in charge of office administration and personnel supervision. He was not very popular with Prashanta, Bhusan, and Amit. Although, from profitability and revenue generation sides, the company was doing very well, there were drainage of money through uncontrolled avoidable expenses on marketing and port operations. Amit was cunningly manipulating Prashanta and Bhusan, taking full advantage of my extensive travel and involvement in a number of port and shipping innovative project development and pursuing expansion and spread of the container feeder service network at the macro level. I also supported and trusted friends on the face value of a few entrepreneurship initiatives with Angel Capital, which not only defocused my attention on my core business but also got us involved in uncalled-for liability creation and capital drainage. Today, in retrospect, I blame myself totally for my major folly in yielding to the emotional pressure of my childhood school friend Malay Chatterji in giving an interest-free short-term corporate loan for his newly promoted civil engineering firm Emakay International and multiplying the same on repayment default in the hope of recovery from his business expansion plan by trusting him without my own domain knowledge in construction business. I had to heavily pay for this with the ultimate liquidation of Emkay International and substantial legal and personal liability clearance later, starting in 2004.

I also had an almost similar experience with another childhood friend, Basab Bhattacharya, who was close to me and our family, and I had to support him when he had a heart attack and needed some stable job support. I took him in my office, as, health-wise, he was not able to continue his business of selling iron vessels (Karai) manufactured in Howrah foundries in the district markets. My single-minded focus on aligning the Indian shipping industry with port infrastructure development made me unconsciously careless in the consolidation of the in-house management of the organization. I did not have the solid team support of my Himalaya building days— no SNR, Shiva, Capt. Ghose, etc. Even Dada's support during the early building days of the Himalayas with Bula Da as our financial consultant was invaluable. Gopal Da's towering presence in the stevedoring and port operations also made the Himalaya's teamwork building invincible. My subconscious was ever alive with my broken dream of a three-decade development plan for Himalaya Shipping. The failings and successes of Capstan's management team building at every stage were making me consciously compare the situation to the canvas of Himalaya's development vision at that particular stage of my life. When the opportunity to take 12 sister NB container vessels on bareboat cum purchase came and was missed by ISS first and then Ibrahim Saraf, I was lamenting on my Himalaya's setback in taking delivery of the new building container vessels, as I was sure to establish the container logistics meticulously planned as Himalaya CEO and a Ship-owner. There was a gulf of difference between a ship-owning company, a shipping agency, and a logistics consultancy corporation. A great deal of my concerted efforts was going towards mind training to accept this reality. I was often reflecting on my own ineptness in conflict management as a spiritually splurged corporate leader, confronting Dada on his weak point of insecurity about the

Samal Harand Marine Division cash cow. Instead of navigating the conflict tactfully for long-term gain, I got into confrontation mode by not allowing Samal Harand a cash cushion for Dada's mental comfort. My faith and surrender to Thakur Ramakrishna gave me a glimpse of quite a few miracles, and perhaps the refinement of my ego took a back seat at that point, ignoring some subtle direction from Thakur for course correction. I write this today as a study point for future management students reading my memoir.

During 1994–1997, for four consecutive financial years, we paid a 50% dividend to Capstan stake holders, and I was generous in offering new cars to all the senior officers. Office overhead became almost 50% higher than what was reasonable for managing the show. Cash drawings against fake invoices were getting cleared despite the junior accountant's objection. I was personally maintaining monthly accounts of the SASCO vessels voyage by voyage with Prashanta's assistance to determine the actual TCY of the vessels, which in average was over USD 6,000 yield per day. Prashanta always justified his support for an unreasonably high salary increase; he was particularly approving of a few senior officers financial indiscipline at Bhusan's recommendation to keep them motivated. According to Bhusan, challenging expense invoices would tantamount to unpleasant confrontations with the officers' integrity. I realized that financial discipline internally was very low, and Bhusan and Amit were taking advantage of Prashanta's weak personality and non-confrontational nature. Capt Philipov of SASCO reported to me that under ICFS management they were finding TCY of the vessels dropping to low USD 3k daily as against USD 6k earlier under Capstan Agency. He wanted me to visit the SASCO office to discuss the reason for this with their accounts officers. Bhusan was dealing with Sanjeev Kakar of ICFS on SASCO operation accounts, and he was made to cooperate with Sanjeev in the ICFS way of account reconciliation and submission between ICFS and SASCO.

This was also justified by Prashanto, Bhusan, and Amit as very necessary to keep our principal happy. I smelled a strong possibility of ICFS losing the SASCO management contract unless they take the vessels on a 4–5-year bareboat charter cum purchase or at least on TC. I knew very well that top-level management bribing arrangements would not be sustainable in Russia for more than 3/4 years as there was frequent change of guards there through political lobbying. I had to talk to DKC at length and requested that he talked to Ibrahim. He was hesitating to talk to Ibrahim to upset the ICFS team and suggested I talk to him directly. I confidentially advised him about the SASCO invitation to me to discuss this matter, and to protect Capstan's interest, I was considering taking the SASCO vessels on a similar BBC cum purchase by Capstan if Ibrahim was not agreeable. DKC was scared to his bones and implored me not to do that, as that would be very harmful for his personal position with Ibrahim, to the extent of losing his very lucrative job. When I talked to Ibrahim, he expressed his respect and admiration for my insightful shipping knowledge but needed some time to discuss the matter with ICFS officers and DKC. He asked me not to worry too much about ICFS losing the management contract as he had high contacts with all the big guns in Russian political dispenzation. He also wanted me to consider opening our Madras office for an ICFS service extension. I gave my consent in principle but wanted to wait a few months for the SASCO vessel situation to stabilize. I was indeed in a dilemma. Meanwhile, DKC called Prashanta out of anxiety and requested that he refrained from making any direct arrangements with SASCO without ICFS. Before my departure for Shakhalyn, I was informed by Aloke Ghose (one of my trusted accounts officers who came to us from J.K. Steel through my friend Gopinath and TT connections) that, in spite of his objection, another tranche of an unsecured loan had gone to Malay Chatterji, who spoke to Prashanta and Bhusan directly, taking my name.

When I asked Prashanta, he said Bhusan was allowed to transfer the funds in view of Malay's very short-term urgency, and he thought Malay had spoken to me. I chided Bhusan and clearly told him that in the future he was to take authorization for fund transfers from two directors and not only Prashanta. Malay called me almost immediately to emotionally explain his urgency and the assured return of the money within a month, which never happened. In retrospect, today I blame myself for condoning many of such indiscipline without taking strong action to set examples for course correction.

My visit to Shakhalyn was eventful, and apart from long sessions with their accounts officers, Capt. Philipov made me meet his boss and one other director when they much appreciated my proposal to give all 12 container vessels to Indian owners on a 5-year bareboat charter and purchase. They promised to watch the situation with ICFS for one more year and then structure a suitable offer for Capstan to consider for a BBC Cum purchase for their twelve vessels. At ground level, they were not happy with Kleiman's role but were silently digesting his influence and manipulating power. I was requested to talk to ICFS to ensure a minimum of USD 5,000/TCY for their vessels after my return to Calcutta.

Although I had to make a quick visit to Dubai, taking Bhusan with me to discuss accounts of SASCO vessels and long-term measures to retain SASCO business, I was not able to convince Ibrahim of a sustainable TC solution. Out of two British officers in ICFS, Howard James had a policeman background with fewer intrigues than his senior Graham Norris. There were a number of other Indian officers in the ICFS team sharing their allegiance between DKC and Graham, with the ultimate focus on pouring sweet gossip into Ibrahim's ear. Ibrahim was like many other Arab sheikhs, prone to lose talks and sweet words of praise from his subordinates, but he was a more modern and intelligent version. After building his empire with family money power and faithful help from DKC, he was arrogantly focused on his money power to retain and expand his business. He had gratitude for DKC and was not grudging in giving DKC freedom on finances and drawings, but he was always having a feeling of insecurity about DKC's international contact level, particularly with the Russians and other Indian clients. He was hiring foreign and particularly Indian officers in his organizations, mostly on DKC's recommendation, but was always suspicious about DKC building independent businesses outside Dubai using his personal contacts. DKC, on the other hand, had a feeling of insecurity in the internal organization and was creating adversaries internally as a result of his effort not to allow grass to grow under his feet. Ravi Chopra (my erstwhile Sinclair colleague who served the Saraf group for a long time) enjoyed the trust and confidence of both Ibrahim and DKC as competent shipping professionals. He took the initiative to arrange a full one-day meeting for me with Ibrahim in Dubai with a one-on-one lunch and dinner to remedy this unhealthy mental misunderstanding much later.

However, coming back to the SASCO story, Ibrahim expressed his genuine surprise about the SASCO vessel accounts mistrust created by ICFS and clearly told his officers to cooperate with me and my accountant to remedy the situation. I advised both DKC and Graham in the presence of Ibrahim and SNR (who was in the meeting more as an observer) that the purpose of my visit was not to do any audit of ICFS accounts but to clearly explain with facts and figures that vessel TCY without ICFS management fees was an average of USD 6,000 per day, which had come down to a little over USD 3000 as per SASCO, and I was called to the SASCO office to discuss this and convey the right message to ICFS.

It was necessary for ICFS accounts officers to mend fences by fulfilling their expectation of a minimum of USD 5,000 TCY or to take the vessels on long-term charter at a reasonable market-compatible rate of hire. I also advised them that I was willing to open a Madras office with 50% expenses shared by ICFS, but for this, we needed all twelve SASCO sister vessels lined up. Very old FESCO vessels deployed by ICFS on the Calcutta-Haldia-Colombo route were found inferior to our service quality with SASCO vessels on the Singapore route.

We left for Calcutta on the same evening after two nights and three days of extensive meetings in Dubai. I shared my concern about the long-term sustainability of this lucrative SASCO business with SNR one-on-one before leaving for the airport. He was to join as MD of South India Shipping Corporation under Essar Shipping with Madras in the next few months. He fully endorsed my concern. He appreciated my affectionate feelings and gratitude for DKC for introducing SASCO to Capstan, but he did not see any option for me but to take up the SASCO vessel's BBC cum purchase offer. He fully agreed with my advice to Ibrahim and ICFS.

Back in Calcutta, I had to spend some quality time preparing for SAIL transloading tender participation through a consortium of LDA-Paris, Maersk-Copenhagen, Capstan, and Clarksons as logistic consultants, and Naresh Kotak of J M Baxi for Indian Agency and technical operation management support at the deep sea location and port terminals. I did not want to invest in further agency infrastructure creation and happily reconciled brokerage and consultancy fees. Clarksons was happy with a fixed commission on revenue. Mr. Bhaskar Basu was handling the tender as Cacutta ED Transport and Shipping of Sail, working under Mr. Arvind Pandey as SAIL Chairman and Director Commercial, Mr. Mihir Moitra, and other Director, Mr. A K Ghose, in Delhi HO. Although the tender was to come out in 1994, during the last quarter of 1993, it was extended up to the first-quarter of 1994, I was making frequent visits to Delhi to discuss complicated operation logistics involving Vizag and Haldia's port infrastructure revamping and, above all, combating deep sea wave height hazards with state-of-the art marine management. We had identified two competitors. Lalit Bhadwar introduced very strong Norwegian ship-owner Western Bulk with Tutu Bose as a local partner. Tutu's hold on SAIL was formidable, particularly with Bhaskar Basu in Calcutta and Bhusanam in Vizag. Initially, on the surface, I was finding both of these gentlemen extremely competent and knowledgeable and eager to discuss and interact with me on project logistics with an open and fair mind. Later, I was cautioned by Mihir Moitra, who was the younger brother of my close college friend Dilip Moitra, and also by A. K. Ghose to be discreet on these fronts as information was leaking out to our competitors. We were also facing strong resistance from Transchart, where Mr. Anchan was in charge after Mr. S. N Banerji (Aku Da) retired. Somnath Da also helped me by writing to FM on the Transchart issue. Capstan was till then a panel broker with Transchart, and my old friend and colleague from Sinclair days, BAL Vashisht, was representing us on a commission-sharing arrangement. At BAL's request, I went and met Anchan to explain the efficacy, including cost and logistics benefit to SAIL, and there was no danger to Transchart of losing fees and commissions for vessels under the framework of the transloading concept unless the end-users decided to deal directly with the owners of the vessels. Anchan directly threatened me to cancel our panel broker registration if I was actively supporting the project. I could clearly see that he was pumped up by our competitor, as Tutu had almost monopoly handling contracts for SAIL-imported coking coal at Haldia and Vizag. He had earlier met Patrick Lescragne of LDA without knowing my closeness to them through Clarksons, and as he later told me in our joint cooperation days, many years after this tender time, He was furious with Patrick when he was advised by both Bhaskar Basu and Bhusanam that Patrick met them with me. There was also some pressure on the Maersk Delhi office to withdraw from the consortium by Transchart, as they were already fixing their vessels for SAIL business through Transchart, as they revealed to us during our consortium team meeting in Paris later in 1994.

My friend Malay Chatterji was frequently visiting Calcutta and creating emotional pressure for fund support at Emkay International, and I yielded to his various emotional intrigues to the detriment of Capstan interest. This included a joint development agreement to construct a three-story building on his less than 3-acre land in Lake Gardens in the expectation of his paying his loans to Capstan. We also eventually invested in a Madras office and guest house during 1994–1995 based on the assurance of ICFS to share 50% of expenses and bringing in SASCO vessels for opening Madras-Singapore and Madras-Clombo in 1995–1996. My friend Mahalingam's brother Swaminathan was looking after our Madras office establishment next to the TPRC Madras office with our Calcutta marketing team, giving him support for local marketing team building. Substantial expenses were incurred in our Singapore marketing efforts. In the midst of all the euphoria of business expansion and building service networks, I ignored the alarm clock clicking in my mind about the vulnerability of an agency house to pursue such projects with a clear vision statement in association with another non-ship-owning organization, as compared to pursuing such projects with a ship-owner's platform like Himalaya Shipping with decision-making and control at our hub center. Also, due to the diversion of attention to multiple dimensions of the shipping business and my particularly unwilling involvement in non-core enterprises other than shipping, I was not able to consolidate Capstan Management. My conscious realization of this urgent requirement was always in my visuals but did not find expression in raw action. We were cash rich during this period from 1992 to 1997 and sufficiently equipped to get into a BBC cum purchase deal for five years for SASCO vessels to establish our ultimate ship-owning target and then expand on other innovative project investments as I earlier planned for Himalaya Shipping in my three-decade growth and expansion plan. Above all, Divinity found fault with many compromises I made naively in accommodating greed and the lack of integrity of friends and associated organizations.

SNR always admired my attitude of detached karma for the development of the Indian shipping industry and port infrastructure with dreams and visions and not to join any big corporate house to compromise honesty and integrity. Back in Madras, as MD of South India Shipping Corp. under Essar management, SNR and I spent a couple of evenings staying with him in his sprawling company bungalow, discussing our journey in shipping together in various capacities. SNR was open and frank in criticizing me as a friend for compromising with Amit's dishonesty, particularly out of parental weakness. One of Amit's brothers-in-law who was a Marine Engineer and batch-mate of SNR advised SNR his concern about Amit and Tumpa's lifestyle and future, unless there was a course correction. SNR also stated 'my repeated advises to DKC in Dubai fell on the deaf ear.' He was almost certain that DKC's greed and multiple side deals with Indian parties at the cost of Saraf organisation would get exposed in few years' time and Capstan should be cautious about potential conflict with ICFS regarding SASCO vessels. He saw no reason in my not going direct with SASCO for DKC's sake. I appreciated his frank talking and offered him stake in Capstan to work together with me for management consolidation. SNR needed few years' time for that. We both agreed that we erred in our strategy for conflict management in dealing with Dada's frog in the well limited visions on Shipping Industry and Dada's feeling of insecurity of SH should have been addressed more maturely to serve the interest of Himalaya's long term growth plan. SNR had respect for PKG as a competent CA and his integral honesty and loyalty to me but he was not a strong management personality with decision making ability.

In my own mind at mid-fifties, I was faltering in fast and unhesitant decision making. There was a silent transformation of mind and attitude happening in my subconscious where my spiritual faith of recognising potential divinity of human beings to get converted from 'Brute Man' to 'God Man' was struggling to handle the pollution of greed and dishonesty of friends, close relatives and colleagues at my work place and joint family home. At the sacred depth of my being 'amar gahan gopon maha apan' in Tagore's words, I was seeking answer to a core question -- whether I was at fault in trusting human as divine soul?

I could share this spiritual restlessness only with two spiritually elevated souls: my mentor Maharaj (Swami Lokeswarananda) and my parent-like legal guardian Pramatha Mitter (Mesho Masai). Maharaj gave me a few sittings and his precious time. With his all-encompassing love and blissful words of wisdom and positivity, he explained to me the difference between the monks who have renounced the world to serve suffering humanity as God with total commitment to Thakur's Mantra of' 'Shiva Gyane Jiva Sheba' and the household devotees who have been assigned by Thakur to do detached karma within the precincts of all attachment to make the world pollution-free and a safe and peaceful habitat for humanity. Human being are to pursue perfection eternally through myriads of creative activities in different spheres of scientific, cultural, and life-elevating innovative activities. He reminded me of Thakur's definition of "Uttam Baidya" and the necessity to be rough and tough on erring individuals for course correction. Self-retrospection is necessary for all spiritual seekers, and blindly trusting any individual without an intuitive evaluation of the ills and wells of the worldly life is not a virtue. Maharaj explained with tender care that Thakur held my hand strongly during the initial building days of Himalaya Shipping in my spiritually splurged detached management efforts with a clear vision of my dream realization for the Indian Shipping Industry. With frugal capital and unwavering faith I was training my mind to swim in Thakur's spiritual world. There has to be always very subtle surveillance of His devotees, where the prominence of the unrefined lower ego over the broader spread of our more refined ego gets course correction through suffering and apparent failures. My fall from heaven on Himalaya's dream run was possibly Thakur's course correction lesson to me for ego refinement. Disciplined spiritual practices and meditation are essential for every human being, particularly devotees enjoying Thakur's blessings for accepting ills and wells with poise and equanimity of mind. I was made to appreciate that a disciplined, spiritually splurged enterprise for wealth creation must have a matching disciplined administration and management system for its humble distribution and delivery of impactful human service. Relaxation and compromise without penance and sacrifice would always have a price to pay in the spiritual world.

I joined Rotary as the Charter President of the Rotary Club of Calcutta Metro South in 1991. In its very first year, RC Metro South was motivated by Swami Lokeswarananda to join hands with Lok Shiksha Parishad, RKM, to participate in and deliver a slum development project at Ram Bagan Slum in North Calcutta with Thakur's blessings by building a block of 16 low-cost flats for the rehabilitation of the slum dwellers. This was lauded by the Rotary World as a path-breaking project. Maharaj cited this as a glaring example of the spiritually splurged delivery of love and empathy by a selfless, motivated team where divinity held our hands. Maharaj, while inspiring me with his kind motivating words, generally stated that helping greedy friends in the guise of their needs without intuitive evaluation of their intentions and intrigues was a manifestation of 'Swakam Karma' and not 'Niskam Karma.' Such services could never be selfless enough to earn divine sanction.

Maharaj was always very concerned about family harmony and expressed his confidence in the strength of my mother's subtle spiritual power and Thakur, Ma, and Swamiji's blessings on our family. He advised me to accept the injustice and breach of trust from my brothers with spiritual resilience. He showered his words of love and blessings to comfort me by saying, 'If you tread steadfastly on the path of truth and perfection, Thakur will always hold your hands.' Pains and sufferings of a spiritually splurged sadhak are always manifestations of Thakur's love, blessings, and direction on the destiny to deliver for humanity with oft manifested divine intervention. My love and affection for my brothers, sisters, nephews, and nieces would ultimately find fruition in a happy and harmonious reunion of the family. Conflicts and frictions in the family were temporary expositions of form, but Thakur's blessings and direction on spiritual course correction have the silent divine power of permanent class. These were words of wisdom from the lips of a Sage, who himself was an infinite reservoir of truth, peace, and bliss.

These few days of sitting at the feet of Maharaj in his RKMIC Monks abode armed me with unspeakable bliss and 'power that is not power' to combat many storms and thunders I encountered later with poise, patience, and focus on spiritual practices to train my mind.

Before I start narrating my intimate and affectionate interaction with Meshomasai (Pramatha Mitter, solicitor, my legal guardian, and validation support of my spiritual faith) elaborately, I must return to happenings in Capstan Shipping during the heydays of

1994 to 1997, before the advent of the cyclonic weather to prevail in my professional life for nearly two decades.

On December 31, 1993, Soma reached Calcutta during her winter break at MIT, and we started living at 171 Shyama Prasad Mukherjee Road with Mani (my mother-in-law) and Kakima (Purnima's aunt) in three flats of the Suryoday Building, 5th floor, in the owners portion of the Gr Plus 5 apartment building constructed under a joint development agreement between owners and the developer. We locked our furnished Elgin Road rooms with Purnima, making weekly visits for cleaning and maintenance under a very strained relationship with the family.

In 1994, immediately after Soma went back to MIT Boston at the end of her break, I had to spend one full week in Paris for the SAIL Tender Participation Meeting of the consortium: LDA, Maersk, Capstan, Clarksons, and J. M. Baxi. LDA hosted the meeting in their office. The three-member Maersk team was led by a charming lady manager of their group. She was competent and incisive in her interactions with tender details. I was somewhat amazed when she casually advised us during one of our lunch get-togethers that she was in her first few months of pregnancy. I am unfortunately failing in my memory to remember her name. Ram Nair and Patrick O'neil came from Clarkson, London, and George Ooman led the JMB team from Bombay with Capt. Chatterji and another officer. I was alone from Capstan, Calcutta. The meeting was very constructive, with in-depth risk, cost, and operation logistic analysis to frame pre-tender questions to be addressed to SAIL by the LDA on behalf of the consortium. Transchart resistance and the strong lobby of the Norwegian competition with Tutu's hold in SAIL were strategically addressed. It was finally decided that all parties would assemble in Capstan Office, Calcutta, 2–3 days before the tender submission date in SAIL, Calcutta Transport and Shipping office at Fairly Place. The team would review and make the final tender document ready for submission without any chance of getting disqualified on trivial technical grounds, and jointly submit and attend the opening of the tender on the scheduled date.

During my absence in the Calcutta office, Purnima was monitoring finance and funds with PKG's consent, as he was far too weak to handle and control Amit's undue pressure with Bhusan's support. On my return, I got a full report of tantrums in the office from Amit and a few of his associates, with Bhusan's support. They identified a few loyal old Capstan staff as Purnima's informers and were openly misbehaving and threatening them. PKG was helplessly shaky, fearing Amit's tantrums as a real threat to the company. Although things got somewhat under control with Purnima's intervention, Amit was spreading loose talk about Purnima influencing decision-making by me and PKG with remote control to subdue Amit's aggressive marketing strategies.

I had dealt with Amit's tantrums, lies, and monkey business from his childhood days and gave him a thorough dressing down on the very first day of my attending office after returning from Paris. I bluntly told him that I had personally trained him in marketing for Himalaya's USA cargo booking on BSC vessels by making him an intern and assistant to Ranjan Mukherji, and while sacking Ranjan for his fraudulent deal-making with Nirmal Pujara, I pardoned Amit with caution. During the struggling days of Capstan in the early mid-eighties, I induced and encouraged him to work with Sinclairs and then P&O, NYK Agents, gaining shipping and marketing experiences and contacts. He was as lazy as always in not following my advice to study the ship-broking course at the London Institute and take the exams. Bubai and Aveek studied, passed exams, and got qualified. I was paying him handsomely with perks to live a comfortable life with his family in peace, and if he was carrying any wrong notion of betraying my trust and affection for his personal gain, then like all other employers and management he worked with earlier, I would be compelled to throw him out. I reminded him that he was thriving in the shipping world, leaning on my professional reputation as my nephew. He was frightened and surrendered with all kinds of assurances. My inherent weakness toward him as an in disciplined child took the better of my professional discretion, and Amit stayed with our organization till 1997 to do bigger damage to the company and spell doom and destruction of his own property assets, which were large, and his carrier in shipping by betraying me later.

From their very childhood, Amit and Renee enjoyed my parental love, affection, and attention. My love and attachment to their parents, Chorda and Chotoboudi, were also very strong. Chotoboudi was a very innocent and loving person who patiently tolerated, out of deep love for Chorda, many of his vices and tortures. Before her unfortunate demise in 1969 under tragic circumstances, she wrote me a note to take care of her two school-going children. This note was received in the morning after she expired in the night due to an overdose of sleeping pills. I would not burden my readers further with such ills and wells of life to justify my Himalayan blunder in giving indulgence to Amit by ignoring SNR's advice and Thakur's 'Uttam Baidya' prescription.

Our Madras office was inaugurated in early 1995 after almost six months of building and interior decor planning by our Calcutta consultant, Debashis Mitra, on ICFS assurance of SASCO vessel introduction in 1995.

SASCO invited me and the Capstan team to attend their Silver Jubilee celebration in the 2nd or 3rd quarter of 1994. They also separately invited the ICFS team. I attended this along with Prashanta, but strangely, no one from ICFS attended. There was a grand reception, which included a daylong picnic at a scenic mountain spot on the island with a flowing river stream, where they arranged for us to go fly fishing. An adequate number of hand-held fishing gears (we call them 'Chhip' in Bengali) were provided. In the midst of abundant fun, frolics, and fanfare in Russian style, we could discuss the deployment of their fleet of 12 sister vessels for feeder operation on the new Madras-Singapore and Madras-Colombo routes. Capt. Philipov emphasized that the deployment of additional vessels must be for a mutually agreed long-term period charter terms and definitely not under the existing ICFS management agreement. They appreciated the results of my talk with ICFS after my last visit to the SASCO office, which increased TCY for their four vessels marginally. They had already appointed a London consultant to evaluate vessels optimum earning potential in the international market and were to receive their full report within the first-quarter of 1995. They were planning to hold a management meeting between the SASCO management team, ICFS, Capstan, and London Consultants to negotiate charter terms for future deployment of the vessels in Indian feeder services. Capt Philipov again recommended Capstan take the vessels on direct five-year TC at USD 4K (+/-) or even consider a bareboat-charter-cum-purchase deal covering actual investment plus interest recovery and 10% profit for determining the BBC daily hire rate. We agreed to offer our full cooperation in this regard.

During our seven-day absence from the office, Purnima was facing continuous emotional pressure from Malay Chatterjee to bail him out of an emergency fund crisis. There was also pressure on fund release from Amit for the setting up of our Madras Guest House at the insistence of ICFS.

I received a message from Howard requesting that I set up joint marketing meetings for ICFS/Capstan at Madras and Singapore to announce the formal inauguration of our Madras-Singapore-Madras feeder service in April 1995. I separately discussed with Ibrahim, DKC, and Graham Norris the necessity of a detailed 50:50 cost-and-profit sharing agreement between ICFS and Capstan for all route feeder services with twelve SASCO vessels and also tying up strong NVOCC support with connectivity logistics outreach covering all major West Asia Gulf ports. This was demanding additional vessel deployment in the Colombo-Dubai-Colombo and Bombay-Dubai-Bombay routes. I briefed them on our SASCO visit and threat from their London Consultant report and proposed a joint conclusive meeting in mid-1995. A minimum of 60–90 days of extensive work on cost and revenue matrix evaluation was required to produce a credible DPR in this regard. Ibrahim advised DKC and Graham to take my guidance for the preparation of the cost and revenue matrix for Madras-Singapore and Calcutta-Singapore services immediately. This was essential before the start of the Madras service, which required pre-operating expenses for proper marketing. Madras office and guest house investment were also essential elements to be included in the cost matrix. We were to reach a consensus within the next 4–6 weeks to proceed further. I had to sit with Graham and the ICFS team in Dubai for a few days to finalize and sign Mou's consensus C&R matrix before starting our joint marketing exercise in Madras and Singapore.

In between, we had 3 days of marathon sessions in our Calcutta office between the SAIL Tender Consortium members, including one session extending beyond midnight for the finalization of our tender documents to meet the target submission date. Apart from our Consortium, Western Bulk, Norway, and ETA, Dubai was declared accepted by the SAIL Tender Committee headed by Bhaskar Basu. Price bids were also opened in the presence of all three parties, and Mr. Bhaskar Basu announced that results and awards would be announced later, after a techno-commercial evaluation of the bids.

During 1994–1995, financial control in our Calcutta office was somewhat restored. One of my other nephews, Ritwik Mitra, who was a young economist and whom I inducted in table tennis during the 5th Asian TT in 1980, expressed his intention to start a shipping career by joining the Capstan Shipping family. I took him in a reasonably senior position at Capstan. This was not liked by Amit at all.

With four vessels of SASCO on the Calcutta-Singapore route, operating with 90/95% capacity utilization, I got busy in preparation of a DPR involving 12 sister vessels of SASCO under a 5-year period TC to Capstan-ICFS JV and their deployment in our proposed JV feeder network covering different routes. I discussed this with the ICFS team and also confidentially with SASCO during our visit.

Since we were indicated an expected TC rate of USD 4K (+/-) daily by Capt Philipov, I advised PKG to run his figures on a basis of USD 4500 per daily TC hire with 10% escalation every 2 years. I became very friendly with PIL, Singapore Chairman Y.C. Chang, through my close German friend Peter Blumbach. I was interacting with him about the possibility of forming a service consortium with equal vessel participation from our JV and PIL on all routes, as proposed in our DPR. PIL was a very reputed ship-owner from Singapore, with formidable fleet strength. ICFS, Capstan's very successful Calcutta-Singapore feeder service, was known to the PIL marketing team. Besides, during my post-Himalaya days at Ceylon Shipping Agency, I met Y.C. and discussed relation building between Capstan and PIL in the container logistics business. PIL was a consortium partner of CSC on the Colombo-Red Sea route.

I was working with PKG and a small team, taking occasional help from Amit, Amar, and others on this project, and it took us more than a month to complete the DPR. Our earlier prepared DPR for ISS on round-the-world container logistics helped with the necessary figures updating.

Although our joint marketing meetings in Madras and Singapore were very successful and our Madras office infrastructure and guest house were satisfactorily set up based on an agreed cost-sharing agreement with ICFS, I was smelling some intrigues in accounting between Sanjeev of ICFS and Bhusan, who was justifying many expenses and fund remittance analyzes from the ICFS side for maintaining good relations with them.

ICFS did not very much like our already agreed 50:50 JV based on taking over all the SASCO vessels on TC. Initially, they were successful in dissuading Ibrahim from getting into this arrangement with tacit support from DKC. However, after my SASCO visit and briefing with Ibrahim and DKC, they had no choice but to get into this arrangement, with DKC supporting me this time. Since then, there has been a divide in ICFS internally, with a few professionally competent Indian officers loyal to DKC supporting him and another group supporting Graham and Howard, who were on the frontlines of the ICFS operation team. The British officers and the group were poisoning Ibrahim's ear with greed and the under-the-table deals of DKC without disclosing their own involvement in such deals. Ravi Chopra was enjoying Ibrahim's trust. Ravi was professionally competent. He understood the gravity of this conspiracy to scuttle the JV arrangement and period chartering of SASCO vessels. He advised Ibrahim professionally to have a one-on-one meeting with me to get my expert and unbiased view on the entire ICFS business and its sustainable future growth. I had to fly out to Dubai for a night and two days at Ibrahim's request for this. In the first meeting in Ibrahim's office, where Graham and Ravi were present, I could find Ibrahim absolutely poisoned against DKC, and he was using abusive words against DKC's betrayal, with Graham gleefully fomenting him. I was a silent listener, and Ravi also made no comments in Graham's presence. I had a 3/4-hour lunch session after this with Ibrahim and discussed at length the details of our JV DPR involving 12 SASCO vessels under 5-year period charter and high ROI over 5-year projections. He was convinced by my analysis of the corruption perpetrated initially by both Graham and DKC's group in ICFS. The reason for one group trying to corner another now to scuttle our JV collaboration was due to the threat of taking away avenues of illicit fringe incomes for the operating officers. When I found Ibrahim respectfully appreciating my analysis and substantially calming down from his anger and disappointment with DKC, I reminded him that DKC had his shipping experience and foundation under me in Himalaya Shipping and helped Ibrahim build his empire with sweat and toil. Other newcomer British officers were short-term wayfarers and more self-serving than DKC. Despite his greed and feeling of insecurity about losing Ibrahim's favor in the organization, DKC would remain ever loyal to Ibrahim, as he was anchored in Dubai with Ibrahim's support. I further elaborated to him on my future game plan to acquire ownership of the SASCO vessels under a BBC purchase agreement to expand our feeder service network under a brand name for international spread.

SASCO vessel operation costs under this arrangement would come down by 7/800 USD per day from our projected USD 4500 daily. I briefed him on our discussion with SASCO and their proposed plan, at the recommendation of their newly appointed London consultant, to hold a meeting of all stakeholders to get into a period TC with our JV at an indicated rate level of USD 4500/day. Ibrahim promised to attend this meeting personally and talk to Kleiman and high Russian contacts for pre-meeting arrangements to bring the rate down in finalizing the long-term charter. He also promised to talk to both Graham and DKC about addressing ICFS account anomalies.

I returned to Calcutta happy after this meeting. When I discussed this visit with SNR, he sounded happy but cautioned me about the frequent whimsical swings of Ibrahim's mind. He advised me to take Ravi Chopra into confidence rather than DKC for tactfully probing account anomalies in ICFS and any mischief or leakage of information going on between Amit and ICFS British officers to scuttle our JV.

I advised DKC to have a frank discussion with Ibrahim to win back his confidence as much as possible and try exposing the ICFS operation team scheming to scuttle our JV project as a follow-up to my talk with him. I kept in constant touch with Ravi Chopra to gather as much input as possible on the ICFS operation front. I briefed him on the gist of my session with Ibrahim, and he was to neutrally interact with Ibrahim on our JV and ICFS operation teams' activities. He was not a trusted man of Graham, who was depending on Howard and Sanjeev in ICFS-Capstan feeder service operational matters.

We started Madras operation in the first-quarter of 1995 with Cacutta-Madras-Colombo service using two Fesco vessels, with limited initial success. ICFS management was emphasizing various decision-making authorities and responsibilities to be determined and divided between JV partners. Graham did not agree to my advice to deploy one vessel only on Colombo service until we establish NVOCC tie-ups and all West Asia Gulf ports service networks after introducing SASCO vessels. Both DKC and RC informed me that the ICFS operating team was not happy with the agreed JV and professional Capstan DPR for the long-term growth plan for the feeder service. With the involvement of other consortium partners like PIL, Dubai NVOCC, and SASCO trusting Capstan, they were anxious about losing much of their free bees and management control. They were keeping in touch with Amit, particularly our accounts people, through Amit to build a case for scuttling our JV. Ibrahim's decision to personally attend the SASCO meeting made Graham a bit uncomfortable, as only Howard was to accompany him with one account assistant.

Graham was concerned about Capstan presenting JV DPR to SASCO, which would harm the ICFS image and credibility. Ibrahim, without time to go into details, was feeling confused.

In the first-quarter of 1995, Purnima and me visited Singapore, Hong Kong, and Seoul on business-cum-vacation and ended up attending World TT in Tianjing, China, as Indian delegate. I had a few MLO meetings to explore feeder tie-ups in Hong Kong and Korea. Kleiman came down from Vladivostok to meet me in Seoul for his personal comfort and advised me he was going to attend the SASCO meeting in the 3rd quarter and suggested we stop by Vladivostok on our way to Sakhalyn. He was concerned about SASCO appointing a London consultant and questions being raised in SASCO management about ICFS accounts. He was very loyal to Ibrahim and DKC and had a substantial commission package, but I felt he was getting disturbed in his mind about the future prospects of the business.

Soma completed her Masters at MIT and came back to Calcutta in the 2nd quarter of 1995 to start her maiden venture, DIAS InfoTech.

I was very happy to have her back and tried to provide her with the best start-up support. On the cultural side, Sunitida wrote the script and directed another less performed Tagore's play, 'Banshori,' with our earlier 'Gora' group of 'Amra Kajon.' Soma played the central character role in the Shruti Natak. About two months of rehearsal kept us gleefully busy in the evenings at our SPM residence. It was performed very successfully at the Kala Mandir Auditorium.

In between, in the 2nd quarter of 1995, SASCO fixed a week-long meeting and discussion between their senior management, ICFS, Capstan, and their London consultant. Kleiman was also to attend this meeting. We planned a travel schedule for Prashanta and me to Sakhalyn, with a stopover at Vladivostok. We were fully ready with JV Project DPR and detailed accounts of the past few years for each individual vessel's actual voyage performance accounts. Howard James came to Calcutta a few days before our departure on the journey to have a pre-meeting discussion and accompany us on the journey together. It was a long journey via London-Moscow and across Siberia with a night halt for few hours at an airport in the midst of Siberia for our Aeroflot Airlines flight.

Howard had a few long heart-to-heart sessions with me in our office before our departure. He even accompanied me to join as a guest in one of our lunch *adda* sessions at the Calcutta Club. Tarun Da (Dutta), the retired Chief Secretary, was impressed with Howard when he shared his past experiences as a senior police officer in Britain. He was genuinely concerned about ICFS losing SASCO vessels if the long-term TC for all the vessels was not finalized. He confessed to me that Graham and Sanjeev were defending a lost cause on the management agreement with SASCO, which was loose-ended. Ibrahim was totally misguided by them on the international charter market evaluation to determine the charter rate for SASCO vessels.

He fully appreciated my view that it would cost us over $5,000 daily to find suitable container feeder vessels on charter. He was comfortable working under my guidance on our JV project to learn more about the intricacies of container shipping logistics without involving himself in the internal politics of ICFS. Howard pleaded with Graham to allow him business class travel with us and felt insulted when this was turned down. He studied our individual vessel voyage performance report, which we were to submit to SASCO, and got worried about ICFS losing its image and credibility. He felt I should not submit this report before the meeting. He was, however, all praise for Amit as a marketing man and was going out with him for golf and evening drinks sessions. My own faith-driven nature got inclined to believe his straight-forward submissions, but my mind was getting alarm bells from the feedback I was receiving from Ravi and DKC. Both of them accepted him as a simpleton policeman, but they viewed him as a weak, insecure pawn in the hands of Graham and his accomplices.

We were in Vladivostok for two nights and flew out to Sakhalyn on the third morning. This eastern modern city town in Russia has a bounty of nature and is beautifully laid out. We were very comfortably lodged in a modern hotel with reasonably good services, unlike in Sakhalyn. In our few meetings with Kleiman, he repeatedly emphasized the necessity of ICFS repairing its relationship with SASCO by signing a period TC contract at a reasonably negotiated rate. He saw potential in SASCO offering more such vessels on TC presently under order with Spanish yards for delivery within 1995, unless orders were canceled by SASCO for lack of gainful employment. PKG was requested by Howard not to submit to SASCO our voyage-wise accounts report on their vessel performance during the last two years, which Howard discussed earlier. At Howard's request, Kleiman also requested that I hold back the report at least till the end of our meetings on rate finalization for TC. I saw logic in this and decided to hold back until the meeting sessions were over. We arrived one day before the meeting's starting date. Ibrahim and Sanjeev arrived on the meeting's starting day, necessitating a slight change in the sessions' schedules.

Prashanta and I managed to have an exclusive session with Capt Philipov's team and their London consultants for nearly 3 hours and could frankly and transparently discuss the actual Capex and Opex of the vessels. and came to the consensus that, with Russian manning of officers and crew, the daily operating cost of the vessels was coming to a little over USD 3000 against an average yield of

USD 4000 (+/-) under ICFS management, even after improvement from the initial low yields of mid-3k. They were very impressed with our DPR and projected 5-year ROI, where we had assumed a USD 4500/TC rate. They confirmed Kleiman's advice to me earlier that they had further vessels on order with Spanish yards that they were interested in providing for our JV project in the future. London Consultants asked me why we needed ICFS in this container logistics project when SASCO provided vessels and Capstan did marketing and all local operation management. Capt. Philipov explained the high level of influence of ICFS owners in Russia and saved me from answering such a blunt question. We were recommended to convince ICFS to close the enblock 12 sister vessels at USD 4500 without too much bargaining in everyone's interest.

Ibrahim had an internal discussion with Kleiman and Howard before meeting me. I found him extremely pumped up about the London Consultants appointment and their intervention in his dealings with a Russian shipping company. As an egocentric Arab sheikh, he was used to ruling the roost, particularly in Russia, with his money power, and he always found high-level decision-makers happily obliging him through his linkmen like Kleiman. I found his pre-meeting arrogance extremely dangerous when he brushed aside my effort to discuss figures and kept on asking Kleiman how much money would be needed to get these London consultants out of the way and settle on a low charter rate. Kleiman was hesitant to argue out of concern for his own pay packet, but I firmly advised him that it was very much essential to finalize the vessels at a reasonable rate for our JV to be successfully launched, and at USD 4500 per daily hire, our projected ROI for 5 years was 25% plus. This would further improve if we took the vessels on BBC purchase terms over 5 years, as I earlier advised him. Ibrahim calmed down a little to say that while he had great respect for my shipping knowledge and wisdom, I must have confidence and trust in his network and influence in Ruissia.

Our meetings went on for four consecutive days with seven members of the SASCO management team: two people from their

London consultant, Ibrahim, Howard, and Sajeev from ICFS, and me and Prashanta from Capstan and Kleiman. London Consultants presented charter market reports from Clarksons, Drewery, and R. S. Plateu in their effort to establish a spot charter rate of USD 5.5k for such vessels and a 2-year period charter rate of USD 5k. They had also expressed views on the return from SASCO investment on such vessels at different levels of period TC rates between USD 4k, 4.5k, and 5k. They were 15%, 20%, and 25%. I allowed Ibrahim to do the negotiation as per his wish. He haggled hard for 3 days, and ultimately it became a stalemate, with Ibrahim going up to USD 4.2K and SASCO at USD 4.5K.

Before our final conclusive meeting on the 4th day, I had a frank discussion with Ibrahim in the presence of Howard and Sanjeev, with Prashanta by my side in the evening. I clearly explained that London Consultants had created a strong foothold for themselves with SASCO management by exposing various weak points in ICFS accounts. They were impressed and convinced on our DPR for container logistics project through feeder service networking and MLO/NVOCC B/L linking concept. SASCO was now ready to commit their fleet deployment support to us with long-term spreading expectations. My own investigation in London about their consultants revealed that they were a small group of brokers trying to get control of Russian vessels for free trading in the London charter market. They had convinced SASCO management of an achievable TC yield for the vessels, and if our negotiation failed, they would fix a few vessels immediately on the 12/18 month charter, and our JV project would badly suffer. On the contrary, if we accepted their rate and closed the deal, London Consultants influence in SASCO would be short-lived. Ibrahim was still upset about Kleiman's allowing these over smart London guys to get entry into SASCO management and polluting their minds against ICFS. While everybody appreciated the urgency of closing this deal, Ibrahim was still emphasizing to me the influence and power of his personal equation with high-ups in the Russian Ministry to throw out these London consultants. He will then deal with the mischief they were playing with him.

It was sheer self-defeating arrogance, and I had to tell him that if this negotiation failed, Capstan would be compelled to take the vessels on charter at the rate offered to save the JV. He requested me not to be unduly hasty, and he would take around 6 months for further evaluation of their offered rate from the ICFS side. That would give him time to explore his Russian contacts in Moscow.

I politely advised him that this would be counterproductive and would give the London guys the opportunity they were trying to create for themselves.

There was a gala party hosted by SASCO on that last evening before our departure, where Vodka flowed like water with Caviar. The party went up to 1.00 a.m. in the morning. I saw Ibrahim interacting with the Russians in high spirits. Howard was flat-out and had to be carried to his room. It took some skilful manoeuvring for me to defend myself against this Russian Vodka assault.

Next morning, before the final meeting, I had a brief chat with Capt. Philipov regarding Ibrahim's intention of taking some time to finally agree to the rate. He advised me to confirm Capstan's agreement to this rate and take the vessels on the Capstan Charter.

I agreed finally to do that but would need GOI DGS approval. This would take a little time after our return. He emphasised on the urgency. Ibrahim asked for some time to get his finance to run figures before agreeing to another US$300 daily hire hike. I could see no body was happy on the other side but I made a blunder in not announcing in the meeting Capstan agreement to take the vessels on Charter in case of any negative response from ICFS. This would have sealed the deal making Ibrahim temporarily upset but could have saved our project with or without ICFS. I planned this in my mind and discussed with Prashanta who was bit hesitant to upset Ibrahim. Before going to the meeting I mentally decided to announce this. Yet I hesitated at the right moment and the opportunity was lost.

We came back empty handed to Calcutta relying on Ibrahim's arrogant assurance without being really convinced in my mind.

Although Calcutta-Singapore service with 4 SASCO vessels were continuing to give us good revenue our Calcutta- Madras -Colombo service with two Fesco vessels were not doing so well despite BKB from our in-house NVOCC agency giving reasonable feeder cargo support for West Asia Gulf ports. I was appreciating the marketing limitations of NVOCC in the absence of consistent Colombo- Dubai link as was envisaged in our JV feeder logistics network project with SASCO vessels. There was good support from SCI for UKC cargo on the Colombo route but with introduction of Madras in our vessels schedule, Calcutta MLO cargo support dwindled. We had already invested substantial funds on our JV account for our Madras office and guest house. Joint marketing meets at Madras and Colombo and substantive consortium discussions with PIL and number of MLOs needed follow up. We had already signed our JV agreement after making our consensus cost matrix for Calcutta, Madras, Singapore and Colombo for the port operation of the vessels part of the MOU. But this was to be converted to a Calcutta Registered separate JV company with RBI sanction. It was very essential for the SASCO vessels to be mobilised for which I was chasing Ibrahim. He was passing it over to Graham to finalise matters. My feedback from DKC was that Graham continued giving wrong advice on Charter Market and various negative feed-back on Capstan's prominence in the JV. SASCO's trust and faith on Capstan was also highlighted by Graham as anti ICFS. We agreed recovery of 50% of ICFS funding for Madras office from ICFS share of the net revenue of Calcutta-Singapore service. There were hitches on trivial issues purposefully enlarged to scuttle full execution of our JV project.

I was overloaded with too many things on my plate. Helping Soma on her Dias Infotech start-up had my top priority. EMKAY INTNL and my friend Malay's emotional pressures was becoming an unbearable burden on our company's coffer. Anwar Shah building was constructed by Capstan on Malay's less than 3 cottah land basis a simple 60:40 profit/ loss sharing agreement to bail him out of his financial crisis by setting up EMKAY Calcutta office in two floors for his independent business generation without disturbing Capstan. EMKAY was to buy over the two floors of the new building at the then Market price specifically for securing a big Swill Calcutta's substantially big contract for a project in Baruch in Gujarat. Financial accommodation provided to EMKAY was a big mistake by me and later cost me big financial losses through his default and breach of trust. Also in spite of LDA-Maersk consortium with Capstan and others becoming undeclared L1 in terms of group strength, techno-commercial quality of our bid, Tutu's influence with SAIL T&S Office in Calcutta using Transchart intervention, as an excuse, canceled the Tender. I had to do lot of running around in Delhi to save the deal but Maersk Delhi office gave up the fight to retain their relationship with SAIL, Calcutta and Transchart. We also invested in a small hotel cum resort project in Santiniketan by purchasing a heritage house in Ratan Palli from Supriya Thakur of Rabindranath's family and popular retired Principal of 'Patha Bhaban.' We named the resort as 'Banshori' after our successful rendition of the Sruti Natok under Suniti Bhose's direction. I had also to give substantial time in pursuing conduct of a World Circuit Ranking TT event in Calcutta where I had to face lot of resistance from the then BTTA President Amiya Gooptu.

I kept up pressure on ICFS for finalization of SASCO 12 vessels charter for which Ibrahim took 6 months' time from ICFS. I was consciously aware that SASCO London consultants were waiting for opportunity to take control of these vessels for deploying them on International spot and period charter assignments. I warned ICFS about the risk they were running by not getting into a proper T/C contract by signing of Charter Party with Indian Statutory authorities also. By successfully marginalising DKC's influence with Ibrahim, Graham was misguiding Ibrahim on ICFS and overall container logistics operations with MLO Agency tie up. Our JV agreement was signed by both parties as a MOU, before we invested on our Madras office, covering in detail all contours of immediate and future routes of feeder service network including MLOs and NVOCC tie ups. There was necessity of registering a JV Company declaring foreign equity and securing necessary Govt approval. This was kept pending till finalization of SASCO vessels Charter. Graham was holding up remittance of their 50% share of Madras office investment and loss sharing due to loss making two ports call Calcutta-Madras -Colombo service by two overage FESCO vessels. When I talked to Ibrahim directly he jubilantly advised me that he had been able to secure Agency of Major MLO MSC for West Asia Gulf Ports and Indian Ports and this would be a big value addition for our JV. He promised to advise Graham to consult me for finalization of SASCO vessels and other JV formalities. DKC was still to regain his foothold with Ibrahim and the organisation. He was keeping in close touch with me and SNR. DKC and few others in his group played some significant role in Ibrahim securing MSC Agency and Ibrahim gave him some prominence in the organisation for this. DKC came to India for a few days and SNR arranged a dinner meeting at his Madras Bunglow for a detail heart to heart interaction on the future of our JV.

DKC poured out his heart in these longish interactions. He regretted trusting Graham in a number of business deals with ICFS, and initially he did not realize that he was poisoning Ibrahim against him. He admitted that after my intervention, Ibrahim went to the SASCO meeting himself without allowing Graham to represent ICFS. Graham did not like this, and he was feeling in-secured about me and Capstan's prominence in the JV and trying his best to scuttle our JV agreement. He was wrongly advising Ibrahim that geared container vessels of larger size and capacity would be available in the international charter market at the same rate as SASCO was expecting for their vessels. Ibrahim also discussed with DKC a proposal from Graham and his ICFS team for establishing a pan-India agency network for ICFS independent of our JV. DKC did not support this, but he warned me that ICFS was secretly trying to allure Capstan marketing team members to join ICFS in their effort to build their pan-India agency network, starting with Kolkata.

DKC, with some hesitation, mentioned my nephew Amit's name as one of their main sources of information from our office. SNR suggested I take SASCO vessels on Capstan Charter and then form a consortium with PIL for running our proposed container service network in different routes through a frank discussion with Ibrahim. DKC feared this would again make his position with Ibrahim suspect, and Ibrahim was still committed to our JV, and by such actions, my personal relationship with Ibrahim would get compromised to the advantage of Graham and his team in ICFS.

In my mid-fifties, I did not have the same intuitively aggressive mind-set as I had in my younger Himalaya days. After this meeting with SNR and DKC, I realized the necessity of an aggressive decision to save the SASCO business and the introduction of the container feeder service project on different routes with 12 SASCO vessels sooner rather than later. But there was hesitation and vacillation in my mind to get into action mode to confront Ibrahim without any further consultation and let down DKC, who introduced SASCO business to us.

There was also continuous nagging from my friend Malay about his EMKAY International business. I committed too many mistakes by compromising with emotions and making wrong non-commercial decisions. I trusted Ibrahim's assurances by ignoring the potential danger of Graham's intrigues.

SASCO vessels were withdrawn from Calcutta-Singapore service after the first-quarter of 1996. Graham was asked to charter suitable vessels to continue the service, and three geared container vessels were introduced into the service at a near USD 5k daily charter hire under our 50:50 JV MOU with an agreed cost matrix for the voyages. My suggestion for getting into an immediate consortium arrangement with PIL for running three vessel services on the Calcutta-Singapore and Madras-Singapore routes with three vessels from our JV and three vessels from PIL was kept pending without any inertia from the ICFS side to continue active dialog with PIL. My own credibility with PIL was being compromised. We continued this profit/loss sharing JV operation for almost one year, up to the 2nd and 3rd quarters of 1997. Calcutta-Singapore 3 vessels service was giving reasonable profit, but Calcutta-Madras-Colombo service was making losses. Even after adjusting the ICFS share of losses from the Madras operation from their profit share in the Calcutta operation, there were substantial losses accumulating for reimbursement from the ICFS side, which they were not remitting. I had to finally insist on ICFS for the registration of an Indian JV company with a clear determination of management structure and equal representation on the board, failing which we needed our dues to be settled to continue further operation. ICFS reacted by abruptly giving cancellation notice of our JV MOU. This was the start of another legal battle for the recovery of our dues of USD 500K plus through international arbitration. We initiated arbitration proceedings at the ICC Paris. Amit and a few of our operations and marketing staff joined ICFS in their Calcutta office. I paid for my own hesitation to promptly accept the SASCO offer. We had to quickly close our Madras office and supporting infrastructure. It was a very costly blow in terms of strain on our finances and time. This was divine direction on me to change the course of Capstan's operation strategy, which I failed to recognize and hastily engaged with a Singapore big group for JV Shipping Company's operation under a newly registered shipping company in Calcutta. Captrans Shipping Ltd. (after securing statutory GOI approvals) was promoted with an equity structure of 40:40:20 between the Singapore Group, Capstan, and the WBIDC West Bengal Government, where Tarun Dutta as Chairman was succeeded by Somnath Chatterjee later. With an eye on a future IPO, authorized capital was kept high, and Rs. 5 crore of immediate capitalization was mooted to start container feeder operations in the Calcutta-Singapore route with chartered vessels. It was originally proposed that we were to make 6–9 months of preparatory team building both at Calcutta and Singapore ends and start the operation after full capitalization of Rs. 5 crore and tie up banking support for capex and opex requirements of the venture jointly between the participating partners. As we were discussing these lines with

Central Bank's Camac Street Branch with their very dynamic and positive-minded manager, Bimalendu Chatterjee, and WBIDC, our Singapore group presented to me the specifications and details of four brand new geared container vessels of 500 TEU capacity that were being delivered to them from the Chinese Shipyard—two of them in the third and fourth quarters of 1997 and the next two by the second and third quarters of 1998. Singapore wanted us to start the operation with two vessels offering a competitively low USD 4K daily charter rate. I suggested full capitalization of Captrans Shipping before starting the operation, and I was confident of securing Rs. 2 crore plus working capital facilities from the Central Bank to take care of fund requirements for the first one-year gestation period to establish our service. Singapore needed a few months to get our JV cleared by their management before capitalization could happen. They had internal issues to be sorted out regarding determining the JV investment source within their group. They would not keep their vessels idle for this period. They had given us the option to start the operations in 1997 by taking their two vessels on a 6-month charter with Capstan's contribution to the equity and working capital facility arrangement with our bank, or wait for their second two sets of vessels to be delivered to them later in 1998, and these two vessels could join after getting free of charter with other charterers.

It was March 1997, when, just after the successful conduct of the World Circuit TT event at Netaji Stadium (where Soma made a very impressive PowerPoint presentation to ITTF Treasurer Hans Gieseck in support of our bid to conduct World TT 1999 team events in Calcutta), I was going to attend the 1997 Manchester World TT as a TTFI delegate with Chauhan. It was a 10-day tour, including a one-night and two-day Paris visit, to discuss a fresh floating crane-based transloading project with LDA, independent of Maersk, which withdrew after the cancellation of an earlier SAIL tender. I had time until May to decide on the Singapore options offered. On my return, I discussed with WBIDC and the Central Bank to mobilize at least Rs. 7/8 crore for chartering the two vessels offered in 1997 and run through the one-year gestation period to save precious time for service establishment. The Central Bank agreed to extend the facility up to Rs. 1.5 crore, and WBIDC did not agree to contribute anything more than 15% of their equity commitment pending full capitalization of the company. Although Capstan had adequate reserves and paid a 50% dividend for a few consecutive years, Prashanta was against risking Capstan's investment in the project before full capitalization. He was running his figures based on 40% capacity utilization of the two chartered vessels and was projecting a need of at least Rs. 7 crore to sustain one-year operation for the vessels; otherwise, there would be short-term financing risks. He was also concerned about the risk of Singapore backing out if their management turns down the JV for some reason. He gave me sound advice to wait for one year, as per Singapore's second option.

Missed opportunities on SASCO vessels were crowding my mind space when, due to my hesitation to take timely decisions, Capstan's dream container logistics project came to an abrupt halt. This time, I made a colossal blunder by ignoring Prashanta's sound advice and deciding to take the vessels on charter and start the service with Capstan funds only before full capitalization of the JV. We had to discontinue the service after running it for about 9/10 months with 25/30% capacity utilization, causing a deep dent not only in Capstan finances but also drainage on my own personal assets. This is a very dark spot in my shipping career. I had a reputation for having a never-say-die attitude among my friends in the shipping industry, and I decided to concentrate on the project consultancy business for Port and Shipping with industry integration for establishing innovative transport supply chain logistics and providing cost and logistics benefits to all stakeholders. I had my 60th birthday on January 3, 1999, but before that, I must narrate a series of other setbacks that befell Capstan and the decision-making errors I was destined to make, which further contributed to Capstan's financial misery.

In the last quarter of 1997, we lost our eviction from the Harrington Mansion case filed against us at the Supreme Court, where the landlord went after losing at the HC Calcutta. There were considerable legal expenses incurred for this, and after eviction, we had to take temporary refuge in Soma's Dias office in the SDF building in Salt Lake for a few months before moving to our new office at Lansdown Court. We took this office at a high rent, increasing our office overhead. Even before our eviction, we hired a very senior and competent CA cum professional finance consultant, Mr. Das Bhowmik, for financial supervision of Captrans Shipping operations and other investment exposures on my friend Malay's EMKAY INTL, where an unsecured loan from Capstan went up to near Rs. 1 crore through Malay's cunning manipulation of Bhusan. Malay used to stay with us during his frequent Calcutta visits during those days and became close to Mani, Kakima (Purnima's mother and aunt), and Purnima. He enjoyed the affection and trust of all of them as my school friend. He knew Purnima was not happy about his continuous emotional pressure on me for support from Capstan and was playing on her natural caring and empathetic nature.

We entrusted Mr. Das Bhwomick to scrutinize EMKAY's A/C and order books, find some ways for the recovery of Capstan's substantial dues, and impose financial discipline in their order servicing. DB was to give special attention to the near $10 million SWIL contract, which EMKAY secured through their Calcutta office in 1997 for the site at Baruch Gujrat. Malay was not particularly happy with our probing through DB but reluctantly accepted this.

He had two competent engineering officers in his Calcutta office, Subhas Basu and Debajit Kar, who were instrumental in securing this Big Swil order. They were both very unhappy about Malay's handling of the mobilization advances from different contracts. They were confidentially advising me about this and requesting Capstan's intervention in EMKAY's finance management and audit. Bhusan was Malay's mouthpiece in the Capstan office, and he was trying to foment Prashanta's ego with DB's appointment and prominence. DB, as a no-nonsense finance man, reported many holes in EMKAY finance management and a lack of proper audit and recommended Prashanta convince Capstan auditor Mrinal Gupta to take charge of the EMKAY audit after consulting Subhas and Debajit. DB found the SWIL contract financially lucrative, and he was impressed with his discussion with Subhas on the technical management of the project. However, for securing a Rs. 2 crore mob advance, there was a necessity of BG from Punjab Sind Bank and some working capital facilities. Malay was not very happy about DB's professional intervention and reported findings, and he suspected Subhas and Debajit were reporting to me about his frequent advice to them to transfer mob advance from projects handled by the Calcutta office to Delhi. DB advised after discussing with the PSB Calcutta office that for providing over Rs. 2 crore in BG for SWIL and other projects, the bank would require adequate collateral security over and above 10% FD pledging as they were not happy with EMKAY's audited accounts for the immediate last three years. Malay was fully conscious of financial irregularities on transfers and spending different project mobilization advances for purposes other than the same project. Realizing the urgency of meeting the requirements of the big SWILL contract, he offered to charge his house in Delhi valued at over Rs. 1 crore as collateral to the bank. PSB still insisted on Capstan providing their balance sheet support by taking 51% equity in the company. All three directors, Prashanto, Purnima, and me, were totally against Capstan's further exposure to EMKAY, a business territory unknown to us and totally outside the scope of our core shipping business and the domain of our expertise and experience. Malay came down to Calcutta and emotionally pleaded with all three of us independently and collectively, projecting a high prospect and potential of scaling for EMKAY, particularly through SWIL contract execution, which would not only secure our recovery of unsecured loans but would also give a high dividend on Capstan investment.

Prashanto and I sat down with DB for a long, three-hour meeting to do risk analysis and take a mature, appropriate decision on this. DB had vast hands-on experience with his long association with the famous Sadhan Dutta and his famed project consultancy exposures internationally. Prashanta expressed his concern about our near Rs. 2.5 crore exposure in Dias of Soma, particularly as Soma was running Dias on remote control from the USA, and there was every likelihood of the West Bengal government loan finance impacting Capstan in case of repayment default. He was always unhappy about the Captrans Shipping investment. Capstan's exposure to EMKAY by way of an unsecured loan and investment in Lake Gardens real estate reached Rs. 1 crore. I did not dispute any one of his concerns and requested that DB give his opinion and view. DB made a very constructive risk and benefit analysis to address each of the concerns voiced by Prashanta. He felt Soma had made a mature decision by moving out to Sillicon Valley for internet product development and the securing of venture capital. She was using the Dias IT infrastructure both in terms of equipment and personnel for proper utilization of the state-of-the art infrastructure created by her at a considerable investment in Calcutta. These investments would have been at a much greater risk if she stayed back in Calcutta and tried to generate revenue and profitability for the company with a 4–5-year gestation period with further loss financing. He felt Soma was a competent, innovative, and dynamic young entrepreneur with the confidence to exploit the Sillicon Valley IT industry paradise of the world. On the Captrans Shipping investment, he agreed with Prashanta that we had taken a hasty decision without adequate risk analysis. The project, being a part of our long-term container shipping transport supply chain logistics management project conceptualized with innovative thinking with multiple links for its global spread over years, needed patience and not haste. It was very important for us to tie up a financially strong shipping group as a JV partner to attract much-needed public equity in the project, as the gestation period was expected to be long with adequate financial sustenance requirements. He politely pointed out that in the case of Himalaya Shipping, we had an approved IPO and tie-ups with consortium partners and MLOs lined up on the strength of our balance sheet and international credibility to pursue this container project.

We tried to replicate this with the ICFS collaboration, which failed due to our signed MOU unfortunately not getting converted into a properly documented Indian JV Company with capitalization and statutory compliances. In the case of Captrans, our Singapore shipping group was collecting charter hire from Captrans without fully committing their JV equity capitalization, placing our investments at considerable risk in the event of their backing out. These were hard and unpleasant truths, and I realized my big blunder and decided to push Singapore for a decision on JV participation and capitalization at the earliest.

On EMKAY investment recovery DB felt our best action point should be to control and discipline Malay in the management of EMKAY Finance by introducing internal audits on all the running projects and big projects like SWILL. He wanted to sit down with Prashanta and a minimum of two senior engineers from the EMKAY team, in addition to Malay, to design an effective MIS document for monthly reporting. He requested that I confront Malay bluntly, without any emotion, about the necessity of this internal audit. Equity participation of Capstan in EMKAY as a pre-requisite for PSB BG and working capital sanction could be considered in terms of the internal audit system design to be agreed upon and documented. Prashanta was still not in favor of Capstan taking any equity in EMKAY and further impacting the Capstan balance sheet, which was also my view. DB argued that we had already taken exposure of over Rs. 1 crore in EMKAY through the internal nexus of Malay with the Capstan accounts team, unfortunately with or without full knowledge of me and Prashanta. He had discussed the SWILL project thoroughly with Subhas, who, according to DB, was a competent project management engineer with professional experience and expertise. Subhas was always by his side when he negotiated and secured PSB sanction for EMKAY's SWILL project. He suggested the recovery of at least 60% of Capstan's dues from the SWILL mobilization advance as a condition for Capstan's converting part of the balance dues into equity in EMKAY. Malay agreed to all the terms, and we recovered 60% of our dues. This was another wrong decision from our side, which proved very costly later.

For Captrans Shipping operations in the Calcutta-Singapore route, we had to appoint Ravi Chopra from ICFS for posting in Singapore using our agents' office. We also appointed Capt. Biswajit Chakraborty in Calcutta for technical supervision of the vessels during loading and unloading at Calcutta and Haldia ports. We also had to take an office in Haldia on rental from Calcutta port as unlike SASCO operation with bigger vessels we were using Haldia for top-up.

Investments in overhead went up, and on the marketing front, Ritwik Mitra and Amar Dutta were doing client servicing with a couple of assistants. Although capacity utilization for incoming cargo from Singapore was over 75%, our outbound cargo from Kolkata-Haldia was hardly 25% during the first 4 or 5 months of our operation. There was a continuous cash loss, and I was pushing the Singapore ship-owner group to clear the JV agreement and expedite the capitalization of Captrans Shipping. Although our banker, Bimalendu Chatterjee of Central Bank, was very cooperative in accommodating our working capital requirement by increasing limits, we had to continuously pump in money from Capstan's reserve beyond our equity commitment of Rs. 2 crore. This adverse liquidity crisis was continuing for over 6 months, compounded by our substantial investment in the new office at Lansdown Court. I was compelled to put our Singapore Shipping Group on notice to sign a JV agreement and complete capitalization within 30 days, failing which our service would be closed and the vessel charter would be terminated. Singapore requested some more time, which made me somewhat doubtful about their final intention. We continued for another 3 months with further cash losses to survive with frequent delays and defaults in payment of charter hires when Singapore sold one of the vessels to Irano Hind Shipping (a SCI JV with Iran with a charter) and threatened us with withdrawal of the other vessel without signing the JV agreement. The operation was closed in the 3rd quarter of 1998, with substantial cash drainage and bank loans outstanding. There were outstanding charter hires both with Singapore Group and Irano Hind (since they became owners of one of the vessels), for which we expressed our inability to pay. The owners waited for us to try to find a suitable alternative JV partner to revive the service, fully realizing that the company would face liquidation if they legally pushed for the recovery of their dues. The loan outstanding with Central Bank was determined as Rs. 90 lacs plus interest accruing until Captran's accounts was declared NPA by the bank.

We started initiating a dialog with SCI Chairman Pravat Srivastav to join as the lead JV partner in our holistic multi-route container feeder service network project, which we planned earlier with SNR/ISS, where the charter cum purchase of 12 SASCO NB sister vessels was envisaged. The SCI Chairman expressed very positive interest and advised Sudhir Rangnekar to do an extensive due diligence exercise on our project report for a quick decision. We presented the project DPR, which we had earlier prepared for ISS and ICFS, with the necessary modifications to Sudhir, who involved Capt. Agarwal and his container department to study and interact with the Capstan team, which consisted of Finance and Marketing cum operation heads. Capt. Agarwal was a very competent and dynamic officer with a positive mindset. He requested that I come to Bombay with the Capstan team for a few days to sit through with him and his team to complete the DD exercise and submit his report to the chairman through his senior Sudhir Rangnekar.

I went to Bombay with DB and Ravi Chopra and stayed in the President Hotel for one whole week, having continuous day-long sessions with Capt. Agarwal and his team in the SCI office. Every evening, we were sitting in the hotel business center to prepare answers to SCI questions and figures emerging from the day's session. Capt. Agarwal hosted working lunch to expedite the process without interruption. We were advised that SCI had already acquired three 1700-TEU-capacity vessels that were deployed on their UKC service route. These vessels were not performing very well. Marketing support in terms of container volume was very marginal from their Calcutta office, which was also overseeing their Bangladesh marketing through agents. The vessels were having multiple calls en route in the round voyage, starting and ending at Colombo, covering UKC ports, Mediterranean ports, the Red Sea, and JNPT.

The market was very competitive in this route, and it was difficult to compete with major MLOs with multiple routes servicing under one window, which helped them to secure volume support at lower freight. Our project concept of a multi-route feeder network covering both feeder service as well as MLO service of SCI made a lot of sense to Capt. Agarwal. We worked on different varieties of voyage economics on Calcutta-Haldia-Singapore, Calcutta-Haldia-Madras-colombo, Madras-Singapore, and Colombo-JNPT-Dubai routes initially with the deployment of 2/3 500 TEU capacity vessels in each of the first three routes and SCI's own 3 bigger vessels in the fourth route with suitable tie-ups with major MLOs based on respective market strengths to eliminate undesirable rate war. My personal marketing reputation was known to SCI from my Himalaya/BSC agency days, particularly in the West Asia Gulf and USA East Coast sectors, and Ravi Chopra, who knew Sudhir well, advised them about Capstan's outstanding performance with SASCO vessels in the Calcutta-Singapore feeder operation. Ravi, as an insider in ICFS, explained their internal conflict as the reason for their backing out of the signed JV MOU with Capstan.

After Capt. Agarwal completed and presented a very positive and favorable DD report to his senior, we had a meeting with Sudhir and Capt. Agarwal on the fourth day for follow-up actions to expedite decision-making. There were frank and elated discussions on the long-term prospect of this JV project when Sudhir wanted us to meet the chairman the next day before our departure to express our appreciation for the great efforts of his department to complete this DD exercise on lightening speed. He, however, felt that, protocol-wise, they should get the report vetted by their Calcutta office before placing it before the board for clearance. Capt. Agarwal expressed his reservation about this, as he strongly felt Calcutta would not like this project and will have grouse against Capstan for by passing them to get the DD done by the HO. Capt. Agarwal had dinner with us that evening. It was four days of intense work for all of us. I had only one evening intimate dinner at my dear friend and younger brother Sabyasachi Hajara and Rintu's place. This was a relaxed evening for the Capstan team after the completion of a satisfying mission. Sabyasachi was heading SCI's bulk carrier and tanker division at the time, and I had initiated interaction with him on Capt. Torsten Olsen's innovative transloading cum barge operation. This concept, he found technology-wise very interesting. He had later arranged for a presentation by Torsten from Scandimar, Sweden, and me from Capstan, Calcutta, at the SCI Board room in the presence of the SCI Chairman and SCI management team.

Capt. Agarwal explained to us that evening (after my mentioning to him that Jayanta Mitter in charge of the SCI Calcutta container department was my cousin) that he had a few interactions with his Calcutta office during the course of the DD exercise and found Jayanta and his team very hostile and non-cooperative. He felt they were getting scared about being exposed to their share of blame for the loss-making SCI container service operation. Knowing Jayanta was my cousin, he hesitantly said that Jayanta's observations about me were not very complimentary. I was a bit perplexed, but I decided to talk to Jayanta on my return to Calcutta. We met Pravat Srivastav next morning along with Sudhir and had a very pleasant and positive talk for nearly an hour. Sudhir was very generous in complimenting me and the project concept. PS, apart from thanking us for our four days of intense work and cooperation in completing their DD exercise, showed a lot of respect to me as a shipping professional. I mentioned to him about my very soul-fulfilling spiritual discourses of 2/3 evenings with Mrs. C. P Srivastav at Bremen in the year 1964, when she was on board Viswa Nidhi with her two young daughters cruising in the Chairman's Owners Suite. He instantly reacted to say that 'one of the young girls is my wife now.' I reminisced about my interview in the SCI office with the then Chairman, Govind Seth, in 1965 and the offer I got to join as an assistant manager, which I could not finally accept. PS quipped to say that if I accepted, I would have been SCI Chairman long before. After this very pleasant meeting, we met Capt. Agarwal and his team to say good-bye.

After returning to Calcutta, I had an unpleasant experience with Jayanta when I talked to him. He expressed his concern about my adverse financial situation and wished I had consulted him before going so far with the SCI Bombay office, spending substantial time and money. The SCI Calcutta container service department was running with professional competence and efficiency, and he had very good relations with D. K. Choudhury and ICFS Dubai and was fully aware of Capstan's present situation. He would never support SCI getting involved in any JV with Capstan. I was shocked and astonished, as I always had a sweet family relationship with him and could relate to no reason for such a reaction. Later, Capt. Agarwal advised me that, as expected, a very adverse report on Capstan was received from their Calcutta office on his DD report, and the project was stalled.

I was formally advised by Sudhir Rangnekar that they would require time to sort out issues raised by their Calcutta office. I was compelled to cut down on the salary overheads of the company by a uniform reduction in salary for survival when some of the staff left but the majority stayed back.

The period 1999–2004 in our Lansdown Court office was our struggle for survival with very frugal revenue generation and acute cash flow problem. I was personally burning mid-night candles in actively pursuing chartering business with a few shipowners and coal import traders in Delhi through my friend Ram Nair of Clarksons and managed to fix Panamax bulk carrier Ratna Deep of ISS/ Ratnakar for a few years period TC, which was generating a steady flow of monthly commission. I kept on pursuing the transloading project with Capt. Olsen of Scandimar and his brilliant concept of a high-performing transloader with auxiliary engines powered by over 20k dwt self-propelled barges with a plug-in plug-out system in the horseshoe-shaped transloader for movement and navigation. Capt. Olsen and I responded to Sabyasachi Hajara's invitation to make our transloading presentation to SCI in their board room. Sabysachi had sent one of their technical officers to Sweden at Capt. Olsen's invitation for a detailed technical evaluation at the Scandimar office and was satisfied with the technical feasibility. Capt. Olsen made a few visits to Calcutta in 1999 and 2000 when we could make presentations to SAIL and Cacutta Port, and Capt. Olsen provided us slides for further presentations without him. I took Ritwik with me to Jamshedpur to make a presentation to TISCO Management, as arranged by Mr. Saxena of their Calcutta office. All the end users, including Calcutta Port, were impressed with the techno-commercial strength of the project. We made a presentation to Mr. Rajwar and his team in ISS, and R. C. Pareekh was entrusted to arrange a joint visit and presentation to Calcutta, Haldia, and Vizag ports, as well as to SAIL, TISCO, and RINL Vizag, along with me and Ritwik. I had been interacting with Capt. Olsen since my Himalaya days. He had been a very strong technical resource for me, with mutual respect for each other.

In 1999, he had already passed 70 years of age, had married a much younger South Indian girl, and had often visited Kerala during the past 7 or 8 years. Mr. Saxena from TISCO visited Sweden and Belgium with him to interact with Scandimar and Bocimar, Belgium, to explore possible ship owners and end-user collaborations on Torsten Olsen's transloading project technology. In my personal assessment of deep-sea transloading operations with year-round weather hazards, Capt Olsen's innovative concept was full-proof to combat weather hazards.. As I have narrated earlier, I had interacted with Luis Dreyfus on their floating crane concept and also with the Klaveness transloading concept with converted panamax. Torsten's Scandimar-Sweden concept was guaranteeing over 4k TPH loading and discharging cadence in their drawings and designs. In spite of the higher investment, Capt. Olsen's DPR, with drawings, designs, and cost lines supported by shipyards and vendors cost-quotes, was giving a high IRR with substantial cost and logistics benefits to the end users. Also, for the ports, there was a substantial augmentation in traffic volume and revenue. I met Sid Sridhar a few years later, when Capt. Olsen was no more, and in terms of technical competence, Sid was the only person close to Capt. Olsen's excellence. Capt. Olsen made his last visit to Calcutta in the year 2000, when he handed over to me his detailed working DPR with many handwritten calculations, vendor lists, and commercial voyage workings with various optional models covering east coast India and prophetically mentioned to me, 'Probir, you would be able to use them with shipowners, ports, and end users in the future as I am not in good health and my age is becoming a handicap.' I was emotionally moved then, and I still keep remembering this. After he went back to Brussels, where he was living with his wife after shifting from Sweden, I had a call from his wife hardly seven days later, informing me with profound grief that Torsten had passed away in his bath tub silently.

During our 6 yrs in Lansdown Court office between 1998 and 2004, we had relentlessly pursued and developed innovative project concept in various port, IWT and shipping related projects like fly-ash export to Bangladesh from Calcutta and Haldia by barges by securing supply contracts from West Bengal Govt power plants of Kolaghat and Bandel, container terminal development project at NSD Kolkata Port with Liebherr, Austria mobile harbour cranes and shore handling equipments with digital port-net system back-up, ship-breaking environment friendly facility development at Geonkhali near Haldia on the river, coal blending project at Haldia for supply of improved quality of blended coal of low ash content and high GCV by 75:25 mechanical blending of local high ash content thermal coal from Coal India with imported low ash content coal from Indonesia to the power plants of PDCL, NTPC, CESC. Mr. Somnath Chatterjee was Chairman of WBIDC during this period, and I received all the encouragement and support from him and the government of West Bengal. Rajarhat Township was getting developed at that time under HIDCO, which was to be much bigger than Salt Lake City. We introduced a quick and efficient land fill and reclamation project technology through Boskalis, Netherlands, for laying pipelines through existing canals (the eastern canal, Keshtopur, Bagjola, etc.) from the Hooghly River for dredging and transporting silt from the Hooghly River to a designated township site. An international tender was invited, and we represented Boskalis, who were finally selected as the L1 party. This project was dragged along for too long by vested political interest and a delay in decision-making by the government bureaucracy in accepting the final price offer of Boskalis, which was very competitive. Unfortunately, by the time HIDCO decided to accept the price, the international dredging market offered much better opportunities for Boskalis equipment to get engaged in other areas.

On the NSD Container Terminal project (which was my concept developed when I chaired the special committee during Bikram Sarkar's time as Chairman of KOPT), I actively worked with Ashim Mukhopadhya OSD and the port's terminal management team with an eye on container traffic augmentation through improved productivity and reduction in composite handling cost by eliminating the then-prevailing stevedores nexus with some of the port officers. The productivity in the terminal was hardly 10 TEU per hour. We projected a fourfold increase in traffic handling with a corresponding increase in port revenue and over a 30% reduction in handling costs. Ashim Mukhopadhya was a very competent and sincere port officer with knowledge and experience, and he provided me with unstinted support from the port side to provide authentic data by coordinating with HOD's as per the chairman's authorization. Utpal Sinha and Ratan Ganguly from the NSD container terminal and the then Traffic Manager, Aloke Chatterji, also lent me extensive support and cooperation. We made a very detailed cost-revenue analysis, comparing existing scenarios prevailing in the port with the projected benefits targeted through this project implementation. We arranged various presentations in the KOPT Kolkata office and also in Haldia by Liebherr Austria on the MHCs of different sizes and capacities and secured varieties of high-tech terminal shore handling equipment for the selection of the most suitable equipment for the project with viable investment cost, and return. We formed a consortium between Capstan and Liebherr, a Mumbai Port project operator with financial credentials (Capstan's financial position, due to setbacks narrated, needed a partner with qualifying financial credentials). Liebherr was a technology partner, committing crane sales to our consortium only and not to any other party participating in the tender. E. C. Bose and Partha also joined us to provide cargo handling support as stevedores.

I had earlier submitted a detailed report on this project concept with all logistics inputs and financial projections to establish a floor price of Rs. 900 per TEU with technical details of cranes and shore handling equipment to give minimum productivity as guaranteed to us by Liebherr. I made several visits to Singapore to interact with PSA, which was keen to join me on this project but did not want to participate in the tender. They explained that their experience with Indian Port tenders was not very pleasant and that they wanted me to participate and secure the tender through the Indian Consortium, and they would consider joining thereafter.

Mr. Sujit Poddar, my dear friend who was very close to CM Jyoti Basu and Somnath Da and an influential CPM member, introduced to me Mr. Choudhury, Chairman of the Mumbai Group, as the lead partner of our consortium with a strong financial and technical background. Sujitbabu was looking after their Kolkata office. We had extensive interaction with Sujit Poddar and their Mumbai senior techno commercial officer nominated for this project in our Landsdowne Court office for the preparation of the RFQ and PRICE BID as per the KOPT tender requirement. I recommended quoting Rs. 900 per TEU minimum floor price to ensure becoming L1. Mumbai party representative (name I am not able to remember due to rusted memory) insisted after talking to his boss in Mumbai to quote Rs. 100 per TEU above the floor price. We were expecting 3 main parties to compete for this tender, although 5 parties were regularly attending pre-bid meetings in the KOPT office. ABG,

Mumbai, TPRC, and Capstan Consortium were the three main parties, and I suspected one of the other two parties was posted by ABG as their backup bid. I was insisting on quoting the floor price, anticipating the ABG ploy. On the bid opening day, the KOPT tender committee opened RFQ bids from four parties including one from Khemka Enterprise, who was a barge operator and fell short of the experience and financial requirements of the tender. On the technical qualification, they were almost copy-pasting the ABG bid. Capstan Consortium was the lone party to submit documents from LIEBHERR as a consortium partner and full technology provider as per the tender requirement. All three other parties, however, submitted letters from LIEBHERR to state their interest in principle in providing technology support in the event of their winning the tender award. We strongly objected to Port considering their RFQ bid based on such letters from LIEBHERR only, which were far short of any firm commitment to become a consortium partner, as was in our case. Other parties claimed that they had selected LIEBHERR equipment as a vendor only and not as a consortium partner. The tender committee was divided in their views but ultimately decided to open all four price bids after 7 days for price evaluation and to decide on this technology issue thereafter. I strongly protested against the Khemka bid as they were not qualifying even on other tender qualification criteria apart from the crane issue. The tender committee appreciated my grievance, and they wanted to discuss it with the chairman before rejecting any bid. Saket Agarwal, owner of ABG, was a very intelligent and smart businessman who I befriended later after this tender incident. Like Tutu, he believed in buying high-level contacts, but he was a bit too fast in his decision-making without in-depth thinking. The then-KOPT Chairman was overly friendly with Saket, which Tutu later discovered and got into a serious legal fight with. On the scheduled price bid opening day, the committee opened all 4 bids one by one. We found ourselves running lowest after the opening of ABG, TPRC, and Capstan Consotium bids, but Khemka Enterprise quoted a floor price of Rs. 900 per TEU to become L1. We strongly protested the tender committee's opening price bid for a party that was not qualified as per the tender committee, but this was the chairman's decision. The tender was awarded to them within the next 48 hours, with ABG backing them up as the upfront operator. Many of the senior KOPT officers felt genuinely sorry and disappointed, as they knew how much toil and sweat I had personally put in to develop this project concept and bring it to the tender stage. The nexus between ABG and the KOPT boss was crystal clear to everybody. Sujit Poddar and his Mumbai technical team regretted their mistake in ingoring my assessment and the Mumbai guy advised me before leaving for Mumbai that they would consider legal action against KOPT for illegally by-passing no. 2 party and favoring no. 3 in the real-term operation of the contract entering through the back door. They indeed served legal notice on KOPT, and it took ABG more than one year to start operation. Both me and Sujit Babu requested that Somnath Da talk to the chairman. Somnath Da, after talking to the chairman confidentially, advised me that the chairman was full of praise for my knowledge and innovative thinking in the development of many port projects and my passionate involvement with port management. He agreed with Somnath Da that if the matter was pursued in court, the tender might get canceled, but that would delay the physical delivery of this innovative container project concept developed meticulously by Capstan. Capstan's lead Mumbai-based consortium partner was an unknown entity for KOPT, while ABG under young Saket Agarwal and his technical support from the Essar Group of his uncles Ruias were already having foot prints in a few Indian ports. While KOPT as PSU were not permitted to appoint me and Capstan as consultants for the port without tender, all port officers, including the chairman, respected me for my detached contribution for the welfare of KOPT. Somnath Da believed him to be genuine when he said ABG or any operators investing in PPP projects of KOPT would value my knowledge and innovative thinking for making commercial consultancy agreements with me. I developed a love-hate relationship with Anup Chanda later, after I was inducted into the KOPT Board as a trustee in March 2004 and served two consecutive terms until 2009. He was a person with super intellect and always enjoyed engaging with me on innovative project discussions, going into minute details, but was very egoistic in some of his fixed ideas. In his conduct and presentations in the board meetings, he never liked to hear critical comments from board members. We often got into arguments whenever any topic on ABG and container terminal operations came up. He strongly supported my transloading project and formed a special trust transloading committee with me and Saxena from Tatatas to lead, along with two other Trustees and relevant HODs of the port. OSD Ashim Mukherji was his man of confidence, who was playing all the coordination and executive roles from the port side in the transloading committee's actions and planning. Capt. Bagchi, DMD, was another very competent and knowledgeable Marine officer in the committee who had given unstinted technical support to the transloading committee.

Before narrating the almost fictional development story of the transloading project from 2004 onwards with KOPT and the end users, I must go back to happenings in the Capstan office between the periods of 1999 and 2003 at the Lansdowne Court office. For these five years, we were struggling and scarcely keeping our heads above water from some revenue generation through the fixing of a three-year period charter of ISS panamax bulk carrier Ratna Deep. We were also introduced to coal trader Kenny Singh and his company by Suniti Da's son, Samik Bhose, who was supplying imported coal to various power plants. With a commission-sharing arrangement with Samik, we fixed many vessels through Clarksons, earning reasonably good commissions. We were also earning agency commissions for NVOCC IAL Dubai for two years until they opened their own office in Kolkata in 2001. We also rigorously pursued the Rajarhat township land filling project of HIDCO West Bengal Govt. with Boskalis, Netherlands, who participated in the tender with their equipment and technology support, signed a consultancy contract with us, and paid Rs. 30 lacs as an upfront advance for government lobbying. We were working on various IWT and port development projects with IWAI, CIWTC, and KOPT, like barge building for operation with shallow draft in the river routes of NW 1 and NW 2, a shipbreaking project at Geonkhali on the Hooghly River near Haldia, and a coal blending project at Haldia with technology support from Humbolt, Germany, through their Kolkata local office. I had also recommended an alternative site at the long abandoned GR jetty near NSD for the coal blending project. We made a joint presentation by Humboldt and Capstan at Somnath Chatterji's invitation at the WBIDC Board room. Somnath Da invited all the power plants: PDCL MD and another officer for all the West Bengal Poower plants; NTPC for their Farakka plant; CESC, both Eastern Railway GM and South Eastern Railway GM; CIL Chairman with another senior officer. KOPT Chairman attended this meeting with OSD Ashim Mukherji. Anup Dutta from Humbolt was a very innovative technical person with very deep domain knowledge on the Indian and international coal markets, different varieties of coal specifications, and their efficacies in usage with different industries as per boiler design. Domestic coals raised by the government, Behemoth Coal India Ltd., from different nationalized coal fields were large in volume but poor in quality in terms of high ash content and low GCV. They were also supplied in chunks to the power plants by CIL in raw form with plenty of outside particles and high moisture content, resulting in expensive grounding and separation processes at the plant site and causing environmental hazards from boiler usage by generating excessive fly ash. The government of India imposed a statutory requirement on coal suppliers to maintain ash content within the limit of 30%, as opposed to 35 to 40% prevailing in the supply source from 90% of the mines. Coal pricing was classified by Coal India under different quality-based coal categories. The coal industry needed very high investment for a permanent solution through coal mines or even higher investment in the liquified supply of coal to plants through the laying of pipelines. In the absence of adequate investments in such processes, all the plants were taking the least expensive blending route of high- and low-quality coal by installing blending and grounding plants at their power plants, achieving limited success in maintaining their statutory obligations on quality. Even then, they were paying disposal fees for fly ash those days. Mainly road building and cement industries were using such fly ash. There were and still are huge volumes of thermal coal and coking coal imports from Indonesia and Australia, respectively, by the power plants and the steal plants. Humboldt's concept of a centralized coal blending plant in different port water fronts with the capacity to supply 10 mmt of blended and grounded coal to the power plants in the region involved the ingress of high-quality import coal from Indonesia with less than 8% ash content, low moisture, and high GCV coal mechanically from ships and barges and receiving the cheapest quality domestic coal by rail rakes again mechanically for blending and grounding processing with different proportions of blending mix to meet the quality specs of different power plants. The finished product had mechanical barge loading and rail car loading arrangements at the blending station for supply to the customers' plant destinations. The project offered huge cost and logistic benefits to the end users as well as CIL by reducing the volume of expensive imported coal and increasing the volume of low-grade CIL coal supply. Benefits for other stake holders were Port and IWT, in terms of traffic volume for port handling and deployment opportunity for barge owners, and also 10 mmt per year traffic handling with perfect logistic match for both-way traffic offerings for rail cars. This was a great boost up for Railways in their 'own your own wagons scheme' they were promoting at that time with leading wagon manufacturers in terms of cost and logistics benefits. However, for such an innovative real-time cost and logistic benefit project for all stakeholders, resistance from vested interest was inevitable. There were millionaire coal traders for import servicing who had a long-term nexus with end-user sourcing departments. There were many such issues with CIL, railways, coal mafias, wagon breakers, etc. After the presentation, we could find support from PDCL, NTPC, IWT, and KOPT. However, between the two railways, CIL and CESC, many negative issues were raised to scuttle its implementation.

During 2000–2001, Malay was in major conflict with Subhas Basu in EMKAY on the handling of the SWIL contract cash. Mr. Das Bhowmik was not happy with Bhusan's way of allowing Malay to take cash out of the SWILL mobilization advance and supported Subhas in his grievance against Malay. Debajyoti Kar had already resigned, and Subhas was holding fort with the Calcutta team for servicing and completing the SWIL contract. There was an acute cash flow crisis in EMKAY's Kolkata Anwar Shah Road office, and they were forced to take shelter in Capstan's Lansdown Court office due to massive unpaid telephone and CESC dues. Malay was handling three projects in Delhi and mismanaging the mob advance from these projects taken against BGs. Subhas was bitterly complaining about Malay taking funds from the SWILL account to Delhi, which was hindering the smooth completion of the SWILL project. Mr. Dasbhowmic supported Subhas and reported to me about Bhushan and PKG's lack of vigilance on EMKAY accounts management, where Malay was taking liberty to create mismanagement of different project finances by misusing mob advance for the projects. I requested that Malay provide the project management progress of all the projects he was handling in Delhi and the financial statements. He came down to Kolkata with sketchy information and advised me that he had been let down by Subhas, Debojit, and a few other project engineers managing different project sites, causing a financial crisis for the company. He had a big fight with Subhas on the SWILL project. Subhas came to my chamber and frankly advised me about his decision to quit. He advised that Malay as MD was mismanaging EMKAY and was not honest and sincere to me regarding repayment of Capstan dues. Subhas was categorical in his statement that EMKAY project profiles were good and all the engineers were feeling unhappy about the lack of integrity of Malay as MD. He was very confident of completing the SWILL project if nearly Rs. 30 lacs, which was taken out by Malay from mob advance, was paid back.

Without prolonging much on this sad story of betrayal and breach of trust from my school friend Malay, which caused the final liquidation of EMKAY by 2004, I will get back to my narrations on Capstan's story during this period of almost 6 years at the Lansdown Court office. We were put into further liabilities and losses by standing guarantor for raising high-interest private loans from EMKAY and other loans from LIC, which we had to repay to get the Anwar Shah Road property released. Malay did not seriously contest the liquidation case filed by a SWILL vendor against EMKAY at Delhi High Court for non-payment of the vendor's bill for the SWILL project.

Later in 2004, Malay started litigation with Capstan in his individual capacity, declaring he had no connection with EMKAY, which was a separate corporate entity, and claiming his 40% ownership stake in the Prince Anwar Shah Road project. He finally recovered from us over Rs. 50 lacs by way of a compromise court order for me to buy over his 40% share with outstanding KMC taxes after prolonged arbitration proceedings.

In early 2000, Soma raised venture capital for a product she developed using her Kolkata DIAS team and office infrastructure in Sillicon Valley, California, and negotiated a full DIAS takeover deal by IT firm Interka of Dr. Ajoy Bose, who used her technical skills and high rating with a MIT background to build Interka and convinced me to sell DIAS shares and investments at a very low price. When Ajoy Bose met me in Kolkata, he went overboard in praising Soma's intelligence, techno-commercial skills, and dynamism. He explained to me that Interka was built by Soma, and he, from his firm Interra, and another friend, Rajiv Singh, only provided start-up funds to raise VC for the product she developed. As a father, I was very pleased, and he was cunning enough to read my pride in my daughter and my parental softness. Mr. Dasbhowmick advised me to demand at least another Rs. 2 crore, which Dr. Bose politely mentioned, was a bit too high for the start-up venture. I took time to discuss this with Soma. Ultimately, he manipulated Soma to make me agree to his price offer, playing on my parental concern by stating that Soma was to run Interka with her DIAS team in Kolkata for scaling business. DB from the Capstan side smoothly handled the takeover of DIAS by Interka by complying with all stautory formalities, the repayment of the total WBFC loan, and the buyback of Webel, Gautam, and my friend Peter's shares in the equity of the company. Capstan was paid Rs. 1.25 crore for the asset value and our share buyback. We were to get some kind of charge on the 4000 sft of office space we secured from the Webel SDF building, which was cleared later by my friend Nandan Bhattacharya, the then MD of WEBEL. I am not able to remember the details. Ajay Bose and Soma came down to Kolkata, for Interka's takeover of DIAS to promote the IT industry in West Bengal. This event was celebrated with great fanfare. Soma always enjoyed much attention from the media; she was already a celebrity in the NASSCOM and Indian IT sectors as a very young emerging entrepreneur. A big launching party was hosted at the Taj Bengal, where CM Jyoti Basu, Somnath Chatterji, and most of the senior officers of the West Bengal Govt IT and Indusrial Ministry were present. Many leaders of IT industry attended. Rita Bhimani handled the event management and ensured large press attendance and coverage. Ajoy Bose gave Soma the center stage, and Jyoti Basu handsomely praised Soma and openly announced that his government would support Soma and take her help in promoting the Kolkata IT sector to Sillicon Valley, and Somnath Da was to lead a delegation to Sillican Valley. Ajoy Bose was happy to be connected with CM, and Somnath Da Courtesy Soma. Later, Interka appointed a Pakistani CEO for their organization, Mr. Oostur, who came to Kolkata instead of Soma to settle with Capstan about a few still outstanding issues to complete the takeover process. He was naive and audacious in telling me about Soma's negative points in corporate management and how difficult it was for him to accommodate Soma in his team. I was shocked and angry and reported this to Soma when she told me Oostur was making her life difficult and Ajoy Bose was not interfering. I got some more money out of Interka for DB to complete the pending takeover issues. Somnath Da led a delegation to Silican Valley later, and Soma anchored the West Bengal government presentation with critical advice and suggestions to Somnath Da's delegation, which was not very pleasant for the senior government officials. I felt relieved that all debts of DIAS with Capstan Guarantee were liquidated and we got a limited span of cash breather.

As a sequel to our coal blending station presentation, we could develop a PDCL fly ash contract for exporting fly-ash from their plants to Bangladesh cement plants. We were picking up fly ash from their Kolaghat and Bandel plants and using Bangladesh barges for this business, and we faced quality hazards and plenty of bureaucratic complications. We continued this business for 3/4 years with a meager return and my old Bangladeshi friend M. A. Jinna, who was a MP in the then ruling party, offering useful support. Capt. Munir was Mr. Jinna's Man Friday and was very able and competent. We did pursue different types of container, tanker, and bulk business in Bangladesh using Mr. Jinna's contacts, which included shipbreaking, which was always a no-go project for western countries, far eastern countries, and the USA for environmental reasons, and green peace activists' strict policing. Alang in Gujarat, west coast India, Bangladesh, and Karachi were the principal markets for the old vessels. These breaking yards were creating pollution and environmental hazards by not complying with pollution norms set up by the World Green Peace Forum for all shipbreaking. The birth and death cycles of different types of ships were like those of human life. The global shipping industry was always facing departure hazards for the old ladies by way of oversupply of tonnage in the market with adverse impact on the freight market. The viability of the new building vessels was being threatened. In the process of evolution in the industry, new building vessels were always facing cost excalation, and prolonged operation of the over-aged vessels was causing disturbance in the eco-system in establishing smooth and efficient transport supply chain logistics management in the international commodity trade. All the OECD countries, including the USA, banned shipbreaking on their watersides to prevent pollution primarily created by the asbestos and other pollutants in the vessels, and the majority of the old vessels were dumped for breaking in India, Bangladesh, and Pakistan shipbreaking yards. China had adapted modern environment-friendly facilities following the norms of the World Green Peace Forum (WGPF). There was a lot of research work going on in Norway on the shipbreaking industry, and some of the more enlightened Indian shipbreakers known to me requested that I talk to WBIDC Chairman Mr. Somnath Chatterjee to support the promotion of a large shipbreaking facility at Geonkhali near Haldia on the river where draft and size-wise empty vessels up to panamax and kamsarmax sizes can be handled. One of the Mumbai ship breakers already made substantial research work by collecting data from Norway and physically visiting China to study their state-of-the-art facility and established some technology collaboration for investment in the creation of such a facility in eastern India. The breaking cost-wise run of the mill Alang facility and also similar facilities in Bangladesh with lesser capacity were much cheaper than a newly created environment-friendly facility, but there was limited scope of an organized industry building where steel products for specific market demand servicing could be produced with total market validation due to its substantially lower production cost compared to such products from big steel plants. Both Somnath Da and KOPT Chairman showed keen interest in the development of a proper shipbreaking industry in West Bengal after we made a power point presentation at the WBIDC board room along with my Mumbai shipbreaker friend and 3/4 Calcutta shipbreakers in the presence of KOPT Chairman and his team. A WBIDC-sponsored SPV was mooted, with the shipbreakers contributing 75% equity. We got in touch with Norske Veritas through the Norwegian Embassy in Delhi, who was keen to promote their R&D work and technology development by collaborating with the West Bengal government on this project. Somnath Da took initiative in making a presentation in Delhi to the Norwegian Ambassador and invited Norwegian technical team to give a boost to this project. There was a strong lobby against this project from the steel industry on environmental pollution grounds, despite the anti-pollution measures in the already-unorganized shipbreaking industry. Both Somnath Da and CM received letters from TISCO MD requesting not to promote this project in West Bengal. We were almost at the delivery stage with an exit solution for a substantial volume of Federal Marine tonnage in the USA. Vested interest from active shipbreakers operating in Alang was also lobbying against this project. Ultimately, we had to abandon this with experience and knowledge gained but zero financial gain.

With EMKAY engineers and a few assistants sitting in our Lansdown Court office and Malay's crocodile tears to save the company by completing the last leg of the SWILL project by a senior engineer, Debajit Chackravarty, I was really getting exhausted in dealing with his account irregularities and financial intrigues. We had a money shark landlord in Vinay Agarwal charging a high monthly rental for our Lansdowne Court office, who lent money and negotiated with Malay other JV deals for EMKAY to take over with high interest and unfair terms. He backed out of the deal when I intervened but was holding me responsible for introducing Malay to him as my school friend. With very small revenue generation from some consultancy and chartering businesses and Bangladesh's export of fly ash, it was becoming very difficult to meet the high overhead expenses. There was also pressure on the sale proceeds of my personal Elgin Road property. We decided to shift over to the Prince Anwar Shah Office in 2004, but for this, we had to pay the substantial outstanding interest claim of Vinay Agarwal from EMKAY to get the property released from him out of charge created by Malay/EMKAY.

We were still pursuing a very lucrative Rajarhat Township land reclamation project with Boskalis. My friend Dick Van Uitert was heading Boskalis India Bangladesh operations. He was a very competent and dynamic technical professional and found interest in my port and shipping knowledge and creative mind to develop the IWT industry with Substantial River dredging in the National Waterways No. 1 and 2. I was interacting with IWAI and the Ministry of Shipping to create multiple riverside jetty facilities with innovative cargo handling logistics both inward and outward to promote economical commodity transportation and trading. Dick attended meetings and presentations with me at IWAI, WBIDC, BIWTC Bangladesh, etc. and introduced a Dutch consultant to me who had already done substantial R&D work for CIWTC when my friend and elder brother Suniti Bhose was CIWTC Chairman. At Dick's initiative, a logistic consultancy agreement was signed between Capstan and Boscalis for pursuing and developing Port, IWT, Dredging, and specifically Rajarhat New Town land reclamation by using Hooghly river silts from river beds identified by Port and Hidco and their transportation to different action areas planned for Rajarhat New Town by Hidco. The tender covering 3000 hectares of land fill by laying pipe lines through canals like the Easten Canal, Bagjola Canal, etc. was saving 5–6 years of land fill time under the prevailing system by digging ponds and soil transportation by Lorries. This cut-and-fill method was causing much delay and pollution problems on the road. There were land mafias and political party nexuses to prolong this as long as possible to sustain earnings through multiple layers of corruption. Dick cooperated with me to wade through all the hurdles, and finally Boskalis became L1.

Hidco Chairman at that time was Minister Gautam Deb, and he retained as his principal adviser a very senior retired PWD engineer, Mr. Gopal Mukherji. Hidco MD at the advent of the project was Mr. Debashis Sen, and then Sumantra Choudhury took over from him immediately after the tender opening. A meeting for further price negotiations was held with Boskalis. Dick from the Boskalis side explained the need for the mobilization of high-cost dredgers and other sophisticated equipment support for pipe line laying through the canals, which would also require substantial dredging and underwater pipe laying. He was sincere in explaining that after meeting Somnath Chatterji with me, he was personally motivated to convince his Netherlands HO to invest in this high-impact township building land reclamation project. Luckily, much of the sophisticated equipment and technical manpower for the project became available after Boskalis completed a few similar-type projects in other nations. Dredging equipment was always in short supply, and international market demand for such equipment and delivery were always time-sensitive and cost-competitive. When the Hidco team, with their bureucratic ego, explained the multiple layers of approvals and sanctions the project was to go through for the final award, Dick politely advised them that Boskalis, or for that matter, any other International Dredging Company's global equipment demands, would not permit their equipment to be committed for more than 3–6 months for any specific project in anticipation of an award. I met Somnath Da with Dick to update him and explained this position. Somnath Da appreciated and spoke to Gautam Deb, who in turn requested that Somnath Da speak to Mr. Chidambaram, the then Finance Minister in Delhi, about clearing the project for the state.

Despite all efforts, this project dragged on for over 10–12 months, and by the time the West Bengal government was ready to invite Boskalis to take the work order, all the equipment was engaged elsewhere, and Boskalis abandoned the project. Dick was transferred elsewhere for other projects, and LCA with Boskalis, which offered a long-term financial revival opportunity for Capstan, was lost due to this project not materializing.

I was inducted as a trustee of KOPT on their board in March 2004 at the initiative of Somnath Da and served two consecutive terms up until March 2009. During this period, when Anup Chanda was the Chairman of KOPT and M. L. Meena was Dy Chairman Haldia, a number of constructive PPP model Port infrastructure development projects were initiated with my very active involvement with both Mr. Chanda and Mr. Meena. As I mentioned earlier, a transloading committee with trustees and relevant port officers was formed, and a global EOI was issued with transloading concept paper on PPP model inviting participation from global parties. This was based on my report regarding techno-commercially viable transloading operations at Kanica Sands during rough weather monsoon months and Sandheads during dry weather months with relatively calm sea. My friends at LDA responded with positive interest with their floating cranes and self-propelled barges of 10,000 DWT. They invested in appointing a consultant or surveyor for exhaustive ocean surveys and preparing reports on weather behaviors at Kanica Sands and Sandshead deep sea ocean locations for year-round operation. LDA made a presentation at the KOPT board room, where, from the port side, all the end users like SAIL, TISCO, CESC, etc. were invited. There was already one mechanical coal terminal on the PPP model (berth no. 4A) operating at Haldia, which was dedicated to SAIL through a long-term 30-year contract. For starting a successful transloading operation at a deep-sea location, substantial logistic matching at Haldia Docks, both within and outside the lock gates, was essential. As a trustee and part of the KOPT-HDC team, I actively shared my concept of two separate coal terminals: one within the dock system with Mobile Harbour cranes and on-shore coal handling equipment for stacking and mechanical loading of 'Railway wagons on the move' basis, which was static in the case of Berth No. 4A. Tender papers were prepared, and invitations to bid were announced within six months. The other one was outside the lock gate near the oil jetty, which involved higher investments with two e-cranes with built-in conveyors for the direct loading of wagons as well as stack-yard delivery where stacker reclaimers for mechanical handling and proper railway linking were conceived. Discharging cadence of over 60k tons per day between the two cranes and the capability of handling two over 20k DWT flat bottom barges were designed for the tender by international consultants. This was conceived to handle over 10 million tons of coal per year. During my tenure of two terms as Trustee on the KOPT Board from 2004 to 2009, there were a number of positive project development initiatives from the KOPT Chairman, who had always respected my experience and innovative ideas, although we had few confrontations in the Board meetings. As an IAS officer with a built-in ego, Anup Chanda never liked to hear any contrary views from the board members. Trustees got used to hearing his monologues in the meeting and gave approval and appreciation of his ideas and initiatives to please him without any serious debates. I was the only voice on the board, asking uncomfortable questions. He was very sensitive to the NSD Container Terminal project awarded to Saket Agarwal ABG through the back door at the floor price, which I worked out for KOPT based on my project concept. There were many complicated issues raised in pre-bid meetings on tender clauses, which were sure to hinder the start of smooth project operation. Breaking the port-stevedore nexus, alignment of operation logistics between the MLOs and the contractor, port net digital system with vessel loading and unloading plan, digitally coordinating call orders, and container movements in the terminal were critical path management issues both for the port and the contractor. In the defensive mindset of most of the port officers, there was a tendency to take the path of least resistance in all decision-making with a saving one's back attitude if this meant sacrificing the port's visible interests. The whole system was corrupt from the Ministry down the line and even honest, clean-thinking officers were living in fear of vested interests ruining their career paths in the organization.

Although, in the back door method, ABG and Saket as L3 took over the contract from the nominee L1 Khemka, they also inherited the low price by blind acceptance of many unresolved KOPT issues that needed deft handling with the cooperation of KOPT officers for satisfactory resolution for a smooth start to the project. Unfortunately, except for the Chairman, Saket was finding his turf difficult, and the project was lingering for a head start even after the mobilization of the Mobile Harbour Cranes and other on-shore equipment. At the request of Somnath Da and Dr. Chanda, Chairman, we did not pursue legal action. We genuinely wanted the terminal operation to start on the concept developed by Capstan with the active cooperation of senior port officers in the interest of all stakeholders. Saket was a dynamic and aggressive young entrepreneur, and I found him eager to absorb and pursue innovative ideas from me in port logistics projects. He was ready to discuss and negotiate consultancy fees for the start of the container terminal project and to further pursue bulk terminal handling and my LDA floating crane transloading project concept with the port and other end users, both steel and power plants. In most of the KOPT board meetings, I raised many of the operational logistic issues regarding the Kolkata NSD container terminal operation commencement delay by the contractor. The chairman was not very comfortable hearing about unresolved KOPT logistic issues that were delaying the process due to his own rigidity and inflexibility, which was the prime cause of the officers' lack of cooperation with the contractor. In one of the board meetings, he went to the extent of directly insulting me by saying I was raising those points out of frustration as the contract was not awarded to Capstan. I was genuinely enraged and raised my voice to say, "You from the chair want to hear your own voice only in the meeting, and your false allegation is not acceptable to me." The majority of the members gave me tacit support. Afterward, Saket got the matter resolved with the chairman, as per my suggestion, and got cooperation from the officers to start the operation. An office space in the land adjacent to a traffic building near NSD docks was allotted to him as a contractor, and there was a vast improvement in the productivity and handling costs of containers in the terminal.

On the transloading project, I introduced Saket to LDA by traveling together to Paris, where Ram Nair of Clarksons joined us for a constructive meeting with LDA and their ship-owning subsidiary, Cetragpa. In response to the EOI of KOPT for the transloading project, LDA already expressed positive interest when Patrick Le-Scragne and another officer from LDA, along with Ram Nair, visited Kolkata port and appointed a professional surveyor for the technical viability study of transloading operations at identified deep-sea locations at Kanica sands and Sandheads in monsoon months and relatively calm weather in winter months, respectively. A KOPT coal terminal tender at berths 8 and 2 was issued for early implementation as a support system for the transloading project. LDA found Saket and ABG a good and reliable partner for pursuing the total transloading project, including participation in the Haldia coal terminal tender with Mobile Harbour Cranes and on-shore handling equipment support for the smooth handling of imported coal by the end-users. In Paris, we signed an LCA between LDA, ABG, Capstan, and Clarcksons with commissions on the cargo volume handled and consultancy fees for the Haldia coal terminal. This project was pursued with the port as well as with end users like SAIL, TISCO, and CESC. Knowing our experience from the past, I recommended to both LDA and ABG to involve Tutu Bose in the project. Tutu had well-established contacts, connections, and necessary arrangements with both the end-users and the port. There was very strong and rigid resistance from Patrick Le-Scragne, as he treated Tutu as responsible for the cancellation of the earlier SAIL tender in 1995, for which LDA had spent substantial time and money. Saket also argued against my practical strategy to secure this long-pending transloading contract award and was egoistic in stating that he was capable of handling port and end users to secure the contract. Tutu was already running a coal terminal at berth no. 4A with strong partnership support from L&T and Kirit Shah of Bangkok, who was a shipowner in his own right. There was a backup SAIL contract of 3 million tons per year for coal handling for 30 years for berth no. 4A. I knew fully well that a peaceful collaboration between LDA, ABG, and Tutu for SAIL coal handling of over 6 MMT PA imports from Australia to be brought to Haldia through the transloading operation could have desirable traction for handling logistics of the daughter vessels between berths no. 2 and 8 of the Haldia terminal tender and the existing terminal of Tutu at berth no. 4A. Three berths together had the potential to handle over 10 MMT PA imported coal traffic from different end users like SAIL, TISCO, CESC, etc. Unfortunately, Patrick Le-Scragne, though very competent, was a bit arrogant and oblivious to the Indian scenario, which was never very straight-forward and simplistic to handle. Patrik found in Saket an equal match between arrogance and ego. After much persuasion, I could organize a meeting at the KOPT board room with the chairman's initiative to invite all the end users. Still, we failed to reach any successful road end for the transloading project. Continuous meetings and interactions between KOPT and SAIL could not resolve the moot point of the controversy as to who would be the ultimate counterparty for the transloading project. KOPT wanted SAIL to award a cargo contract to the transloading service provider with KOPT concessional rates and logistic backup for handling the daughter vessels at Haldia coal terminals. SAIL, as PSU did not find this workable, and they wanted KOPT to appoint a transloading contractor against a long-term minimum cargo guarantee per annum from them with requisite BG security. All efforts by Saket at the Shipping Ministry and Steel Ministry in Delhi, with the number of visits from LDA and Clarksons, failed to yield any results as Tutu's lobby was very strong. Ultimately, LDA and ABG decided to participate in the berth 2 and 8 Haldia terminal tender as a JV consortium. LDA wanted to close our consultancy agreement for transloading cum Haldia coal terminal by paying lumsum one-time fees to Capstan and Clarkson, as Patrick did not want to pursue transloading anymore and found no role for Capstan and Clarksons in their JV for Indian Port terminal projects with ABG. The proposition and fees offered were not to my liking, but I accepted the same at Clarksons request and Saket's advice that Patrick did not like my closeness with Tutu and my recommendation to them to collaborate with Tutu. For me, trandloading was my dream concept, and I already explored many better technology options, like the Scandimar of the late Captain Torsten Olsen, as I already narrated, and the Panamax-size converted transloader from Klaveness Shipping, Norway. The floating crane concept of LDA was not my preferred option, but I accepted it as LDA committed investment while others were only offering concepts and technology. As a KOPT Trustee, I always tried to convince the Chairman and the board, even by going up to the Minister, to invest in the transloading project as a part of the KOPT-HDC mobile virtual port extension at a deep-sea location with substantially lower investment than building a deep sea port with integrated rail, road, and IWT logistics, breakwaters, and state-of-the-art cargo terminals for handling capacity building. Such high technology and investment would require 10–12 years of lead time and very competitive traffic generation for its viability. MVP Transloading operation with a 12–

18 month lead time and low investment was tailor-made to generate multiple benefits to KOPT in terms of cargo volume, IWT industry spread in the river, and rail/road integration for a robust and wholesome development of a transport supply logistic chain management offering huge scaling potential for all stakeholders. The future sustainability of the KOPT-HDC as dedicated IWT ports for river-ocean linking was also to be established over 10–12 years, which was the lead time required for Deep Sea Port to come up with attractive investment incentives for private and public corporates through developed wholesome logistics infrastructure. After LDA-ABG backed out of the transloading project, my close old friend Lalit Bhadwar, a very competent and knowledgeable Delhi-based shipbroker and shipping consultant, introduced to me Sid Sridhar, an extraordinarily innovative and experienced technocrat from Seabulk, Vancouver, Canada. Sid had very deep domain knowledge of transloading operations and a reputed background in designing, building, and handling 5–6 million tons of iron ore loading at Goa by a Cape-size transloader. Bocimar Shipping Group, Belgium, one of the world's largest bulk shipping companies (Lalit's Shipowner Principal), had partnered with Seabulk to invest in transloading projects with their large fleet of Capesize, Kamsarmax, and Panamax vessels. My friend, who was like my very own younger brother, Sabyasachi Hajara, had just become Chairman of the Shipping Corporation of India at that time. Sabyasachi agreed for SCI to join a strong transloading project consortium with our team of Bocimar, Seabulk, Capstan, Lalit, and Tutu, jointly pursuing with KOPT and the coal importers, particularly SAIL and TISCO, for the delivery of this comprehensive transloading project, which included investment in Capesize transhippers, second-hand Panamax vessels for feedering import coal between mother vessels directly through transloading operations, and storage of part cargo in the transloaders' hold at a reduced permissible Haldia draft. In view of the over 10 MMT PA handling capacity of import coal in the Capesize transhipper project concept, we included in the project investment a larger state-of-the-art coal terminal outside the Haldia lock gates at

the identified location near the 2nd oil jetty, which was already on the KOPT-HDC drawing board for tendering, as I narrated earlier. Later, Saibal De and ILFS were brought into the consortium by Mr. Patnaik, who was in charge of the Seabulk, India, office in Delhi. It was planned that both Bocimar, with their large bulk carrier fleet of capesize, Kamsarmax, and Panamax-sized vessels, and SCI, who had already ordered Capesize and Panamax-sized new buildings at Korean shipyards, would offer scheduled bulk carrier loadings at the Australian loading ports of the steel plants as per the requirements and nominations of both SAIL and TISCO to ensure the scheduled arrival of two mother vessels at the transloading point at a frequency of every three days. All the consortium partners had to invest substantial time and quality manpower in pursuing this project to bring it up to the stage of tendering by KOPT, duly covering the roles and responsibilities of all stakeholders. From the end user's side, KOPT was to secure a minimum cargo guarantee against BG, which made it almost obligatory for SAIL and TISCO to get into scheduled COAs with shipowners where a strong SCI-Bolimar combination of requisite vessels had an edge over the competitors. There was obvious resistance from Transchart and other foreign vessel owners, which were getting marginalized due to SCI's presence in the consortium. There were other vested interests in the internal chartering departments of SCI as a shipping behemoth as well as in SAIL, the two Navaratna PSUs, which had to be overcome. The consortium participated in the KOPT tender and secured the bid. They were asked to bid for the Haldia coal terminal outside the lock gate.

In the preparation of the techno-commercially viable tender document, I had major differences with the KOPT-HDC technical team who were limited in their vision with the concept of a mobile harbor crane, already implemented basis the other tender award on berth no 2 & 8 inside the lock gate. The merry-go-round direct loading of rail cars with railway logistics built up at the back yard of the terminal with smooth mainline linking was also having lack of vision and courage of the port officers to go for.

The concept that I proposed as per the designs and drawings of Sid Sridhar / Seabulk was to have two e-cranes with conveyor shoots to reach up to the stackyards. The conveyor was also designed for the direct loading of rolling railway wagons apart from a backup of stacker reclaimer for mechanical wagon loading from separate stackyards. Stacking different grades of imported coal both for steel plants and power plants of adequate holding capacity was also in the plan design. An International Standard coal terminal capable of loading and unloading two daughter vessels at a time giving over 40k ton per day discharging cadence was conceived. This was designed for handling over 30 MMT PA coking and thermal coal and also loading smaller barges for river transportation to the power plants of NTPC at Farakka and CESC at Budge Budge. Although the investment was high, handling costs were substantially reduced for the end users after achieving substantial traffic and revenue augmentation for the port. The project had over 20% IRR for the investors. This was found acceptable to our consortium team. In the internal working of the consortium team investment preference of the partners in the transloading MVP, both transloader and conservancy equipment at the Sandheads and Kanika Sands anchorage locations, and the long-term investment on the custom-built shallow-drafted over 25k DWT self-propelled barges and the Haldia coal terminal outside the lock gate were discussed and settled between the consortium partners. Transloader and conservancy equipment was treated as an independent profit center project, IRR-wise, where Bocimar had the majority equity holding with a token minority holding of SCI. In the daughter vessels, both initial panamax vessels and long-term custom-built barges, SCI had the majority holding and Bocimar had a token minority. In the Haldia coal terminal, the majority holding was to be from ILFS, with token minority holdings from SCI and ISHPL of Tutu (already operating berth no. 4A coal terminal). We arranged a meeting between ILFS engineers and the KOPT-HHDC technical team to discuss the entire terminal investment planning and financial figures to secure optimum cost and logistic benefits for end users like KOPT and investors. In the Indian Port Industry,

KOPT needed TAMP approval for formulating their port handling charges. For this, they were required to send full project details with a benefit analysis to TAMP. Haldia port officers raised various negative issues, like the difficulty in shifting HDC staff quarters to the backyard of the terminal for the implementation of the Merry Go Round Rail Car Loading proposed in our project with mainline linking, and almost convinced ILFS to abandon Sid's technology and terminal layout. Port officers were used to low-productivity cargo handling operations until then (dealing with vested interests with total involvement). The 40k ton per day productivity per crane and systemic terminal operation for handling 30 MMT PA cargo was a pipe dream for them. Ultimately, they overruled my decision to send their proposal to TAMP for rate approval, sticking to mobile harbor cranes and conventional terminal handling equipment with lower investment as well as productivity. I was compelled to meet TAMP officers in Delhi and present our proposal with higher productivity and investment, achieving lower cost and logistic benefits to the end users with a gain to port in terms of traffic and revenue augmentation. In the subsequent TAMP hearings at the KOPT guest house, KOPT officers had to face uncomfortable interactions from the TAMP Chairman and his team, and they were upset with me for giving an independent proposal to TAMP under the Capstan banner. This matter dragged on for a few months, and in the meantime, strong objections from the Orissa government for starting transloading operations at Kanika Sands surfaced. According to the Orissa government Kanika Sands was outside the KOPT operation zone. OG challenged Ministry clearance for this project and the matter went up to the Supreme Court to determine the jurisdictions of the states on the coastal high seas. There was also a door-to-door delivery proposal tender issued by SAIL covering the loading of the cargo at the source Australian ports and delivery of the cargo up to their plant site through a railway logistics link-up. At this stage, I had involved Ramesh Maheswari and Texmaco in the consortium with the consent of all, i.e., SCI, Bocimar (through Lalit Bhadwar, MD of their Indian office), ILFS, and Sid Sridhar-Seabulk (his

Indian office head was Gokul Pattanayak). Sid came down to Kolkata, and we arranged a full project presentation at the Texmaco works board room, where Ramesh Maheswari and his technical team went overboard in complementing Sid for his total technology presentation covering transloading MVP equipment at a deep-drafted high-seas location, feedering logistics through daughter's vessels, and the state-of-the-art coal terminal design concept at Haldia outside lockgate-identified location. With their high-level connections with Indian Railways and wagon manufacturing capacity, Texmaco was well equipped to meet SAIL's tender requirement for delivery up to the plant site. There were considerable interactions and joint presentations between KOPT and SAIL. I arranged the visit of KOPT Dy Chairman and ED Transport & Shipping of SAIL to Texmaco Works at RM's request, which were all very productive with the firm belief that Texmaco would be a major investor, which was the impression gathered by all. In the Texmaco organization, after KK Birla's demise, his son-in-law, Saroj Poddar, was the chairman, and he was not as dynamic as Ramesh Maheswari in his corporate thinking. The project dragged on at both the Texmaco and SAIL end on the issue of railway logistic management. Beaurocratic unrealistic expectations from the SAIL side and Texmaco Chairman's hesitation to extend investment in logistics beyond their core area of rail car manufacturing were having unending travel on the project pathway without determination of destination. This became a sore point for all other consortium members, including KOPT as the counterparty. In the preparation of the techno-commercially viable tender document, I had major differences with the KOPT-HDC technical team, who were limited in their vision with the concept of a mobile harbor crane, already implemented for the other tender award on berths 2 and 8 inside the lock gate. The merry-go-round direct loading of rail cars with railway logistics built up at the back yard of the terminal with smooth mainline linking was also lacking the vision and courage of the port officers to go for it.

There was also a door-to-door delivery proposal tender issued by SAIL covering the loading of the cargo at the source Australian ports and delivery of the cargo up to their plant site through a railway logistics link-up. At this stage, I had involved Ramesh Maheswari and Texmaco in the consortium with the consent of all, i.e., SCI, Bocimar (through Lalit Bhadwar, MD of their Indian office), ILFS, and Sid Sridhar-Seabulk (his Indian office head was Gokul Pattanayak). Sid came down to Kolkata, and we arranged a full project presentation at the Texmaco works board room, where Ramesh Maheswari and his technical team went overboard in complementing Sid for his total technology presentation covering transloading MVP equipment at a deep-drafted high-seas location, feedering logistics through daughter's vessels, and the state-of-the-art coal terminal design concept at Haldia outside lock gate-identified location. With their high-level connections with Indian Railways and wagon manufacturing capacity, Texmaco was well equipped to meet SAIL's tender requirement for delivery up to the plant site. There were considerable interactions and joint presentations between KOPT and SAIL. I arranged the visit of KOPT Dy Chairman and ED Transport & Shipping of SAIL to Texmaco Works at RM's request, which were all very productive with the firm belief that Texmaco would be a major investor, which was the impression gathered by all. In the Texmaco organization, after KK Birla's demise, his son-in-law, Saroj Poddar, was the chairman, and he was not as dynamic as Ramesh Maheswari in his corporate thinking. The project dragged on at both the Texmaco and SAIL end on the issue of railway logistic management. Beaurocratic unrealistic expectations from the SAIL side and Texmaco Chairman's hesitation to extend investment in logistics beyond their core area of rail car manufacturing were having unending travel on the project pathway without determination of destination. This became a sore point for all other consortium members, including KOPT as the counterparty.

In 2009, my second term as trustee of KOPT ended. During my tenure as trustee between 2004 March/April and 2009 March and a short break of a few months for the changeover of the board after the 1st term, Anup Chanda was chairman, and despite little egocentric board confrontation, Dr. Chanda was a super intelligent person with a cultural and spiritual bent of mind. He was thinking big for the port and always gave me a lot of respect for my professional shipping knowledge and innovative ideas. I will narrate a few of the projects he supported and implemented, as well as a couple of projects he seriously supported but remained incomplete at the end of his tenure. For the Haldia Coal Terminal project covering berth nos. 2 and 8, at the tender preparation stage, he involved me extensively in the MHC concept and went out of his way to arrange an interactive meeting with all the HODs and technical officers of KOPT and HDC, including HDC Dy Chairman Mr. M. L Meena at KOPT with me on a holiday as I was leaving for the USA for three weeks on the same late-evening flight of Singapore Airlines. Although, in the final tender document, all my suggestions at the concept discussion stage did not find reflection, a major part of them was included.

My prime difference with him was on the issue of the port taking on a bridge counter-party role between the contractor and the end-users with a load on the bid-winning contractor's price rate. My argument was for the port to remain happy with the traffic augmentation and enhanced revenue generation from port charges, both port-related and cargo-related, and not burden the end users with a marginal cost increase that could make the port uncompetitive with neighboring ports like Paradeep, Vizag, etc. Dr. Chanda was fending for additional revenue for the port, even at the risk of taking on multiple logistics handling obligations for the port. At the concept discussion time, I arranged an evening meeting between Dr. Chanda, me, and Tutu Bose (from the handling contractor side) in his office, which lasted nearly 3 hours. Neither I nor Tutu could finally convince him to change his mind on this issue.

There were more than four participants in this tender, which included ABG LDA JV, TMILL (Tata), and Tutu's ISHPL consortium. After extensive pre-bid discussion, ABG LDA JV got the bid award at a competitive rate. As the then consultant to Tutu, I advised both Dibyendu Bose of TMILL and Tutu about a bid price for winning the tender based on the financials and figures we prepared for this project, which was giving over 22% IRR for 10-year projections. Tutu wanted to quote this rate, but Dibyendu found it much too low. Ultimately, Saket won the bid at a price that was Rs. 5 per ton more than my suggested price and over Rs. 10 per ton lower than Dibyendu's quoted price.

Dr. Chanda also had some differences with me on the KOPT-NSD container terminal, which was awarded to ABG finally in spite of this structural issue but finally implemented by Saket by taking me on his side at Dr. Chanda's suggestion.

Dr. Chanda made a major contribution to Howrah Bridge lighting with beautiful changing of colors using legendary lighting expert Tapas Sen in his very old age during my tenure on the KOPT board. Howrah Bridge was under the management of KOPT always, but unfortunately, no other chairman took such ideas of maintenance and beautification as Dr. Chanda. Huge idle real estate properties in KOPT, including Strand Road warehouses and jetties, were also suitably developed and beautified as Millennium Park.

Dr. Chanda also collaborated with Ramakrishna Mission Seva Pratisthan in the major uplifting of the Kolkata Port Hospital, and Swami Sarbalokananda, who was the then Secretary of RKM Seva Pratisthan, in his speech on the occasion of the inauguration of the upgraded and renovated hospital, profusely praised Dr. Chanda for this initiative. With my close association with RKM and Maharaj, I was very happy to be a part of this project as a trustee of KOPT.

At Dr. Chanda's request, I shared my own concept of corporate vision and port infrastructure development for KOPT-Haldia, emphasizing a nation-building platform. He appreciated the concept and, for practical implementation, obtained clearance from the ministry to appoint an international port consultant through global tendering. The consultant, Haskinson, submitted a comprehensive report to the KOPT board, but it fell short of fully exploiting the potential of ocean-river-rail-road linking as envisioned in my concept paper. Later, during Mr. Kahlon's tenure as Chairman of

KOPT, I presented an updated version of the concept paper in article form, detailing international and Indian port and shipping scenarios. This article was published in one of the KOPT journals, and Mr. Kahlon shared it with the Ministry of Shipping.

For my readers, I'm giving here the full article to benefit posterity.

***

CORPORATE VISION 2020 FOR KOPT-HDC – POSITIONING INFRA SERVICE PRODUCT BASED NATION BUILDING PLATFORM

By Probir Mitra

My vision for Kolkata/Haldia Port is to position it as a privatized corporate entity that will encompass in its fold an integrated infrastructure service product at the macro level as the true gateway of eastern India, including neighboring countries such as Bangladesh, Nepal, Bhutan, and Myanmar.

The ambit of KOPT-Haldia's Corporate Service Management Domain will include deep-drafted anchorage in the high seas within a 150-nautical-mile range on the coastline, the entire river infrastructure from Sandheads/Sagar up to Diamond Harbour-Kulpi-Kolkata-Haldia, National Waterway No. 1 up to Patna, Allahabad; National Waterway No. 2 up to Guwahati via Bangladesh; and the development, upkeep, and linking of ports to rail and road systems with the National Grid.

The service product will be designed on a multimodal platform to offer a source-to-destination transportation logistic solution for end users, both importers and exporters.

Implementation of this Mega Vision Statement will be primarily focused on a management structure where a CEO with a missionary zeal will be leading from the front with a highly motivated decentralized management team capable of independently leading and delivering various links of the total chain with entrepreneurial innovative service product concept management at different layers of connectivity like state-of-the Art mechanical jetty and terminal infrastructure to achieve optimum productivity, revenue earning potential, and substantial cost savings through best operational logistic management. This can be through outsourcing or in-house investments after an in-depth analysis of the product's management strength, marketability, and scaling potential.

Bulk cargo handling, POL/oil products, and containers will all be targeted to achieve traffic volume to their full potential.

In traffic planning, it is to be kept in view that India's overseas seabound trade has increased almost seven times from the late '80s until the 1st decade of 2000, i.e., up to 2010. It is further predicted to increase another four times by 2020.

The global containerization trade growth was over 10% from 2010 to 2010, and this suddenly came down to 6% in 2011.

From now until 2020, the growth rate forecast is over 9% per year. The world merchandise trade, which is primarily containerized, was over USD 25 billion in 2009. This is likely to grow to the level of USD 37 billion by 2015–2016.

India's container and merchandise trade, which had a 10-fold increase during the two decades between 1990 and 2009, is expected to grow between 4 and 5 times between 2014 and 2020.

There is continuous innovation in container ship design, and over 50 mega-post-Panamax ships in excess of 10,000 TEUs in capacity joined the world fleet in 2012. The concept of "Round the World Container Service" for mega-ships in clockwise and anti-clockwise modes by different major consortia of container shipping companies is likely to establish feeder networks all over the world for servicing shallow draft river ports in the interior in its Door to Door Service Concept.

The volume of international sea-bound trade at the end of the first decade of 2000 was a little over 8 billion tons, of which over

30% is oil cargo for tankers and nearly 70% is dry cargo, which includes both bulk carriers and containership cargo.

The container trade has seen the largest growth as the level of containerization is taking place at a rapid pace in the merchandise commodity sector.

The bulk cargo sector reflects the future energy requirements, which are integrally linked with development economics, particularly in non-OECD countries.. The development demands of non-OECD countries will require expanding consumption of all types of fuels. In this sector, coal will remain the single largest contributor to the growth of power sectors.

The oil sector, which is the other sector for energy fuels, will have interesting demand mapping over the next 10–20 years.

Growth in demand will come from non-OECD countries like China, India, and the Middle East.

Supply sources will primarily come from OPEC, where the largest increment will be from natural gas liquids as well as conventional crude from Iraq and Saudi Arabia.

From the non-OECD countries, India will contribute over 30% of the global growth during the next 2 decades, and India's share of global coal consumption will have a 6–8% jump during this period.

It is also interesting to note that India's massive port infrastructure requirement during the past 2 decades was met mainly by the major ports (over 70%) and balanced by the non-major ports, which have recently come up in Gujarat, Orissa, Andhra Pradesh, and other states.

A very substantial increase is expected in traffic volume in major ports. From a little over 550 MMT PA in 2010–2011, it is estimated to go up to 1031 MMT PA within the next 5 years, and by 2020, it is estimated to reach over 1200 MMT PA.

Non-major private ports are not only matching up with the major ports in their traffic growth, but by 2020 they are expected to overtake major ports' traffic volume.

This clearly establishes the delivery potential of the private sector over bureaucratic red tape in public sector management.

The purpose of my giving this brief overview of the trade and economic scenario, both globally and nationally, is to highlight the high demand potential of the KOPT-HDC Integrated Infrastructure Service Product, both traffic volume-wise and revenue-wise.

The service product, as said earlier, will be primarily structured around creating a deep-drafted MVP (mobile vessel port) at an identified anchorage location for trans-loading operations and then catering to the handling of custom-built, specially designed daughter vessels and barges commensurate with the draft availability at various locations of the river, starting from Sagar Island to Diamond Harbour in Haldia-Kulpi—various locations in National Waterways No. 1 and National Waterways No. 2 in Bangladesh rivers, etc., to ensure seamless traffic flow—bulk cargo as well as container cargo, oil products, etc.

If investment in MVP and custom-built crafts come from private parties, then KOPT-HDC's private corporate investment will be on a compatible cost-revenue model for river engineering like capital drilling, regular maintenance drilling, pilotage, and other necessary state-of-the Art infrastructural support to guarantee committed drafts, night navigations, an optimal level of pilotage, and lockgate operations.

The present continuous polemic on the dredging operation, where the Dredging Corporation of India (DCI) is not always in sync with the KOPT Marine Deptt in meeting the demand for dredgers of the requisite types, is always of prominent focus. Delays and indecisiveness from the Ministry and Planning Commission are major hindrances to deploying global contractors who can build and invest in the right type of dredgers with systemic utilization of capacity. This can always be overcome by private port management.

There is a government decision to build port infrastructure on Sagar Island, mostly by reclaiming land. However, the popular phrase "Deep Drafted Port at Sagar Island" as mentioned in the media is a misnomer.

Through adequate capital and maintenance dredging, the best draft achievable at Sagar Island may never exceed 12.5 meters; more realistic figures are between 11.5 and 12 meters.

KOPT-HDC, as a private corporation, will have the freedom to introduce an all-comprehensive dredging system through global tendering, which will include Sagar Island, the entire stretch of the Hooghly River (this will include Eden Channel bypassing Auckland Channel, Rangafala Balari, and other critical points), NW-1, and NW-2, where it is important to guarantee over 3 million metric tons of draft all through for commercial river craft operations.

The silt removal by expensive dredgers has not been addressed so far with a systemic focus on innovative management. The introduction of private investment with a holistic approach will be able to ensure that silts are not dumped at the mouth of the river by expensive dredgers and are allowed to come back to the river again on its natural flow. A stationary dredger at its dredging point with shallow-drafted bottom open hopper barges that can get into the interiors of the adjacent lands and well-laid-out pipelines for proper utilization of the silts for land reclamation will be a win-win economic proposition.

For a riverine port like KOPT-HDC, continuous dredging operations need to be established on technologically viable norms, whereas a large global dredging company has to invest in a fleet of dredgers of different sizes and types with innovative equipment designs. There will not only be huge potential for the development and employment of trained personnel in this dredging industry, but it will also create institutional training facilities with river engineering as an independent discipline in the whole of Eastern India.

There will be scope for startup entrepreneurs to provide a technologically viable outsourcing facility to the main contractor throughout the long and wide reach of the river system this dredging industry is supposed to serve.

The Jetty Infrastructure Development is essential at Sagar-Haldia-Diamond Harbour-Budge Budge-Kulpi within the comparative deep drafted zones of the river system and comparatively smaller barge jetties and terminals at different points at NW No. 1 and NW No. 2 like Tribeni, Katwa, Farakka, Baharampur, Jangipur, Bhagalpur, Semaria, Doriaganj, Ballia, Ghazipur, Varanasi, Chunar, and Allahabad. A 1,620-kilometer stretch along NW-1 will need to be dredged, deepened, and rendered navigable by ATBs and SPBs. Similarly, an 891-kilometer stretch along NW-2 needed to be upgraded and maintained, along with its fixed terminal at Pandu and floating terminals at Dhubri, Jogighopa, Tezpur, Silghat, Dibrugarh, Jamgurhi, Bogibil, Saikhowa, and Sadiya.

Each independent jetty, terminal infrastructure, fully mechanized, semi-mechanized, and partially manual facilities will have to be created based on a professional traffic survey assessment.

All the jetties can be built on the PPP model with proper road and rail linkages between the port system and the national grid for servicing the entire hinterland of eastern India, NE India, and neighboring countries.

The financing model will have a fixed minimum IRR target for the private parties in the PPP model and also for the port as an independent private corporate entity.

The supply chain logistics of the bulk trade and the merchandise trade (both import and export) will be addressed separately, with the target of reaching the optimum peak over the next two decades. The oil fuel requirement of the energy sector and other industrial sectors needs to be addressed through a combination of pipelines laying for specialized products up to the end users' points, SBMs, both crude and product handling facilities, and infrastructure creation on the PPP model.

The present global recession, particularly in the USA and other OECD countries, has brought to the fore a major gap in the middle tier of the pyramid. The peak of the pyramid is witnessing the accumulation of wealth at the top. The bottom of the pyramid is being addressed in the Development Economics Project of various international bodies like the World Bank, ADB, etc.

Middle-tier SMEs have not been effectively addressed so far, which is creating a gaping void in the total global economic system.

KOPT-HDC Mega Transportation Logistic Service Product will offer huge opportunities for the SMEs to get launched as startups and then create value-added service products in the chain in the spheres of export-import trade, agriculture, and food chain, small and medium-scale manufacturing industries with the optimal potential to scale up and reach consumers and end users through healthy competition.

Entrepreneurship Incubation Centers will be created through technology and management institutes like IITs and IIMs, effectively collaborating with the corporation on a genuine need-based platform. This will promote inclusive growth in the national economy with nation-building support from the youth and student communities.

There is no better way of exploiting the demographic divide of our nation to its maximum potential.

There is huge scope for expanding the shipbuilding, bargebuilding, and repair industry through the revitalization of existing facilities already available, like Hooghly Docking, Shalimar, and various other small and medium barge building facilities on the river, and this includes idle capacity in KOPT dry docks.

This private port project will also create a huge opportunity for the IT industry to make inroads by creating various innovative digital products for logistic management through effective data storage and management with integrated links.

IT and IT-enabled services with adequate customer satisfaction focus will automatically improve port management efficiency. Portnet systems for various container and bulk cargo terminals, port operation management, effective EDI systems among the port community, executive information systems, facility management services, and ERP (energy resource planning) are some of the IT product services that will be developed both as products and services. This will be a continuous, evolving process on an innovative platform of products and services.

Considering the worldwide crisis of water supply—for industrial use, agricultural use, and municipal supply for drinking water—desalination of seawater through the reverse osmosis process has gained huge international spread through active technology development and commercial initiatives of leading organizations like Energy Recovery Inc. (ERI), USA, a global leader in energy recovery devices for desalination and other industrial processes. It may be noted that China's top economic planning agency, the National Development and Reform Commission (NDRC), included in the country's 5-year plan a tripling of China's desalination capacity by 2015 to more than 2 million cubic meters (528 billion gallons) per day of water.

The KOPT-HDC-HDCvate port may introduce a high-potential water desalination design and development partner for major energy-saving technologies in conjunction with municipal and industrial enterprises in the country.

The drying up of the river water sources in the mountains will, in the long run, require technology development for tapping seawater resources through an energy recovery process.

China and many other countries have recognized the need to protect the interests of the people and reduce the harmful overuse of underground aquifers and water tables.

By partnering with organizations like ERI or equivalent, the KOPT-HDC project will be able to scale new horizons by introducing different water desalination plants throughout its long outreach of ocean-river connectivity through the introduction of contractors on the PPP model.

This is going to be a major nation-building exercise to achieve inclusive growth through a high-tech integrated water management system.

Durgapur Canal, built 5–6 decades ago by DVC, has been dysfunctional for ages. Frequent flood havocs, particularly in the eastern and NE parts of the country, have always been termed natural calamities, and the release of water by different dams when they are crossing danger lines has been accepted in the government management system as a necessary evil. No management system has so far addressed water scarcity for industry and agriculture in adequate measure. Therefore, the spread of water desalination technology as an independent industry with techno-commercially viable investment and IRR structuring will be a big revenue center for the port.

Financial Modeling of the KOPT-HDC Corporate with a major JV partner like Rotterdam Euro or the likes in the USA or SE Asia with experience and expertise in integrated port management involving sea, river, and a multimodal transport chain will aim at phase-wise scaling of primarily traffic linked revenue on the cargo sector. There will be infrastructural-linked revenue from dredging, ship building/ repairing water management, and the tourism industry.

A robust HRD system with networking of specialized training institutes – IITs, IIMs, and ITIs will also need structuring on a Return-Based Investment Platform.

The primary focus of this HRD system should be to follow Swami Vivekananda's MISSION MAN MAKING and accept Swamiji as the Management Guru and Ramakrishna Mission Monks in different Training Centers as Motivators to achieve Integration of Body, Mind, and Soul through 4 YOGAs/Value-Based Discourses and Character Building Exercises among the students of all the Institutes in the network.

This is my vision for realizing the full potential of this major riverine port with peace and productivity as its end product.

***

From the Capstan side, we worked closely with the then SCI Chairman Sabyasachi Hajara, Saket Agarwal, ABG, and KOPT for the introduction of a Sagar Lightening Cum Container Barge Service for Kolkata Haldia Port to accommodate larger, higher-capacity container vessels coming from Singapore to a floating container operation system specially designed by German technocrat Mr. Malcho of Hamburg with a shallow drafted river-specific flat bottom fully equipped container barge with storage capacity and cranes for fast loading and unloading of containers between mother-daughter barges at Sagar Island. Dr. Chanda supported this project, but ultimately, my friend Sabyasachi Hajara could not get this cleared by his board.

I interacted with IWAI and NTPC for a long time to develop and implement the project of imported thermal coal supply to the NTPC Farakka power plant with the transloading of mother vessels at Sandheads to daughter vessels up to Sagar draft and then further transfer from the daughter vessels to a flotilla of smaller barges, either ATB (powerful tug pushing shallow drafted dumb barges) or SPB (self-propelled shallow drafted 2500 tons cargo capacity barges custom built and designed with a broad beam and a short length of 3-meter draft). A fully mechanized barge jetty with the capacity to handle two barges at a time was designed with two unloaders and a conveyor system to reach the plant. Each of the two unloaders was designed to give more than 1000 tph unloading productivity. This was also included in our report to IWAI and NTPC for the purpose of tender document finalization. This document was finalized by us after many meetings and presentations we made to IWAI, particularly quite a few to NTPC and KOPT. Chairman NTPC was a close personal friend of Sabyasachi Hajara, and there was strong support from him for the project. Apart from Sid from the Seabulk side providing strong technical support, I had gone to Bangkok with Tutu to meet Kirit Shah, a ship owner from Bangkok, to join the SCI, L&T, Gimpex, Chennai, and ISHPL consortium to invest in this project. After extensive R&D work, I thought the IWAI Chairperson, who was a very intelligent lady, was convinced about the total concept of techno-commercial logistics we presented to her with 10-year financial projections at a floor price of Rs. 1300 per ton for a 3mmt pa take-or-pay cargo contract for a minimum of 8 years from NTPC. Mr. Meena Kopt, chairman, agreed to provide concessional port charges for the project.

While preparing the tender document, IWAI reduced the floor price to Rs. 950/- to allure NTPC by making them believe that there would be no need for secondary transloading by deploying larger daughter vessels at the Sandheads, Kanika Sands transloading point. They assumed that by building ocean-going smaller barges (within a 3-meter draft), there could be direct loading from the mother vessel at the transloading point. This was technically absurd, and our consortium did not find it worthwhile to participate, and we explained to NTPC the reason for our non-participation. TMILL from Tata Group also independently quoted a little over my floor price based on an independent viability exercise with secondary transloading by larger daughter vessels at Kanica Sands and Sandheads.

Jindal Group's shipping logistics arm secured the tender award at Rs. 1050 per ton with an 8-year back-to-back contract for handling 3 mmtpa of coal imports from the deep sea transloading point to the NTPC Farakka thermal power plant. They hired an officer from the

TMILL team for logistic handling. The project was messed up due to a lack of shipping knowledge and internal bickering.

Sid Sridhar and Seabulk refused to take the transloading contract at a low rate due to a lack of technological and commercial viability.

Capt. Rajesh Mehrotra of Sula Shipping, USA, with an old converted Panamax transloader belonging to their associated Dutch owner, ventured to take the transloading contract but ultimately had to withdraw their transloader due to continuous payment defaults from the Jindal side. Later, I became very intimate with Raju through the introduction of my friend Sabyasachi Hajara. Sula had to ultimately create a separate SPV for logistics handling by his Indian office, with a very competent Master Mariner, Capt. Srikant, at the helm of their Indian office. Raju made some adjustments to his dues from Jindal with the condition of full Sula Control in the logistic management of this contract. Sula signed a logistic consultancy agreement with Capstan covering both the NTPC contract and the bigger transloading contract with KOPT for imported coking coal for steel plants and thermal coal from other power plants at Haldia through the introduction of two more Panamax transloaders. The project was loaded with substantial investment by Jindals in building over 20 small, 2500-ton self-propelled barges for sea-river operation at Goa. These barges were wrongly designed, which made them incapable of carrying more than 60% of their capacity at the permissible river draft. There was also a technical lacuna and a cost overrun in the building of the barge jetty at Farakka with conveyor unloaders for delivery up to the NTPC plant site. The investment was not justifying the revenue structure.

Both Raju and Srikant were trying hard to repair the logistics mess up by the earlier Jindal team by combining both transloading projects under the NTPC contract subsidized by the KOPT contract, but they were not getting much cooperation from Jindals. The overload of cuts and kickbacks on the barge building and the jetty building were substantial. There was also an undercurrent of resistance from the Jindal side to give freehand to Raju and his team for decision-making in logistics handling. I had provided them with my contact support in KOPT at the chairman level and relevant officers who had always given me respect and cooperation. I also introduced Raju to my friend Ramesh Maheswary of Texmaco for project funding support when Jindal management was showing apathy to invest further. Saibal De of ILFS, who was part of our earlier strong consortium with SCI, Bocimar, Seabulk, and others, confirmed their interest in joining the KOPT transloading project but not the NTPC Farakka project.

Jindal finally appointed PWC as a financial consultant for the entire project accounts audit, financial restructuring, and finding a buyer to take over the project SPV from Jindal. Ramesh Maheswari showed interest in the project, and at his request from Capstan, we invested substantial time and money in presenting project financials with a long-term projected IRR. We also arranged various meetings and interactions at their works in Belghoria with KOPT-HDC, SAIL, ILFS, Sula, PWC, Jindals, etc. Texmaco Rail had an interest in and synergy in the railway logistics part of the project. I had many meetings with Texmaco Chairman Saroj Poddar and even arranged for Raju to meet Saroj in Delhi. My personal relationship with the Poddar family was strong for a long time. Ramesh was K K Birla's man of complete trust and chief architect for building Texmaco as the leading Wagon manufacturing and engineering firm of the nation. After the demise of K. K. Birla, Saroj Poddar, as his son-in-law, became Chairman of Texmaco, and earlier, freedom of Ramesh Maheswari in decision-making got somewhat curtailed. Although Saroj was fully dependent on Ramesh at the ground level and made him vice chairman with all facilities, Ramesh did not enjoy the same level of trust and confidence of the chairman as he had always enjoyed with K. K. Birla. Ramesh was both a highly intelligent businessman and a very competent professional manager. For the Jindal project revival, he was moving fast and made me and my team work very hard with financial presentations, the preparation of technological and financial feasibility reports, arranging meetings and presenting to KOPT, SAIL, IWAI, Jindals, and their appointed consultant, PwC. We introduced Saibal De of IL&FS as their consortium partner in the project and invested time and money in traveling and securing inputs for them from NTPC, SAIL, PwC, and KOPT. We also worked hard on providing a technological concept for transloading operations. This included onshore terminal logistics, including rail, ocean, and river integrated services for the NTPC contract, which was poorly designed by Jindal. Also, input on transloading operation logistics and presentations to different steel and power plants were provided to the Texmaco team. Ramesh, with his outstanding communication skills and project technology grasping capacity, provided confidence to all the clients. He showed interest in real value addition by expressing his interest in investing in railway logistics with railway collaboration by supplying custom-built wagons for pilferage-free delivery up to the clients' plant sites. Unfortunately, Saroj Poddar was not K. K. Birla, and I could appreciate Ramesh's embarrassment when the Texmaco chairman walked out of this project and was not prepared to pay any consultancy fee to Capstan for the huge volume of work done on this and other projects spanning over 5 or 6 years.

Later, Jindals got into a legal battle with both the KOPT and NTPC when I tried to mediate a solution. Ultimately, as Jindals were devoid of any shipping knowledge or genuine intention to fulfill their contractual obligations with Kopt and NTPC, KOPT terminated their contract and revoked their BG. Sula and Raju Meherotra withdrew completely. KOPT, after the unfortunate politically motivated framing of Chairman Kahlon on corruption charges by the West Bengal government, went leaderless for a good span of time before the Chairman of Vizag Port was given dual charge of Vizag and Kolkata. It took another couple of years for the Ministry to appoint a permanent chairman to take full charge.

I have always been critical of the port infrastructure building and management of Indian ports by the politicians in power at the Ministry and the corrupt bureaucratic system that was depriving the Indian port and shipping industry the opportunity to fully exploit the huge potential of our nation in global trade and industry. The chairmen who were joining to lead and manage ports for a limited span of time were all competent and intelligent professionals but had very limited scope to drive their dreams, visions, and innovative thinking to the ultimate stage of fast policy framing and decision-making with a target delivery timeline. In my long experience as a port user as well as a port consultant and trustee of KOPT, I found dreams, passions, and commitments with most of the chairmen and port officers for the port as an institution, but the vested interest lobby, political pressures, and risk of their job security and often designed false framing of corruption charges were restricting them to a job safety first attitude at the cost of the growth and development of the port.

As a Trustee, I had convinced the then Chairman, Dr. Anup Chanda, to pursue a holistic policy for logistics integration of port services in the areas of state-of-the-art container and bulk cargo terminal buildings linking ocean, river, rail, and road infrastructure development on a viable cost optimization model for smooth and efficient traffic flow of finished products and raw materials. I also included in my draft project paper the creation of SBM in the high seas for retention and expansion of oil traffic to Haldia, which was facing a serious risk of shifting to neighboring ports to suit the oil company's logistic convenience.

The outcome was the appointment of a global consultant after lobbying and horsetrading on fees. The final report, which came to the board of trustees from a Hong Kong consultant, was devoid of a comprehensive plan and was referred back for further review, resulting in precious time loss. Later, at Chairman Kahlon's request, I revised my report with more details and content additions in the form of an article..

My long five-decade entrepreneurial journey in the Indian port and shipping industry was always loaded with dreams, vision, and innovative thinking for establishing a robust and smooth transportation supply chain logistics management system for creating a globally competitive product value for commodity trade and raw material cost benefits for India's manufacturing industries. In post-independent India, the nation was suffering from a mindset of inferiority complex as a legacy of the British Raj. We were prepared to easily accept our poor developing country tag globally and accept our destiny to sit in the back row of the comity of nation-states. My concept and dream for a robust Indian port and shipping industry that offers potential opportunities for multiple ancillary industries and MSMEs sprouting throughout the nation could have a real-time impact on the global economy if realized. I was consciously aware that this was not easy to wade through the myriads of hurdles and hassles on the pathway created by the greed and lust of the politicians and self-seeking vested interests infested with lower attributes of human nature. The evolution of humans in the world to become humane has happened through decades and centuries of sustained human efforts. It was to happen through the eternal pursuit of truth and perfection.

My faith and surrender to Thakur Ramakrishna kept me moving with a 'never say die' attitude of positivity in all my detached karma to pursue my dreams and visions fearlessly.

I have always accepted my sorrows and sufferings, hurdles, and hassles as happening through divine design for my ultimate good and the cleaning process of my mind temple to create and maintain a happy habitat for my soul to manifest in full bloom.

In these twilight hours of my mortal life, I end my memoirs of a long sojourn by staying steadfast on Swamiji's beautiful and inspiring Words of Wisdom:

> Change not thy nature, gentle bloom,
> Thou violet, sweet and pure,
> But ever pour thy sweet perfume
> Unasked, unstinted, sure!

IndiePress

The best route your story can take.

To publish your own book, contact us.

We publish poetry collections, short story collections, novellas and novels.

contact@http://indiepress.in/

Instagram- indie_press